The Army of Maximinus Thrax

The Roman Soldier of the early 3rd Century AD

Dr. Jan Eschbach and Stefano Borin

(Translated by the author)

ZEUGHAUS VERLAG GmbH

Res ad triarios rediit.

Livy, Ab urbe condita, VIII, 8, 8 f.

Author: Dr. Jan Eschbach
Illustrations: Stefano Borin
Editor: Christine Young
Maps: Bernhard Glänzer

Publisher: Zeughaus Verlag GmbH
Knesebeckstr. 88
10623 Berlin, Germany

Telephone: +49 (0)30/315 700 30
Email: info@zeughausverlag.de
Website: www.zeughausverlag.de

Bibliographic information from the Deutschen Bibliothek: The Deutsche Bibliothek lists this publication in the German National Bibliography; detailed bibliographic information is available at http://dnb.ddb.de

Printed in European Union
Originally published in German as
Heere & Waffen No. 34 "Das Heer des Maximinus Thrax"
(Berlin: Zeughaus Verlag, 2020)

ISBN: 978-3-96360-025-8

The cover illustration shows an early 3rd century AD infantryman of the Praetorian Guard on campaign. The shield on the back cover is the so-called Amazon shield excavated at the Roman frontier fortress of Dura Europos.

Contents

Picti
Hiberni
Oceanus Germanicus
Mare
BRITANNIA INFERIOR
BRIT. SUPERIOR
Albis
Cherusci
Colonia Agrippina (CCAA)
Chatti
GERM. INF.
Rhenus
Oceanus
Agri Decumates
Marcomanni
BELGICA
GERM. SUP.
LUGDUNENSIS
NORICUM
Mare Cantabricum
AQUITANIA
RAETIA
Aquileia
ALPES
NARBONENSIS
ITALIA
TARRACONENSIS
CORSICA
Roma
LUSITANIA
SARDINIA
BAETICA
SICILIA
Carthago
MAURET. TINGITANA
MAURETANIA CAESARIENSIS
NUMIDIA
AFRICA
Garamantes
23 Legio I Parthica (Singara)
24 Legio XIV Flavia (Sura)
25 Legio IV Scythica (Oresa)
26 Legio III Gallica (Raphanea)
27 Legio III Cyrenaica (Bostra)
28 Legio VI Ferrata (Caporcotani)
29 Legio X Fretensis (Aelia Capitolina)
30 Legio II Traiana (Nicopolis)
31 Legio III Augusta (Lambaesis)
32 Legio VII Gemina (Legio)
33 Legio II Parthica (Albanum)

The Roman Empire and the deployment of legions ca. AD 230.

Silver *denarius* from Maximinus' reign bearing the Emperor's portrait with the inscription IMP MAXIMINVS PIVS AVG *[Imperator Maximinus Pius Augustus]*; the reverse side bears an allegorical depiction of Peace, with the inscription PAX AVGVSTI (Author's collection).

CHRONOLOGY

AD 161	Marcus Aurelius ascends the throne of the Caesars together with his co-emperor Lucius Verus.
AD 162-66	Lucius Verus leads victorious campaign against the Parthians. Roman troops returning from the East bring plague epidemic to the Roman Empire.
AD 167-180	Marcomanni and Quadi invade Roman Empire. They reach northern Italy before being beaten back. Wars against Marcomanni, Quadi and Sarmatians on the Danube. Imperial frontiers are restored. Lucius Verus dies in 169 AD.
AD 180	Marcus Aurelius dies in camp at Vindobona, presumably of plague. He is succeeded by his son Commodus.
AD 192	Commodus is assassinated. Aided by Praetorian Prefect Laetus, urban prefect Publius Helvius Pertinax becomes emperor.
AD 193	The Praetorians murder Pertinax and raise Marcus Didius Julianus to the purple. The governors of Syria and Pannonia, Gaius Pescennius Niger and Lucius Septimius Severus, are acclaimed emperors by their troops. Severus appoints Decius Clodius Albinus, governor of Britain, his co-emperor (*Caesar*) and marches on Rome. Didius Julianus is murdered; Severus disbands and reraises Praetorians.
AD 193-194	Pescennius Niger is defeated at Issus. He is killed while fleeing to the Parthians.
AD 196-197	Albinus rises against Severus. Severus defeats Albinus at Lugdunum (Lyon). Albinus is killed.
AD 197-199	Parthian War. Parthian capital Ctesiphon taken and sacked. Founding of the Roman province of Mesopotamia.
AD 208-211	Severus campaigns in Britain. He dies at Eburacum (York), bestowing power on his two sons Caracalla (actually Marcus Aurelius Severus Antoninus) and Geta.
AD 212	Geta is murdered. Caracalla passes the *Constitutio Antoniniana* granting Roman citizenship to all free-born inhabitants of the Empire.
AD 213-214	Caracalla campaigns against Germans and Dacians.
AD 216-217	Campaign against kingdom of Adiabene. While preparing his „Alexandrian" campaign against Parthia Caracalla is assassinated by a bodyguard at Edessa. Praetorian Prefect Marcus Opellius Macrinus is proclaimed emperor. He is the first emperor of non-senatorial rank. Three-day battle against Parthians at Nisibis ends in a draw.
AD 218	Macrinus is defeated and killed by the forces of the pretender Varius Avitus Bassianus, known as Elagabalus, alleged son of Caracalla.
AD 222	Elagabalus is killed by mutinous Praetorians. He is succeeded by his thirteen-year-old cousin Marcus Aurelius Alexander Severus. His mother Iulia Mamaea acts as his effective co-ruler.
AD 224-226	The Parthian Arsacid dynasty is overthrown by the Persian Ardashir. Founding of the Sassanid Empire.
AD 231-233	Following Persian incursions into Roman Mesopotamia, Alexander Severus campaigns against the Persians. Initial Roman successes are brought to nothing by Roman defeat outside Ctesiphon.
AD 233-234	Alamanni raid Rhine provinces and Gaul, causing severe damage.
AD 235	Alexander Severus marches to Rhine frontier. His attempts to negotiate with the Alamanni cause Roman troops to mutiny. Alexander Severus and his mother are killed by soldiers at Mainz. End of Severan dynasty. The legions proclaim the Thracian officer Gaius Iulius Verus Maximinus emperor.

AD 235-236	Maximinus leads his troops on a campaign to the River Elbe. Germans are beaten in battles in the Elbe marshes and at the Harzhorn pass. Rhine frontier secured.
AD 236-237	Maximinus fights and defeats Sarmatians and Carpi on the Danube.
AD 238	Year of the Six Emperors: rebellion against Maximinus in North Africa. The octogenarian proconsul Marcus Antonius Gordianus Sempronianus and his son are declared emperors. Capelianus, governor of Numidia, remains loyal to Maximinus and defeats the pretenders' army outside Carthage. Gordian II dies in the rout, Gordian I commits suicide. The Senate elects two of its members, Marcus Clodius Pupienus and Decimus Caelius Calvinus Balbinus, joint emperors. Maximinus invades Italy. His advance is checked at Aquileia, which he unsuccessfully attempts to besiege. Mutinous soldiers of *legio II Parthica* assassinate Maximinus and his son. The Praetorians kill Pupienus and Balbinus and raise the grandson of Gordian I, Gordian III, to the purple.
AD 238-244	Persians occupy Roman province of Mesopotamia but are defeated at Rhesaina in AD 243. The Roman counter-offensive meets with disaster when Gordian III mysteriously dies at Mesiche. His Praetorian Prefect Marcus Iulius Philippus, the Arab, succeeds him to the throne. Philippus makes peace with Persia but is forced to accept unfavourable terms.
AD 245-246	Philippus campaigns against Carpi on the Danube.
AD 247	Philippus lavishly celebrates the 1,000-year anniversary of the founding of Rome.
AD 249	The governor of Pannonia, Gaius Messius Quintus Traianus Decius, repulses recurrent Carpi incursions into Roman territory on the Danube. He is proclaimed emperor by his troops. Philippus loses the battle of Verona against Decius, and his life. Decius is the first of the so-called „Illyrian Emperors".
AD 250-251	War against the Goths. Decius is defeated by Gothic king Kniva. Decius and his son and co-ruler Herennius are again defeated and killed at Abrittus in AD 251. Decius is the first Roman emperor to die in battle. The governor of Moesia, Trebonianus Gallus, is acclaimed emperor by the Danube legions. He concludes a costly peace treaty with the Goths.
AD 252-253	After arrears in Roman tribute payments, Shapur I invades Roman East. A Roman force is defeated outside Antioch, which is sacked by the Persians. The Roman governor of Pannonia, Marcus Aemilius Aemilianus, defeats Goths under Kniva. He is proclaimed emperor by his troops. Trebonianus Gallus is assassinated by his own troops before the governor of Raetia and Noricum, Publius Licinius Valerianus, can gather reinforcements to aid him against Aemiianus. Aemilianus is murdered as Valerianus' army approaches, Valerian becomes emperor. He appoints his son Gallienus co-emperor.

INTRODUCTION

A savage battle between Romans and barbarians rages on the so-called Ludovisi sarcophagus dating from the second half of the 3rd century AD. Discovered in a vineyard outside the gates of Rome in 1621, it is now on display in the Museo Nazionale Romano in Rome. The twisted bodies of men and beasts are locked in a grim struggle as standards fly above the ranks and a trumpeter sounds the charge. While legionaries and cavalrymen go about their gory business, the general hovers above on his rising steed, his right arm flung out in a gesture of blessing[1].

The sculpture's propaganda is simple and straightforward – defeated and asking for mercy, the barbarians cower; Rome remains victorious. If one takes a closer look however, this triumphal monument carved in marble (a cast may be seen in the Römisch-Germanisches Zentralmuseum in Mainz) can be understood as pointing to a profound crisis. The Romans are actually fighting two enemies simultaneously. While the enemies crowding in from the right are easily recognisable as Germanic tribesmen by their beards, nudity and breeches, the enemies on the left half of the relief are probably Parthians or Persians. They wear baggy oriental breeches and belted tunics, some have donned Phrygian caps.

In a dramatic if flattering manner, the sculptor depicts the Empire's geopolitical situation at the beginning of the 3rd century AD. Indeed the outlook was not as promising as the sarcophagus suggests. On her northern and eastern frontiers, Rome was facing two powerful enemies. Along the Rhine and the Danube massive and coordinated attacks by German tribes had become alarmingly frequent, and in the East the Parthian Empire had been replaced by the far more aggressive Sassanid Persians. When the young emperor Alexander Severus was unable to contain this double threat, his soldiers brutally murdered him. He was succeeded by Gaius Iulius Verus Maximinus, a professional officer from Thrace[2]. His rise to power ushered in the era of the Soldier Emperors, a time of deep internal and external crisis for the Empire. For the next five decades enemy invasions, civil war, disease, usurpations and economic decline were to determine its fortunes, before Diocletian's reforms brought back a certain degree of stability.

All over Europe the Harzhorn battlefield, excavated since 2008, has rekindled interest in this time of upheavals. While by no means claiming completeness, this work seeks to introduce the general reader to the events and the people involved in shaping the beginning of this era, the protagonist being the emperor Maximinus. Since the Roman army at this time was undergoing far-reaching changes and experiencing complete political and social revaluation, its organisation, equipment and weapons will be examined with the aim of creating a basic idea of the soldiers from whose ranks the men came who henceforth were to determine the Empire's fate. The soldiers on the Ludovisi sarcophagus shall accompany us through much of this story. This work shall also be dealing briefly with the events surrounding the battle of the Harzhorn.

Special thanks is due to Dr Mario Küßner from the Archaeological Institute of the Federal State of Thuringia at Weimar for patiently and enthusiastically sharing and explaining his results regarding the excavation of the Roman marching camp at Hachelbich. I am equally indebted to Dr. Michael Geschwinde, head of division at the Braunschweig branch of the Archaeological Institute of the Federal State of Lower Saxony, for his kindness and patience when it came to explaining the Roman march and the battle of the Harzhorn to me. I should also like to thank my dear friend and colleague Andrea Getz-Güdelhöfer, whose classical expertise helped when my own occasionally wore thin. Needless to say that all mistakes are my own.

My special thanks goes to my brilliant artist Stefano Borin for his detailed and expressive illustrations that helped bring the army of Maximinus Thrax to life. A big thank you goes to Bernhard Glänzer, who drew the maps. I am grateful to Stefan Müller of my publisher Zeughaus-Verlag, who faithfully and patiently accompanied my work. Finally, I would like to thank my family, who has learned to live with my obsession on a daily basis *cum tranquilitate animi*.

I should like to dedicate this little book to my sons Justus and Jonas, but also to Peter Connolly, Rosemary Sutcliff, and – perhaps *mirabile dictu* – to René Goscinny and Albert Uderzo, whose works got me interested in all of this as a child.

1 KÜNZL, Ernst, *Der Traum vom Imperium. Der Ludovisisarkophag – Grabmal eines Feldherrn Roms*, Regensburg/Mainz 2010, p. 67.

2 The name *Thrax*, probably derogatory to indicate his supposedly barbarian *origins*, seems to have first appeared in late antiquity.

Plate I

Battle frieze on the Ludovisi sarcophagus

(Museo Nazionale Romano)

ROME IN CRISIS – THE THIRD CENTURY

The Severan dynasty

What were the main political events that determined the third-century army's existence? Trajan's campaigns at the beginning of the second century AD marked the conclusion of a long period of territorial expansion of the Empire. While the reigns of Hadrian and Antoninus Pius had been marked mostly by consolidation and a certain degree of prosperity, the end of the second century saw the first signs of a crisis that in the third century was to bring Rome to the verge of collapse. Marcomanni and Quadi launched a large-scale invasion across the Danube and managed to reach northern Italy. In a succession of prolonged and bloody wars Marcus Aurelius was able to restore the northern frontiers. Previously it had taken considerable effort to defeat the Parthians in a war over Armenia. Although this conflict was resolved to Rome's benefit, the returning legions brought the so-called Antonine Plague to the Empire (in fact possibly smallpox), which would ravage the provinces for years to come.

The assassination of Marcus Aurelius's son Commodus resulted in a struggle for power from which in 193 AD the governor of Pannonia, the North African senator Septimius Severus, finally emerged victorious. The founder of the Severan dynasty undertook numerous campaigns, which took him to Mesopotamia, Africa and Britain, where he died in AD 197. While Severus had dealt mercilessly with his political enemies, he was generous to the soldiers, fully aware that it was to them that he owed his elevation to the throne. He raised their pay by a considerable degree (something which had not occurred for nearly a century), creating an economic upsurge especially in the Danube provinces[3]. This profound financial and political revaluation of the soldiers however would lead to a dangerous and harmful development whose consequences Severus would hardly have been capable of foreseeing.

After Severus's death his elder son Marcus Aurelius Antoninus, also known as Caracalla, murdered his brother Geta and declared himself sole ruler. Caracalla (his nickname derives from a Gallic type of hooded cape he was especially fond of wearing) had as a child been witness to the gory struggle for power which had made his father Emperor of Rome. Grown suspicious and ruthless in consequence, he took to heart the the admonitions of his father that the security of his rule was primarily based on the soldiers. Caracalla again raised their pay (which almost caused the bankruptcy of the Imperial revenue) and when amongst his soldiers gave himself the air of a *commilito*, a simple comrade, by marching, dressing in simple garb and sharing their rations. Presumably in order to replenish the Imperial coffers, Caracalla in 212 AD issued the *Constitutio Antoniniana*, by which he granted Roman citizenship to all free-born inhabitants of the Roman Empire. He thus eliminated not just a century-old social framework but also the basic social difference between the auxiliaries and the legions.

To further secure their allegiance, Caracalla led his troops on a campaign against the German tribes in the Main region in 213 AD. Considering himself the successor of Alexander the Great, Caracalla then began to plan a campaign against Parthia, which was at this time torn by internal strife. Things took a different course. Shortly after his departure from Edessa in April 217 AD Caracalla was assassinated by a bodyguard as he was relieving himself by the roadside. One of the conspirators, his Praetorian Prefect Macrinus, became the new emperor.

Following the brief interlude of the rules of Macrinus (217 AD) and Elagabalus (218-222 AD) the last member of the Severan dynasty, the young Alexander Severus, mounted the throne of the Caesars. Raised by the Praetorians, this erudite and modest young man succeeded with the help of his prudent mother and circumspect advisors to stabilise the situation at home and induce economic recovery. He was however soon confronted with a number of problems which would maintain the Roman Empire in an almost constant state of crisis for nearly a century: the new Sassanid dynasty proved a more aggressive and formidable enemy in the East than the Parthians had ever been. Considering themselves the successors of the Achaemenids, the Sassanids now claimed all Roman territory between the Tigris and the Mediterranean for themselves, and they meant business.

After some futile attempts to settle the matter by diplomatic means, the Emperor and his legions marched east. The Persian campaign was costly and indecisive. Receiving the news of a Germanic invasion of the Northern provinces, Alexander Severus decided to march to the Rhine. As he had done in the east, he attempted negotiations. Rumours spread among the soldiers that the Emperor was trying to buy the Germans off. These rumours distressed and angered the local landowners as well as the troops[4]. The latters'discontent manifested itself in murder: angry at not being permitted to fight and feeling that they were being denied their share of the spoils by an emperor they had come to consider a coward, mutinous soldiers killed

3 PFERDEHIRT, Barbara/SCHOLZ, Markus, „Die Epoche der Severischen Kaiser", in: Archäologisches Landesmuseum Baden-Württemberg (ed.): *Caracalla. Kaiser, Tyrann, Feldherr*, Darmstadt/Mainz 2013, p. 33-52, p.37, 43, 60; David S. POTTER, *The Roman Empire at Bay AD 180-395*, London/New York² 2014, p. 130.

4 LEHMANN, Gustav Adolf, *Imperium und Barbaricum. Neue Befunde und Erkenntnisse zu den römisch-germanischen Auseinandersetzungen im norddeutschen Raum – von der augusteischen Okkupationsphase bis zum Germanien-Zug des Maximinus Thrax (235 n. Chr.)*, Vienna 2011, p. 101.

Plate II

Bust of the Emperor Maximinus I

(Palazzo Nuovo, Musei Capitolini, Rome)

the twenty-six-year-old Emperor and his mother in the Imperial camp at Mainz-Bretzenheim[5]. The troops proceeded to declare an officer named Gaius Iulius Verus Maximinus the new Emperor of Rome.

Sensitive and introverted, Alexander Severus had never managed to command his troops' affection as Septimius Severus and Caracalla had done. Increases in pay and generous donatives, combined with internal unrest and mounting crisis on the frontiers, had begun to spawn a new self-confidence in the troops which henceforth would be difficult to control. The beginning of the 3rd century AD marked the rise of a new political and military culture. For the first time, the legions had made one of their own an emperor. In what was to follow, the legions were to prove both a blessing and a curse.

The sources

Compared to other periods of Roman history, we know fairly little about the time of the soldier emperors (also termed barrack emperors), because the amount of sources at our disposal is limited. The two main sources we may rely on are the historic works of Herodian (born ca. 178 AD) and Cassius Dio (b. ca. 163 AD). Both works were written in Greek. Dio's originally quite extensive history has only survived in a number of fragments, and comes to an abrupt end at the beginning of the period concerned. It breaks off in the year 229 AD. It is obvious that Dio's work served as a source for Herodian. Other historic works help us to gain a fairly satisfactory view of events and provide interesting details. One of these is the *Historia Augusta*, written presumably in the fourth century, a compilation of biographies of the Roman Emperors from Hadrian to Numerian (r. AD 117-285). We are as yet unclear about authorship, and considerable doubt has been cast on its reliability. While some passages of the *Historia Augusta* can certainly be regarded as fictitious and a degree of caution is therefore advisable, it is evident that the author, or authors, of this work could draw on important contemporary sources.

These sources are supplemented by the (mostly lost) works of the Athenian writer Dexippus, whose work related the period until the death of Claudius II Gothicus (d. AD 270), and of Eusebios and Nikostratos of Trapezunt. Another work, now entirely lost, was a history composed by the Italic senator Asinius Quadratus. Other written sources include so-called breviaries, short historic treatises which are mostly considered reliable and can be traced back to one and the same unknown original source. These breviaries were written by Eutropius and Aurelius Victor. There are also the anonymous works entitled *Epitome de Caesaribus* and *Chronica Urbis Romae*. We may gain further insight into the period by consulting various other works by early Christian and Byzantine authors.

Maximinus I and the time of the Soldier Emperors

The new emperor, upon whose shoulders his soldiers placed the purple *paludamentum* as Alexander Severus lay dead in his tent, was a provincial[6]. He had been born around the year 173 AD in the Dobruja in central Thrace[7] and was able to look back upon a remarkable military career. Apparently of immense physical strength (the sources claim he was a wrestling champion and capable of drawing a fully packed cart single-handed[8]), he entered the cavalry under Septimius Severus and rose to command the Imperial horse guards (*equites singulares Augusti*). He belonged to Alexander Severus's circle of military advisors and will have held a high-ranking position in the Persian campaign, possibly even acting as commander-in-chief. There are clues indicating that he held the rank of *dux ripae*, the local Roman commander responsible for securing the frontier along the River Euphrates, whose base was Dura Europos[9]. An inscription found in North Africa seems to indicate he was governor of Mauretania. He later followed Alexander Severus to the Rhine, where he probably took an active part in the conspiracy, since the young emperor's vacillations will have disgusted his soldier's sense of honour. At this time Maximinus was probably already an *evocatus*, a veteran still serving on account of his experience and expertise[10].

At the time of his elevation Maximinus held the rank of *praefectus tironibus*, making him the officer in charge of training the recruits. This specially created position demanded a high degree of professionalism, leadership and profound military knowledge. Maximinus Thrax was an experienced old soldier, and it was his own men that offered him the purple cloak in the training ground.

The beginning of Maximinus' reign marked a breach in several respects. He was the first professional soldier on the throne and thus his ascendency proved a political novelty, even though his contemporaries were probably not particularly aware of this. Maximinus was also not a member of the Senate. If we discount Macrinus' con-

5 The sources give the location of the emperor's camp as *in vico Britannico* (cf. LEHMANN, p. 101). The outcome of the coup d'état was far from certain since Maximinus was not in the imperial camp but based in a different camp. Had Severus succeeded in motivating his troops to resist the usurper, the course of history might have been very different.

6 Maximinus is also commonly referred to as Maximinus I (to distinguish him from Maximinus II Daia, Caesar of the East from AD 305 to 311, Augustus of the East from 311 to 313).

7 DEPPMEYER, Korana, „Maximinus Thrax – vom thrakischen Soldaten zum römischen Kaiser", in: PÖPPELMANN, Heike/ DEPPMEYER, Korana/STEINMETZ, Wolf-Dieter, *Roms vergessener Feldzug. die Schlacht am Harzhorn*, Darmstadt 2013, p. 104.

8 Historia Augusta, *Duo Maximini*, VI.

9 DEPPMAYER, ibid., p.105.

10 DE LA BÉDOYÈRE, Guy, *Praetorian. The rise and fall of Rome's imperial bodyguard*, New Haven/London 2017, p. 243.

spiracy against Caracalla (which probably involved only a few men), the events at Mogontiacum were also remarkable in that for the first time the soldiers had staged a *coup d'état* and raised one of their own to the purple. The quick succession of rulers that was to determine the next five decades stood in stark contrast to the dynastic and adoptive principles which had hitherto formed the basis of the Principate[11]. The precarious strategic situation on the frontiers required the presence of the Emperor in the field, and thus the military background of the so-called soldier emperors was a reaction to the political and military realities of the moment. Although many of these men were still of senatorial rank, this was no longer considered a prerequisite of the purple. The army had begun to replace the Senate as the Empire's determining political factor. In view of the rapidly changing political and geostrategic circumstances this was hardly surprising.[12]

When he was acclaimed Emperor at Mogontiacum, Maximinus was between fifty and sixty years of age. He was probably an equestrian and hence a representative of the increasingly professionalised social class which in the coming decades was to replace the members of the Senate in the army's high command. Around 215 AD he married Caecilia Paulina, a woman from a senatorial family, which shows that his origins were not as humble as some written sources would make us believe. His full name, Gaius Lucius Verus Maximinus, proves that his family had already held Roman citizenship for a while and did not owe it to Caracalla's *Constitutio Antoniniana*[13].

The surviving busts of Maximinus show us the grim and furrowed features of a seasoned soldier. His massive skull has a strong neck and a square jaw, and his hair and beard are both trimmed short in military style (contrasting the rich Greek beard of the philosopher Emperor Marcus Aurelius). The emperor's gaze has a determined note, his demeanour indicates sobriety and deliberation. As LEHMANN has shown, this depiction became a stylistic icon which was to influence the imperial portraits of an entire epoch[14]. The sources characterise Maximinus as brave, cruel, wary and strong-minded, but also as modest and just. He would hardly have been able to win his troops' affection if it had been different.

The new Emperor quickly set about keeping his troops happy. He doubled their rations, remitted punishments, and promised them plunder and glory. A mutiny which had spread among the élite Osrhoenian archers in the Imperial army was quickly put down (Historia Augusta, *Duo Maximini*, XI, 3 f.). Maximinus paid the customary *donativum*, the grant due to the troops at every Imperial succession, doubling the sum for those units which had been instrumental in his acclamation. The civilian population likewise received a special payment, the *congiarium*. These payments were a tremendous strain on the Imperial finances, but Herodian's allegation that Maximinus' generosity was ruinous is not particularly convincing: he was merely continuing the policy of his predecessors. Macrinus and Alexander Severus had both attempted to restrict the amount of *donativa*, which had resulted in severe unrest among the troops. To economise in this respect was clearly suicidal.

Maximinus finished the pontoon bridge begun by his predecessor at Mainz and led the army into free German territory. When exactly this happened, remains unclear. While some scholars as well as the sources point to a rapid departure even in the year 235 (Alexander Severus's vacillation had, after all, cost him dear), others are inclined to believe that preparations and deployments delayed the beginning of the campaign until 236[15].Far from Roman territory, the army marched to the Elbe where it won a resounding victory, returning to winter quarters in the Rhine garrisons via Lower Saxony and northern Hesse. The Romans laid waste to all hostile territory, plundering and torching German settlements. On its return march the army was ambushed at the Harzhorn pass but was able to repulse the attackers.

After the German campaign Maximinus, now famed as *Germanicus Maximus*, marched to Sirmium on the Danube, from where he conducted several campaigns against the Sarmatians. Unfortunately, not much is known about these campaigns. The campaigns were evidently successful, but nevertheless expensive. In order to finance these military operations and the rewards for the soldiers, he increased taxes and levies in the entire Empire and reduced the corn supply for the population of Rome. This of course made him highly unpopular, especially among the wealthy Italic senatorial families, who still found the barbarian's putsch in Mainz impossible to stomach. Never before had an Emperor been acclaimed without the approval of the Senate.

Open resistance against the Thracian's rule began in the province of Africa, one of the most prosperous areas of the Empire. These provinces had come to feel the Emperor's taxes particularly heavily. The local governor was killed and the aged proconsul Gordian and his son of the same name were proclaimed joint Emperors. By confirming Gordian's appointment, the Senate openly sided against Maximinus. The vanquisher of the Germans and Sarmatians had become a public enemy.

Meanwhile Capelianus, the governor of Numidia, had marched to the Gordians' residential city of Carthage with *legio III Augusta*. The Gordians' "Praetorians", hurriedly

11 The images of Maximinus and his son on coins suggest that Maximinus attempted to present himself in the tradition of the Severan emperors.

12 DEPPMAYER, ibid., p. 103-104.

13 SOMMER, Michael, *Die Soldatenkaiser,* Darmstadt^3 2014, p. 29.

14 LEHMANN, p. 101

15 WOLTERS, Reinhard, „Der Feldzug des Maximinus Thrax in das Innere Germaniens 236/236 n. Chr. In der numismatischen Überlieferung", in: PÖPPELMANN, Heike/DEPPMAYER, Korana/ STEINMETZ, Wolf-Dieter, *Roms Vergessener Feldzug. Die Schlacht am Harzhorn*, Darmstadt 2013, pp. 116-123, p. 116.

raised from the young men of the city's local élite, were easily routed by the legionaries, the survivors slaughtered by pursuing cavalry outside the city walls. Gordian the Younger was killed in the fighting, his father took his own life. It appeared that the revolt had been crushed.

Maximinus, who had never entered Rome, led his army south in forced marches. The Senate was clear about the consequences should the Emperor reach Rome. It appointed from its midst two joint *Augusti*, Pupienus and Balbinus. Gordian I's grandson, Gordian III, was to be their *Caesar*.

Maximinus had begun to lay siege to Aquileia in northern Italy. He was met with determined resistance, disease and supply problems began to take their toll on the besiegers. Meanwhile Pupienus and Balbinus were raising troops. Pupienus hurried to Ravenna to raise an army with which to relieve Aquileia. Time was running out for Maximinus. Fearing for the safety of their families at their base at Albanum, soldiers of *legio II Parthica* stormed the Emperor's tent in May 238 AD. They killed Maximinus and his son and sent their heads to Rome. There it was decreed that his memory be obliterated (*damnatio memoriae*). Maximinus' name was erased from all inscriptions, his statues destroyed.

Maximinus has been criticised for laying siege to Aquileia since the operation cost him valuable time and ultimately his soldiers' affection. On the other hand, Maximinus was an experienced soldier who appreciated Aquileia's strategic value. The city, where several important trade routes converged, formed the entrance to Italy from the northwest, that is from the strategically vital Alpine provinces. The Emperor was probably keen on securing his lines of communication before marching south to fight.

Maximinus' image was until quite recently determined by negative characterisations and depictions. This is mainly due to the fact that most biographical accounts rely heavily on Herodian, who as a member of the senatorial class was biased against the Emperor, whom he considered a barbarian upstart. Herodian viewed the reign of Marcus Aurelius as a golden age which was followed by decline under a succession of incompetent tyrants. His depiction of Maximinus' allegedly simple and half-barbarian origins (he was supposed to have spent his childhood as a shepherd boy in the mountains of Thrace), his superhuman strength and cultural and mental primitiveness was intended to create the image of a man unworthy of the throne of the Caesars. Thus we have good reason to suspect the apocryphal nature of the *Historia Augusta*'s relation of Maximinus' appearance at the games which Septimius Severus hosted in honour of his son Geta (HA, *Duo Maximini*, II-III). Maximinus' entrance onto the world stage resembles a fairground lark, with a coarse rustic simpleton beating the wrestling champions of the assembled legions, running as fast as the Emperor's steed, and gobbling down vast quantities of wine and meat. Impressed by such physical prowess, Severus is supposed to have received him into his bodyguard. The *Historia Augusta* paints the picture of a cruel, bloodthirsty and ignorant buffoon suitable for terrifying young children, but hardly worthy of a skilled military leader (Historia Augusta, *Duo Maximini*, VIII). His name, which may be translated as "big little one", has led to speculation whether this might actually be a derisive nickname poking fun at his herculean physique and supposedly feeble mind. This is highly unlikely however.

In view of all these anecdotes and unreliable accounts we tend to overlook that Maximinus must have been an intelligent, experienced, dutiful, charismatic and strong-minded military leader who was honestly concerned for the security and stability of the Empire and whose campaigns on the frontiers were extremely successful. Monuments indicate that the construction and maintenance of the Empire's roads was an additional undertaking Maximinus seems to have pursued, presumably for strategic reasons. Maximinus Thrax – soldier and innovator, but also political precedent.

The year 238 AD had seen no less than six emperors. Maximinus was the first of the soldier emperors who were now to determine the Empire's fate in breathtaking succession. Of these twenty rulers (if we take into account the renegade Gallic Empire that existed from 260 to 274 AD) only two died natural deaths, the other were assassinated by their own soldiery, were killed in battle, or – as was to happen to the unfortunate Valerian – died in captivity.

In political matters, the military eclipsed the Senate; in rapid succession the legions proclaimed rulers and pretenders, and disposed of them. Although Michael SOMMER has pointed out that throughout its existence the Roman Empire lived in a state of almost constant crisis and that some areas remained untouched by the developments described, the 3rd century was remarkable even by these standards[16]. The Empire staggered as civil war and enemy incursions drained it of its resources. In the east, the Persians went onto the offensive with the Goths ravaging the Balkans. Parts of the western Empire seceded. As a consequence of inward and outward strife many provinces fell into economic decline, inflation soared. Landscapes became deserted as people fled to the towns and cities for greater safety. This was aggravated by a climate change, which caused the problem of food to become precarious in many parts of the Empire. Strong rulers like Gallienus, Aurelian, Probus and Diocletian prevented complete collapse. Diocletian's far-reaching reforms initiated revival and secured a new phase of recovery, relative stability and a certain prosperity towards the end of the century. Under Constantine the Empire would flourish once more during a final era of glory in late antiquity.

This book will seek to present the soldiers who during five decades defended the Empire against its enemies from abroad and self-confidently determined its political fate.

16 SOMMER, p. 96 ff.

THE ROMAN ARMY AT THE BEGINNING OF THE THIRD CENTURY AD

Be harmonious, enrich the soldiers, and scorn all other men.
Advice of the dying Septimius Severus to his sons

The legions

In spite of some reforms and changes which will be duly addressed, the basic structure of the Roman army had remained unchanged since the early days of the Principate. Roman tactics and strategy still relied mainly on the heavy legionary infantry, supported by more lightly armed auxiliaries. The cavalry was still largely recruited from provincials. This was supplemented by units specialising in specific combat techniques, mostly recruited from peoples well-schooled in the use of certain arms and skills, e. g. Syrian archers or Balearic slingers.

That said, the Roman Army at the beginning of the 3rd century AD was starting to undergo a phase of change, both regarding tactics and equipment. The reforms of Septimius Severus triggered many of these developments, as we shall see. The army of Maximinus Thrax was in many respects a product of his predecessors.

At the army's core remained the *legio*, an infantry unit consisting (on paper) of ca. 5,500 troops recruited from Roman citizens; we must suppose however that it was never up to full strength due to detachments serving elsewhere (*vexillationes*), sick cases and soldiers being away on special duties and business abroad. Each legion consisted of ten cohorts, of which the first was double strength. Each cohort was subdivided into six centuries of approximately 80 soldiers each (the first cohort's centuries numbering 160). Each century in turn was subdivided into ten *contubernia* mess groups of eight soldiers each[17]. At this time each legion still had 120 horsemen at its disposal, who served as scouts and despatch riders[18]. They were allocated to the individual centuries and commanded by a *centurio*. With the exception of the Egyptian legions (Egypt was an Imperial province since it provided the corn vital for the food supply of Rome) and the three new legions raised by Septimius Severus all legions were commanded by a senatorial *legatus*, who was aided by a tribune also of senatorial rank (*tribunes laticlavius*), and six equestrian tribunes (*tribuni angusticlavii*)[19]. Third in command was the camp prefect (*praefectus castrorum*), who was normally an equestrian and a professional soldier. Then there were the legion's fifty-nine centurions, those of the first cohort being the most senior (*primi ordines*). The many junior officers (*principales*) ranked below the centurions, among them the eagle bearer (*aquilifer*), the standard bearers (*signiferi* and *vexillarii*), the centurions' deputies (*optiones*), doctors (*medici*), officers in charge of the camp hospitals (*optiones valetudinariorum*), and officers of the watchword (*tesserarii*). Soldiers with special duties included musicians (*cornicines* and *tubicines*), medical orderlies (*capsarii*), apothecaries (*seplasiarii*), vets (*veterinarii*), drill masters (*campidoctores* and *exercitatores*), scribes and clerks (*librarii*), military police (*statores*), intelligence officers (*speculatores*),and soldiers in charge of their unit's administration (*cornicularii*), to name but a few. Soldiers with special qualifications were excused fatigues and were hence named *immunes*. According to qualification and rank, these soldiers received either double pay (*duplicarii*) or one and a half times the normal soldier's pay (*sesquiplicarii*). The common soldiers (*milites gregarii*), being simple *munifices* ("workers"), could only hope for the next *donativum*.

Severus' decision not to place the newly raised legions *I-III Parthicae* under the command of a senatorial legate soon became common practice. The *legati* and senatorial *tribuni laticlavii* were still often enough men who did military service as part of their political careers (*cursus honorum*). Hence they often lacked the military knowledge and experience that was increasingly vital in such positions. The notoriously distrustful Severus also seems to have viewed them as something of a liability. He preferred equestrian officers, whose inferior social standing and ambitions obliged them to him. At a time in which the legions were constantly forced to send detachments (*vexillationes*) to fight in different campaigns, it was normally left to the equestrian *praefectus castrorum* to command the rump force that held the garrison. The received official command structure was thus not yet officially abolished but was becoming increasingly obsolete as strategic circumstances changed[20]. Tackling the mounting pressure on the Empire's frontiers required professional soldiers, not political careerists. We last hear of the rank of *tribu-*

17 According to SYVÄNNE, each *contubernium* in fact consisted of ten men, the section being commanded by an appropriately named *decanus*. The *contubernium* thus would have consisted of eight soldiers, one recruit (*tiro*) and one servant (*calo*). The latter two would not have gone into action but tended to the soldiers's equipment and the mule, and helped to guard the baggage train (SYVÄNNE, Ilkka, *Caracalla. A Military Biography*, Barnsley 2017, p. 9 f.).

18 SYVÄNNE, pointing to relevant sections in John Lydus (*De Magistratibus*, I. 16 and I. 46) and Pseudo-Hyginus (V. 30) claims that the legionary cavalry numbered 600 men in 22 squadrons of 32 horsemen, each commanded by a decurion (SYVÄNNE 2017, p. 8-9).

19 To be counted among the equestrian order (*ordo equester*), a citizen had to own assets amounting to at least four hundred thousand sesterces in the official census. They wore a narrow stripe on their togas (*angustus clavus*), and a golden ring.

20 STROBEL, Karl, „Strategy and Army Structure between Septimius Severus and Constantine the Great", in Paul ERDKAMP (ed.), *A Companion to the Roman Army*, Maldon/Oxford/Victoria 2007, p. 267-285, p. 272.

nus laticlavius in the year 249 AD[21]. After this point it was equestrian officers who were to determine the army's and the Empire's fate, though at the time of Maximinus Thrax' reign this development was still very much in its early stages. Gallienus officially abolished the senatorial ranks in the army's command structure around the year 260 AD[22].

In the course of the 3rd century AD, provinces exposed to acute military danger required commanders who could take independent action if a large-scale enemy attack occurred. The imperilled frontier defences were thus frequently put under the responsibility of so-called *duces*. A *dux* had originally been an officer assigned temporary overall command in a desperate situation, but *duces* took over in most frontier provinces as the century progressed. Maximinus himself had served as *dux ripae* in Mesopotamia, with the fortress of Dura Europos as his headquarters.[23]

The increasing professionalisation of the army's command structure offered numerous chances of social advancement. Provided that they could show a certain degree of education, experienced soldiers that had risen from the ranks by merit and had become *primi ordines* were able to become members of the *ordo equester* and command legions and auxiliary units[24]. These old hands would have kept an expert's watchful eye on the actions of their imperial commanders-in-chief. There are hints that the early third century saw the emergence of a kind of general staff, a cadre pool called the *protectores*, from which officers were selected to lead vexillations and other formations[25]. In the course of this development the army became a new social élite which was to provide the Empire with numerous rulers.

Maximinus' proclamation underscored the increasing importance of Rome's Danube legions, of which there were no less than eight. Ragnar HUND stresses the fact that the crack Danube forces rose to become the cream of the Roman army henceforth. Brought in to deal with all kinds of crises and threats, these legions fought in various campaigns on various fronts[26]. This was due not only to their efficiency but also to the fact that the location of their garrisons enabled them to swiftly reach both the eastern and western provinces.

The Severan period saw the first *numeri* established from legionary infantry. They must not be confused with the auxiliary units of the same name. Legionary *numeri* were former *vexillationes* which instead of returning to their parent legions were permanently stationed in other regions, often where they had last been on campaign. These new units were henceforth often named simply after their garrison town or region[27]. This practice proves the dire circumstances which forced the Empire to constantly dispatch troops to areas under threat without completely exposing the frontier provinces, a measure which was proving both ineffective and costly. Here we may discern the first steps in the direction of a reorganisation which was to reshape the Roman army in late antiquity. Indeed the constant military conflicts of the third century had as a consequence the fragmentation of the traditional ten-cohort legion, which ultimately created new types of legions in the army of the fourth and fifth centuries. The employment of entire, full-strength legions became increasingly rare even though it was not altogether discontinued. The result of the continuous dispatch of vexillations to often remote theatres of war was a gradual corrosion of the parent units' numbers and the emergence of new, smaller legions that originated from these vexillations, or *numeri*[28]. A look at the *Notitia Dignitatum*, an administrative handbook dating from the fifth century, shows that the origins of several units based in different regions may be traced back to one and the same original parent legion. It remains a matter of debate whether the considerable increase in the number of units also meant that the number of soldiers serving in the army rose accordingly.

In the year 197 AD Rome had at its disposal thirty legions, a number which was augmented that same year by Septimius Severus with the creation of three more legions (*legiones I-III Parthicae*). Two of these legions were intended as garrison troops for the newly-created province of Mesopotamia, where they were at first stationed at Singara (Iraq) and Rhesaina (Syria). *Legio II Parthica* was garrisoned at Albanum south of Rome. It consisted of seasoned troops drawn from the Danube legions which Severus was able to trust with keeping an eye on both the fickle Senate and the unruly population. The size of the force based in Italy was also considered a deterrent to any potential usurper. The stationing of troops on Italian soil constituted a political affront, Italy being (Rome and its garrison excepted) an area troops were only permitted to enter with the Senate's explicit consent. *Legio II Parthica* became an élite unit, receiving something like guard sta-

21 Ibid., p. 271.

22 SOMMER, p. 94.

23 ELTON, Hugh, „Military Forces", in SABIN, Philip/VAN WEES, Hans/ WHITBY, Michael (Hrsg.): *The Cambridge History of Greek and Roman Warfare, Vol. II: Rome from the late Republic to the late Empire, Part II: The Late Empire*, Cambridge 2007
, p. 270-309, p. 273.

24 SOMMER, p. 94.

25 STROBEL, p. 273; SOUTHERN claims this corps was established only under Gallienus and Valerian (*The Roman Empire from Severus to Constantine*, Abingdon/New York^2 2014, p. 179). The name *protectores* was used for Imperial bodyguards and members of the Imperial retinue.

26 HUND, Ragnar, „Maximiniana. Zu einem ehrenden Beinamen militärischer Formationen im frühen 3. Jahrhundert n. Chr.", in PÖPPELMANN, Heike/DEPPMAYER, Korana/STEINMETZ, Wolf-Dieter (eds.), *Roms vergessener Feldzug. Die Schlacht am Harzhorn*, Darmstadt 2013, p. 108-116, p. 112.

27 PFERDEHIRT/SCHOLZ, p. 43.

28 COWAN, Ross, *Imperial Roman Legionary AD 161-284*, Oxford 2003, p. 18 f.

tus. The stationing of a legion in Italy was not simply a novelty in political terms, it was also unusual in that nearly all other legions were stationed along the frontiers[29]. This strategy's flaw was the fact that the core of the Empire was extremely vulnerable to enemy attack once this defensive cordon had been breached. The Marcomanni had succeeded in getting as far as northern Italy before being repulsed. The creation of a Roman mobile field force in the course of the third century may be viewed as a reaction to this decisive strategic weakness. The stationing of *legio II Parthica* in Italy as a fast-moving Imperial striking force for military emergencies constitutes a first step in this direction. Karl STROBEL sees these changes at the beginning of the third century as the nucleus of the later mobile field armies, a sustainable position if we consider that the successors of Septimius Severus employed a core of troops in numerous campaigns in different areas of the Empire, e. g. Alexander Severus in Persia and Germany, Maximinus in Germany and on the Danube, and in northern Italy. This became common practice under their successors. The armies of Gallienus and Valerian were no longer completely dissolved after the end of a campaign but served as a basis for further developments under Aurelian, Probus, and Diocletian.[30]

Regarding recruitment, the third century seems to have formed something of a turning point. Septimius Severus had created a precedent when he had disbanded the Praetorians, who had hitherto been recruited mostly from Italians, and replaced them with soldiers from the Pannonian legions that were loyal to him. Like the Praetorians, the legions were the prerogative of Roman citizens, while free inhabitants of the Empire could join the auxiliaries, which gave them the chance to win Roman citizenship for themselves and their descendants after 25 years' service. We shall further discuss this in the context of the *Constitutio Antoniniana*.

Right into the second century AD, Italians had dominated in the legions, but in the wake of the consolidation of the Empire and the stationing of legions in permanent garrisons these troops also began to recruit provincials. Roman citizenship spread as veterans settled locally. The remark *origo castris* ("from the camp") often to be found in Roman recruiting lists of the 2nd and 3rd centuries points to the recruitment of the sons of local veterans, but may also be a phrase indicating that in times of crisis the regulations were not always scrupulously observed[31]. Of course the legions did not merely rely on the garrison's immediate vicinities for recruitment but drew potential soldiers from the entire province in which they were stationed; the sources show that recruits also travelled from other, more remote parts of the Empire to join their legion. Constant postings saw to it that individual army units eventually developed into a quite heterogeneous ethnic mix[32].

Since vexillations did not always return to their parent units, they were often forced to develop a completely new recruiting system at their new base, as they lacked the refined and long-established logistics and administration at the disposal of their original garrisons. What is more, these vexillations were often on the move for years, fighting in different campaigns in various parts of the Empire. Until his elevation to the throne, Maximinus had held the position of *praefectus tironibus*, the staff officer responsible for recruitment and training in Alexander Severus's army. We may conclude from this that the legions on campaign did not simply draw replacements from their parent units but also relied on training recruits locally in a camp immediately attached to the field army's current garrison. In this context STROBEL observes that Maximinus initiated a recruitment programme for men from the Italic cities, obviously to bring his army up to strength[33].

From the second century onwards, most non-Italic recruits hailed from the "old" provinces of Gaul, Baetica in Spain, Africa and Macedonia. Towards the end of the century men were increasingly recruited from the Danube provinces of Illyria, Thrace and Pannonia. This development intensified when the breakaway Gallic Empire (260-274) made large parts of the western Empire inaccessible to Imperial recruitment. During his reign, Maximinus Thrax attempted to reform the recruitment system by again trying to integrate the populations of the Italic cities (s. above), but this seems to have been an ephemeral measure. In the early third century, legionaries from *legio II Parthica* did indeed come from Italy, but a very large number of its soldiers hailed from Thrace and Illyria. The Danube provinces henceforth formed the social and military backbone of the Roman army of the third and early fourth centuries. In the turmoil of civil wars and campaigns against the Empire's foreign enemies its officers rose to the highest positions, and ultimately were to reach for the imperial purple.[34]

In the first and second centuries legionaries had served for 25 years. Since soldiers were discharged every two years only, this meant that many effectively served for 26 years. Under Septimius Severus the legions discharged soldiers annually; nevertheless, the length of service seems to have remained at 26 years.

What can be said regarding the legionaries' pay? Unfortunately, historians are far from unanimous regarding the question of the soldiers' income in the third century, and which emperor raised the soldiers' pay by which amount. It is also extremely difficult to clearly ascertain the Roman currency's purchasing power at this time. On entering

29 With the exception of the Spanish provinces.

30 STROBEL, p. 269 f.

31 SOUTHERN, Patricia, *The Roman Army. A History 753 BC-AD 476*, Stroud 2014, p. 225; LE BOHEC, Yann, *Die Römische Armee. Von Augustus bis zu Konstantin dem Großen*, Stuttgart 1993, p. 88.

32 SOUTHERN, *Roman Army* (2014), p. 224.

33 STROBEL, p. 170.

34 Ibid., p. 278.

Plate III

Legionary *lanciarius*

This legionary 'light bob' wears a bronze helmet of Rainau-Buch type, decorated with a horsehair crest (*crista*). In contrast to helmets of Niederbieber type, the crossed reinforcements protecting the skull are not attached but simply embossed. Over his *subarmalis* with attached *pteryges* he wears a *lorica segmentata* of Newstead type, which at first glance may seem an odd choice for a light infantryman; however, while not seriously impeding movement, the *lorica segmentata* offers more freedom of movement for the legs. A strip of metal from a *lorica segmentata* from an unknown site has two coins riveted to it, one of the Emperor Domitian, the other of the Emperor Maximinus Thrax. Whether this was simply a reliable means of transporting one's financial reserves, or a talisman, or a make-do repair, remains impossible to tell.

For improved manoeuverability, the soldier prefers puttees (*fasciae crurales*) to greaves. This is confirmed by pictorial contemporary sources. He is armed with the *spatha*, a heavy dagger of Künzing type for close-quarter fighting, and several javelins (*lanceae*) for skirmishing with enemy infantry and horsemen. A well-known if rather crudely executed grave stele of a *lanciarius* of the Second Parthian Legion discovered at Apamea (SYR) shows the deceased carrying a large quiver of javelins in his right hand. The mode of carrying the quiver slung across the back is conjectural yet appears feasible in view of the weapons' length. Since shields were often dished, the javelins could not be carried in the left hand due to the shield's cavity.

The *lanciarius*'s shield is of the conventional oval type though smaller, since the Apamea stele shows a much smaller shield. Nevertheless, fast-moving light infantry had to rely on shields for protection when there were no comrades to guard their flanks. The unwieldy heavy infantry *scutum* would have proved utterly unsuitable for the *lanciarii*'s daring task. The shield motif follows an example excavated at Dura. It is of interest that the deity depicted wears a similar helmet to those of the gods on the fresco depicting the religious ceremony of *cohors XX Palmyrenorum* at the Bel temple at Dura.

S Borin '19

Plate IV

Centurion

A grim-faced centurion surveys his men on the march. He wears a helmet of Niederbieber type with a transverse crest (*crista transversa*) indicating his rank, and a *lorica segmentata* of Newstead type over a padded *subarmalis* with double rows of fringed leather *pteryges*. His legs are protected by a pair of simple iron greaves. His *vitis*, the dreaded gnarled vine stick of the centurions, was being replaced at this time by a straight rod with a mushroom-shaped knob frequently depicted on contemporary centurions' grave steles. The legion being on the march, our centurion is not wearing the leather harness displaying his military decorations (*dona militaria*). He will don these for battle and on parade, the bracelet (*armilla*) on his right arm serving as the only hint that this man is a highly decorated, battle-scarred veteran who will lead his century from the front when they go into action. Despite the appalling brutality many of these officers exercised to instil discipline, they were also prepared to sacrifice themselves for their men and to die where they stood when circumstances demanded. Every legion possessed fifty-nine of these highly experienced leaders, who guaranteed a constantly high degree of military efficieny, training and professionalisation within the ranks.

To protect himself from the cold, the centurion wears a dark red fringed *sagum* with tufts as attested by pictorial evidence. On parade he would replace this cloak with the ceremonial red *paludamentum* to be draped over his shoulder and left arm. His tent and equipment are being carried by a mule tended by his two *calones* (servants).

the army, the recruit received a bounty of 300 sesterces. Soldiers were paid three times per year, but there were deductions for food, clothing, equipment and weapons. These deductions seem to have decreased in the 2nd century, and the Emperor granted an additional subsidy for the above-mentioned expenses. The soldiers' pay was regularly supplemented by considerable benefits (*donativa*) on specific occasions. On discharge, the legionary was paid a certain sum according to rank and length of service; under Caracalla, this was 20, 000 sesterces for legionaries and 25, 000 for Praetorians[35]. The soldier was also able to sell his equipment to his unit's armoury.[36]

Septimius Severus raised the soldiers' pay considerably (whether he doubled their incomes or merely raised them by 50 per cent remains a matter of debate[37]). This was supplemented by the afore-mentioned *donativa*. Junior officers like the *tesserarius* received one and a half times this amount and thus belonged to the salary group of *sesquiplicarii*. Standard bearers and *optiones* received double pay (*duplicarii*). The centurions were paid according to rank. Under Domitian a centurion of the *primi ordines* received the sum of 27, 000 sesterces, which was double the amount of a regular legionary centurion. The *primus pilus* received the proud sum of 54, 000 sesterces per annum. Although these specific sums had become obsolete by the early third century, we may assume that the relations between the salaries had not.

With his father's advice on his mind, Severus' son Caracalla on his accession again doubled his soldiers' pay. Maximinus in turn seems to have doubled this amount once more, which is a likely explanation for his unpopular fiscal measures[38]. It should not be overlooked that the third century was a time of soaring inflation, and the content of silver to the *denarius* decreased dramatically. The above-mentioned raises of the soldiers' pay must be viewed in this context. What at first glance appears to us as a pay raise of astronomical proportions may in fact merely be an adjustment to accommodate contemporary realities. Nevertheless, the soldier's profession in the early third century seems to have been a profitable one.

35 Cf. RATHBONE, Dominic, „Welfare and the State: A: Military Finance and Supply", in: SABIN, Philip/VAN WEES, Hans/WHITBY, Michael (eds.), *The Cambridge History of Greek and Roman Warfare, Vol. II: Rome from the late Republic to the late Empire, Part II: The Late Empire*, Cambridge 2007, p. 158-197, p. 158 ff. There were four sesterces to a *denarius*, 25 *denarii* forming the equivalent of one *aureus*. The *Antoninianus* introduced by Caracalla had a nominal value of two *denarii*, but was probably worth only 1, 5 *denarii*. Its value rapidly declined due to its constantly diminishing content of silver.

36 SPEIDEL, Michael, „Pay and Income: Principate", in LE BOHEC, Yann (ed.), *The Encyclopedia of the Roman Army*, Chichester 2015, p. 738-740, p. 739.

37 Cf. PFERDEHIRT/SCHOLZ, p. 44, COWAN (2003), p. 10.

38 S. above; SPEIDEL claims that Caracalla only raised the soldiers' incomes by half.

Regarding the development of the soldiers' pay, HAYNES puts forward the following figures for the late 2nd and early 3rd century (p. a. in denarii)[39]:

Emperor	legionary	auxiliary infantry	*cohors* cavalry	*ala* cavalry
Septimius Severus	2,400	2,000	2,400	2,800
Caracalla	3,600	3,000	3,600	4,200
Maximinus	7,200	6,000	7,200	8,400

One of Septimius Severus's better-known measures is his reform of the soldiers' position regarding their families. Relying on Herodian, many scholars once held the view that the Emperor abolished the army's ban on marriage. This viewpoint is now widely considered as an over-simplification. Historians now believe that Severus merely allowed the soldiers to live with their women outside the walls of the camp. The ban was still in effect, but it ultimately caused the soldiers' reluctance to serve in areas situated far away from their garrison towns, since it meant leaving behind loved ones without any securities to fall back on should they fail to return.[40]

The *auxilia*

The Roman army's second pillar were the *auxilia*, infantry and cavalry units recruited from free-born inhabitants of the Empire (*peregrini*), which were commanded either by prefects or tribunes. Ever since the days of the Republic Rome had received allies and foreign troops into the ranks of its armies in order to increase their effectivity as a fighting force or to compensate for tactical weaknesses, e. g. as cavalrymen or light infantry. A few occasions of severe crisis excepted, the legions were closed to non-citizens. The chance to receive Roman citizenship for oneself and one's descendants after completion of service was a strong incentive for recruitment into the auxiliaries. This grant of citizenship was documented in the form of a bronze tablet (*diploma*) signed by witnesses, several of which have been found on military sites. In this context the *Constitutio Antoniniana* poses a specific problem. The granting of Roman citizenship to all free-born inhabitants of the Roman Empire made obsolete the most obvious distinction between the legions and the *auxilia*. It is reasonable to assume that the legions continued to recruit citizens but were now able to choose from a much wider range of potential recruits. The *auxilia* were now also in the position to recruit Roman citizens but were probably

39 HAYNES, p. 48. Cf. below.

40 PFERDEHIRT/SCHOLZ, p. 43.

also open to men from beyond the Empire's frontiers[41]. To speak of a "barbarisation" of the Roman army in this period (or any other at that) would be a complete misconception.

33 legions would not nearly have had the sufficient manpower to control the Empire and guard its frontiers. It was left to the auxiliaries to protect and control the frontiers in times of peace. The number of auxiliaries in relation to the legions was approximately 1,5:1. It is very hard to estimate the overall number of auxiliaries however; estimates vary between 180, 000 (SPAUL) and ca. 281, 000 (HOLDER). These considerable divergences result from the fact that we have several units with identical names whose presence can occasionally be ascertained in different places at one time, and estimates that a much higher percentage of units was part-mounted even though their names do not define them as such (some scholars claim that sources indicate about 70 per cent of all auxiliary foot units actually being part-mounted). Historians believe that Septimius Severus increased the army not just by raising three new legions but also by forming twenty new auxiliary cohorts.[42]

Since the early Principate the *auxilia* had been organised into cavalry regiments (*alae*, "wings"), infantry cohorts (*cohortes peditatae*) and part-mounted cohorts (*cohortes equitatae*), with the cavalry numbering about one fifth of the latter units' overall strength. These regular units were supplemented by irregular auxiliary *numeri*, who were often commanded by their own chieftains and supported the regular troops by scouting and patrolling the frontier regions. The organisation of the *auxilia* in comparatively small units made it possible for them to be employed much more flexibly and with less logistical effort than the unwieldy legions; they could be dispatched and transferred at short notice and with comparative ease, their smaller numbers making them ideally suited for garrisoning the frontier defences, patrolling and policing the frontier, and keeping an eye on the hinterland. The principle was based less on concentration than on even distribution. It is a well-known fact that in earlier times the Romans had raised auxiliary regiments from the defeated tribes and frequently employed them far from their homelands in order to remove the military threat of rebellion and to prevent fraternisation between the local populace and occupying forces. Risings of well-trained and well-equipped auxiliaries could pose a serious threat, as the Batavian revolt on the Rhine in AD 69 had shown.

In the second century we may assume the following (ideal) unit strengths:

Ala milliaria	722 horsemen in 32 *turmae* (768 including officers)
Ala quingenaria	480 horsemen in 16 *turmae* (512 including officers)
Cohors peditata milliaria	800 infantry in 10 *centuriae*
Cohors peditata quingenaria	480 infantry in 6 *centuriae*
Cohors equitata milliaria	1040 soldiers (800 infantry in 10 *centuriae*; 240 horsemen in 8 *turmae*)
Cohors equitata quingenaria	600 soldiers (probably 480 infantry in 6 *centuriae*; 120 horsemen in 4 *turmae*)

The majority of auxiliary units consisted of regular medium cavalrymen and foot soldiers, but in contrast to the legions the strength of the *auxilia* lay in their tactical flexibility and variety. The mixed composition of the *cohortes equitatae* of both foot and horse, for example, allowed for various effective modes of employment, especially in the frontier regions, where forts and walls had to be manned, minor incursions contained and roads policed. On campaign the cavalry contingents of several *cohortes equitatae* were combined to form larger battle units.

In the ranks of the *auxilia* could be found numerous specialists, whose weapons derived from the traditional fighting techniques of their native peoples and whose skills now augmented the Roman arsenal. For example, Thracians, Pannonians, Gauls and Germans were renowned for their audacity and skill as horsemen, the Syrian and Arabian tribes supplied recruits for the *cohortes* and *alae sagittariorum* (foot and horse archers), Palmyrenes and Arabs served in the *dromedarii* (camel corps[43]), Moors and Numidians in the *Mauri* (North African light horse), and Alpine Raetians in the *cohortes gaesatorum* (units armed with the *gaesum*, a heavy Celtic barbed lance). There were regiments of mounted archers and the first units of extra-heavily armoured cavalry modelled on Parthian and Persian units. These troops were at first recruited from cap-

41 In the third century AD the Roman army for the first time had within its ranks entire units of soldiers from outside the Empire's borders, e. g. a regiment of cataphracts from Sarmatia stationed in Deva (Chester) on Hadrian's Wall. These soldiers were probably former prisoners of war taken in Marcus Aurelius' Marcomannic Wars. Even before the *Constitutio Antoniniana* entire units of auxiliaries had received the honorary title of *civium Romanorum*, e. g. the Second Raetian Cohort based at the Saalburg fort in Germany.

42 PFERDEHIRT/SCHOLZ, p.43.

43 There were both complete *alae* of *dromedarii* and smaller contingents assigned to the *cohortes equitatae* in the east. These did not nominally belong to the cohort's cavalry section but served as scouts and patrolmen.

Plate V

Cavalryman of *Ala II Flavia Pia Fidelis*

Stationed at Aalen in modern Baden-Württemberg in Severan times, the milliary *Ala II Flavia Pia Fidelis* was the élite cavalry formation on the Raetian *limes* and as such would have taken part in Maximinus' German campaign. Its camp was the largest on the Raetian frontier. It gained the epithet *Pia Fidelis Domitiana* for its loyalty to the Flavians during the Saturninus revolt in 89 AD, losing *Domitiana* after Domitian's *damnatio memoriae*. The Severan epithet *Alexandriana* is given on an inscription found at Aalen (AE 1986, 529). It is highly probable that *Ala II Flavia* abandoned this epithet after Alexander Severus' murder in AD 235.

The *alae* formed the cream of the Roman cavalry arm. Equipment was testimony to the soldiers' military pride, status, and efficiency. The horseman wears an elaborately worked masked helmet of *mater castrorum* type, excavated at Straubing. These helmets were once considered precious accoutrements in the context of parades and cavalry sports manoeuvres, but recently have been identified by some scholars as part of the cavalry's battle equipment. Alternatively, he could be wearing an open-faced helmet of Heddernheim or Niederbieber type. The soldiers' neck is protected by a simple scarf (*focale*). As his fellow soldier in the *equites singulares*, the horseman can afford an elaborate scale cuirass whose protective qualities are enhanced by leather *pteryges*. According to military fashion he wears breeches and boots with spurs, the knees and shins being protected by a pair of decorated greaves (*ocreae*) discovered at Regensburg-Kumpfmühl. He wears a military decoration in form of a bracelet (*armilla*)

The cavalryman, shown here on outpost duty, is equipped with a *spatha* and lance for close quarter fighting; the lance (*hasta*) could also be thrown. When skirmishing, he will resort to a quiver of javelins hanging from the saddle at his right side. The cavalry practised the throwing of javelins as part of the spectacular *hippika gymnasia*. The oval, slightly concave shield has been painted with the unit's name and mascots, and various allegorical images (Mars, Hercules, busts of Minerva and Roma, Pegasus). His rolled-up cloak (*sagum*) has been tied to the saddle and is just visible behind the shield.

The horse equipment follows the depiction of the horse of an unknown member of the Imperial horse guard found at Rome (cf. plate XII). The horse's hind quarters are protected by a series of studded leather straps passing under the tail. The chamfrom was found at Straubing.

ALA II FLAVIA P F
S. Bojin '19

Plate VI

Auxiliary Infantryman of *Cohors II Raetorum Civium Romanorum*

From around 135 AD to the fall of the *limes* defences in 260 AD, the probably part-mounted Second Cohort of Raetians formed the garrison of the Saalburg fort which guarded the strategically important route across the ridge of the Taunus hills into the Rhine and Main valleys. Previously the cohort had been stationed further north at Butzbach. Originally the cohort had been recruited in the 1st century AD among the warlike Celtic mountain tribes of the Alpine province of Raetia. At some time the cohort was summarily granted Roman citizenship; other attested epithets are *Antoniniana* (awarded by Caracalla) and *Severiana* (awarded by Alexander Severus).

Knotting his scarf (*focale*), a glum-faced infantryman prepares for sentry duty or patrol on a winter's day. It was these soldiers' duty to man the watchtowers and forts along the *limes* and to control the traffic passing to and fro along the border. They patrolled the walls, palisades and frontier roads, and contained enemy incursions until reinforcements arrived. The garrisons of the *limes* fortresses suffered heavy losses as a consequence of the Germanic invasions after 233 AD and will have welcomed an emperor who meant business when it came to dealing with the troublesome barbarians.

The soldier wears a bronze helmet of Niederbieber type. The unusual attachment of the peak and the perforated cheekguard are attested from various finds. Helmets with the peak pointing upwards have been excavated at Friedberg and Osterburken. Over his padded *subarmalis* he has donned a mail coat with long sleeves. Coats like this are shown on reliefs on the arch of Diocletian. His simple ring buckle belt, sword and baldric reflect the comparatively lowly status of the men of the *cohortes equitatae*.

His heavy dagger (*pugio*) is worn on a separate baldric. A hoard of these weapons was excavated in the headquarters building (*principia*) at the fortress of Künzing (Quintana) on the Danube *limes*. Daggers like this seem to have formed part of the troops' standard equipment.

Over his woollen breeches the soldier wears a pair of simple iron greaves also found at Künzing. To protect his feet from the cold damp he might be wearing woollen socks (*udones*) inside his military boots. He has put on his heavy woollen fringed military cloak (*sagum*) against the effects of sleet and snow. The wool fat will keep him warm and prevent rust damaging his armour.

The soldier is equipped with a stout spear, which he has propped up against his dished shield. The outside surface is colourfully painted with his unit's device, and he has inscribed his name on the inside to avoid confusion in the confinement of the barrack's small equipment room when the trumpets sound the alarm.

CO

Plate VII

Cavalry standard bearer of *Cohors I Germanorum Civium Romanorum*

At the beginning of the third century AD, the First Cohort of Germans formed the garrison of the Upper German *limes* fortress located at Jagsthausen in Baden-Württemberg. Previously it had been stationed at Bad Wimpfen. *Cohors I Germanorum Civium Romanorum* was a quingenary cohort and very probably part-mounted (BAATZ (1974), REUTER/THIEL (2015)). The painting shows the standard bearer (*vexillarius*) of the cohort's cavalry section (each *turma* would have had a separate *signum* standard). Similar to 18th century grenadier battalions composed of troops from several regiments, the cavalry squadrons of several *cohortes equitatae* would have been combined to form cavalry units of *ala* size on campaign.

As a junior officer (*principalis*), the soldier wears equipment of a quality generally superior to that of the rank and file. His most conspicuous piece of armour is surely his bronze helmet of Guisborough/Chalon type, excavated at Rusovce (SLK). Its unusual crenellated shape is reminiscent of a tower with an eagle perched on the battlements. Eagles also adorn the cheek-guards. The browband is decorated with the depiction of a warrior god flanked by winged victories holding laurel wreaths.

His mail coat, damaged by a glancing thrust from a German *framea* javelin, is decorated with several rows of bronze rings at cuffs and hem. The *subarmalis* has twin rows of red *pteryges* with yellow or gold fringes attached at the sleeves. The chestplates follow examples found at Orgovány (H). His belt buckles and baldric decorations are reconstructed according to various finds from Central Europe and the Middle East. The sword hilt follows finds from Roman *limes* fortresses at Buch and Niederbieber; the elaborate disc chape was also excavated at Niederbieber. The soldier wears the regular woollen breeches (*bracae*), and puttees for warmth and protection – being financially less well-off than the troopers of the pampered *alae*, this veteran cohort horseman makes do without greaves. His cloak sports a broad stripe and fringes, a fashion attested by fresco depictions at Luxor (EGY) from the late 3rd century. His rank is further emphasised by his red tunic decorated with purple stripes; it may well be a reward for valour, since the sources mention red tunics being awarded for bravery in the 3rd century[44].

The slightly dished oval shield has a decorated bronze or iron boss (obscured by the cloak), the simple rawhide binding stitched with red leather. The shield blazon is conjectural but follows general contemporary evidence.

Again we choose to follow the grave stele of an *eques singularis* found at the Via Labicana in Rome when reconstructing the horse harness. Since some of the neck straps depicted on the stele appear too tight to comfortably accommodate the horse's head, buckles have been added; this is mere academic guesswork however. To avoid slipping and sagging, the straps were probably attached to the horse's bridle. The bridle bit follows depictions from the 1st century AD; similar bits were in use in the 3rd century.

The *vexillum* standard consists of a spear with a red-painted shaft and a decorated iron point with a flag (*flammula*) suspended from a cross-bar. The flag itself follows the depiction of *cohors XX Palmyrenorum*'s standard on a fresco at Dura. It bears the inscription EQ COH I GER C R (*equites cohortis primae Germanorum civium Romanorum*). The Pegasus device is speculative but not unlikely as a badge for a mounted unit.

44 Emperor Valerian awarded the future Emperor Aurelian several red tunics in recognition of his skills as a general (*HA, Aurelian*, 13, 3)

EQ COH I
ERM C R
S. Bojin '19

tured Sarmatians (*cataphractarii*, or *clibanarii* [45]).While the regular cohorts and *alae* eventually began to recru it men from the immediate surroundings of their garrisons, the specialists continued to recruit men from their native lands [46]. The *Historia Augusta* records the presence of foreign auxiliaries in Maximinus' army when he crossed the Rhine (they had come with Alexander Severus from the East) [47]. The crack Osrhoenian archers and the Moorish javelineers excelled at the guerrilla warfare that was necessary to tackle the lightly armed German tribesmen in their native terrain.

The increased appreciation of military efficiency as a personal asset created new prospects for the *auxilia*. The career of decurion Barsemis Abbei, documented by an inscription excavated at Intercisa (H), may serve as an example in this respect. Barsemis was an Osrhoenian, his native country only having been recently incorporated as a regular province into the Empire by Septimius Severus. Barsemis joined an Osrhoenian *numerus* and was later made a decurion in the *ala Firma catafractaria*, so now served as a heavy cavalryman. The next step in his career was his appointment as a training officer of *cohors Hemesenorum sagittariorum*, another specialist unit. Barsenis' professionalism as an officer and his profound knowledge of weaponry had evidently been recognized and appreciated by his superiors. This military career may serve as proof that service in the 3rd century Roman Army offered even provincials without Roman citizenship a wide range of military careers, and, above all, considerable social advancement. [48]

The *alae* formed the cream of the *auxilia*, while the *cohortes equitatae* ranked oddly low in the military hierarchy. This lowly status is ascertained by a famous speech delivered by Hadrian to the Roman garrison at Lambaesis during a tour of inspection of the African provinces. He was present at a joint training exercise of the Third Augustan Legion, *Ala I Pannoniorum*, and *Cohors VI Commagenorum*. In his comment on the soldiers' performance, which is recorded in the form of an inscription at Lambaesis, Hadrian explicitly praises the cohort's cavalrymen, who had acquitted themselves well despite the previous manoeuvres of the *ala*'s glittering horsemen. The Commagenians' versatility under arms was much appreciated by the Emperor. In this context, Hadrian mentions the cohort cavalry's equipment, which he notes as inferior in quality to that of the *ala*, and their smaller horses. [49]

Since we know that the soldiers were required to purchase their own equipment, we may deduce from Hadrian's words that the troops' differing prestige manifested itself in their pay. A Praetorian received more pay than a legionary, who in turn was better off than an auxiliary. Auxiliary cavalrymen were better paid than their infantry counterparts, their equipment being more numerous and expensive, and each cavalryman had one or two grooms (*calones*). As stated above, we only have reliable sources for the 1st century AD regarding the soldiers' pay, while the 3rd century is largely a matter of conjecture. The frequently quoted formula according to which an auxiliary drew about one third of a legionary's pay (SPEIDEL assumes a quota of 5:6) [50], is an oversimplification which must be treated with caution in view of the differences between auxiliary cavalrymen and infantrymen, and between the *alae* horsemen and the troopers of the *cohortes equitatae*. We also do not know if the *auxilia* were entitled to the *donativa* which supplemented the legionaries' income, and whether they received a payment on discharge, or if (at least until the *Constitutio Antoniniana*) Roman citizenship was their only reward. To what extent the *Constitutio Antoniniana* influenced the auxiliaries' pay, is likewise more or less guesswork. GOLDSWORTHY holds the opinion that the *auxilia*'s pay may not have been standardised at all but instead varied according to province and ethnic background of the troops. [51]

45 The first unit of extra-heavy cavalry in the Roman army which can be ascertained is the *ala Gallorum et Pannoniorum catafractaria* in the early 2nd century AD (*HA* mentions this regiment in Alexander Severus' army). *Cataphractarii* and *clibanarii* were presumably differently armoured and equipped. The name *cataphractarii* is probably merely a general term. Since the Greek word κατάφρακτοσ (*kataphraktos*) simply means "covered" or "armoured", this has led to tremendous confusion. Nearly all Roman cavalry wore armour, thus almost every Roman horseman could call himself *cataphractarius*. However, the adoption of the Greek word seems to suggest some difference. Be that as it may, a *cataphractarius* was not necessarily a *clibanarius* on an armoured horse (gravestones show cataphracts on unarmoured horses). The word *clibanarius* is an etymological puzzler. It may have derived from a Persian word, or is an example of soldier's humour, *clibanus* meaning field oven, or baking pot. A telling name for a cavalryman sweating in his heavy armour!

46 Cf. HAYNES, Ian, *Blood of the Provinces. The Roman* Auxilia *and the Making of Provincial Society from Augustus to the Severans*, Oxford 2013, p. 145 ff.

47 *Historia Augusta*, XI, 7 f.

48 HAYNES, p. 92.

49 GOLDSWORTHY, Adrian, *The Complete Roman Army*, London 2003, p. 94 f.

50 ELLIOTT, Paul, *Legions in Crisis. Transformation of the Roman Soldier AD 192-284*, 2014, p. 26; SPEIDEL (in LE BOHEC 2015), p. 739.

51 GOLDSWORTHY, ibid.

The Roman garrison

Large numbers of troops with different tasks were based at the capital. The urban garrison was not a homogeneous group but consisted of various troop types. [52]

Pride of place goes to the *cohortes praetoriae*, the soldiers responsible for guarding the Emperor and his retinue. In the times of the Republic picked soldiers had guarded the general's tent (*praetorium*). During the civil wars generals had relied on élite troops from the legions and the *auxilia* for their personal safety. At the beginning of the Principate Augustus established the Praetorian cohorts as an integral part of the regular army. They were commanded by one or occasionally two equestrian Praetorian Prefects (*praefecti praetorio*) and thus removed from undesirable senatorial influence. The Praetorian Prefects were often given independent military commands.

To avoid the compromising of political sensitivities the Praetorian cohorts were first stationed in towns around the capital. Tiberius finally stationed them in the newly-constructed Praetorian camp (*castra praetoria*) in the north-eastern part of the city. The barracks were also the base of various other troops of the urban garrison, of whom more anon. The Praetorian infantry was supplemented by a cavalry contingent; one other horse guard unit were the crack *equites singulares Augusti*, Maximinus' old regiment[53]. Preserved documents (*laterculi*) suggest that the Praetorian cavalry (*equites cohortium praetoriarum*) were nominally assigned to the individual centuries. As was the case with the legionary cavalry, the Praetorian horse do not seem to have been organised in *turmae* and did thus not form an administratively independent unit[54].

The number of Praetorian cohorts (each was commanded by a *tribunus*) varied a good deal throughout the imperial era and has caused much controversy among historians. Although the Praetorian cohorts were recruited exclusively from Roman citizens and until the reign of Septimius Severus consisted almost entirely of Italians, they were not organised like the legions, but at first into nine cohorts (one short of a legion's ten). The reason for this number may possibly be found in Augustus' feel for the politically apt: in order to refute any kind of accusation that he was raising a private army, he sought to avoid organisational and numerical parallels[55].

As for the number and strength of the Praetorian cohorts, we are forced to rely on contradictory evidence. In the first century AD, the number of cohorts varied between nine under Augustus and sixteen under Vitellius; the notoriously tight-fisted Vespasian reduced their number once more to nine. Later the number of cohorts possibly rose to ten, maybe under Domitian. Cohort strength is difficult to ascertain, even if one takes into account the capacities of the Praetorian camp for accommodation. A majority among historians tends to assume that the cohorts were milliary units, every cohort consisting of six double centuries. Every cohort would thus have numbered 960 men, which would have made the *cohortes praetoriae* the equivalent of two full-strength regular legions. This view is encouraged by the fact that apart from guarding the imperial palaces, the Praetorian cohorts had numerous other tasks to fulfil, and they also accompanied the Emperor or members of his family on campaign[56].

As a reaction to the chaos which had ensued after the death of Commodus, Septimius Severus instigated a far-reaching change in the Praetorian cohorts' composition and organisation. In order to chastise them for the murder of his predecessor Pertinax, he dissolved the cohorts, only to immediately re-raise them with members of the Danube legions. The well-known tale according to which after Pertinax's death a decadent and greedy soldiery had auctioned off the imperial purple from the battlements of the *castra praetoria* was construed by the senators Cassius Dio and Herodian by exploiting a familiar cliché and is probably apocryphal. [57]

Severus not only changed the composition and strength of the Praetorians by raising cohort strength to 1,500, he also doubled the number of soldiers in every other unit of the Roman garrison; the strength of the *equites singulares*, the emperor's horse guard of hand-picked auxiliary cavalrymen (hence the name), rose to 2,000, which required the erection of a new camp to accommodate them, the *castra nova* on the Lateran hill. [58]

In our era, Praetorians seem to have served for 18 years; this is suggested by inscriptions[59], but due to the different recruitment method introduced by Severus this span of time must probably be regarded as the total amount of time spent serving in different branches of the army (s. below). A soldier might be recruited into the guard from the legions and posted back with a higher rank.

The method of forming the Praetorian cohorts from experienced and reliable soldiers from the legions was maintained after Severus' death and remained thus until the final disbanding of the guard by Constantine. Even though as a crack force the Praetorians had never been the emperor's lily boys, Severus had now formed an élite body based exclusively on merit and courage. Comparable to Napoleon's Old Guard, henceforth a Praetorian had

52 BUSCH, Alexandra, *Militär in Rom. Militärische und paramilitärische Einheiten im kaiserzeitlichen Stadtbild*, Wiesbaden 2011, p. 19.

53 This troop had first held the name of *Germani corporis custodes*; later they were called *Batavi* after their recruitment area.

54 BUSCH, p. 20.

55 BINGHAM, Sandra, *The Praetorian Guard. A HIstory of Rome's Élite Special Forces*, London/New York 2013, p. 52.

56 BINGHAM, p. 55f.

57 Ibid., p. 44 f.

58 PFERDEHIRT/SCHOLZ, p. 43; SPEIDEL Michael, *Riding for Caesar. The Roman Emperors' Horse Guards*, London 1994, p. 59.

59 COWAN, Ross, *Roman Guardsman 62 BC-AD 324*, Oxford 2014, p. 21.

Plate VIII

Praetorian guardsman on campaign

The depicted guardsman of *Cohors III Praetoria Pia Vindex* is a battle-hardened veteran of the Danube legions. The high quality of his equipment reflects his status as a member of an élite corps. The most conspicuous item is surely his magnificent bronze bipartite helmet of Worthing type with added crest. He wears a *lorica segmentata* of Newstead type over an arming doublet (*subarmalis*) with attached red leather *pteryges* and a red *tunica manicata*. His legwear under campaign conditions consists of the simple woollen breeches (*bracae*) and laced boots (*calcei, perones*) common to almost all units on the northern frontier at the time. His military belt (*cingulum*) is fastened with a square bronze buckle, the straps ending in two bronze pendants according to contemporary military fashion. The baldric (*balteus*) decorations follow various finds from different parts of the Empire (Zugmantel (D), Silistra (BG). The ivory eagle head hilt of the *spatha* has been reconstructed according to various gravestones of members of the guard. His other sidearm, a comparatively simple *semispatha*, is a souvenir of his service as a legionary on the Danube defences. The dolphin-shaped scabbard clasp was found at South Shields (GB). His golden bracelet (*armilla*) is a military decoration.

His double-weighted *pilum* follows a depiction on the contemporary grave stele of Praetorian guardsman Lucius Aurelius Lucianus. *Pila* could have up to three of these weights, as shown on the grave stele of Caius Monnenius Secundus, soldier of *cohors XIIII urbana*, now in the collection of the Palazzo dei Conservatori in Rome. The rectangular *scutum* with red leather binding is modelled on the famous example excavated at Dura Europos (SYR). The shield boss (*umbo*) was found in the River Tyne and is of slightly earlier date. The shield's dark blue painting is based upon the (admittedly conjectural) assumption that earlier Praetorian shields displaying stars, crescents (*lunulae*) and winged thunderbolts were painted to resemble the night sky. Eagle, victories and lion follow the Dura *scutum*, but then a series of coins issued by the Emperor Gallienus confirms that the lion was also a badge of the Praetorian Guard. The shield is also emblazoned with another Praetorian device, the scorpion, once sign of the Emperor Tiberius.

CO HIIIPR PV
S.Barin '20

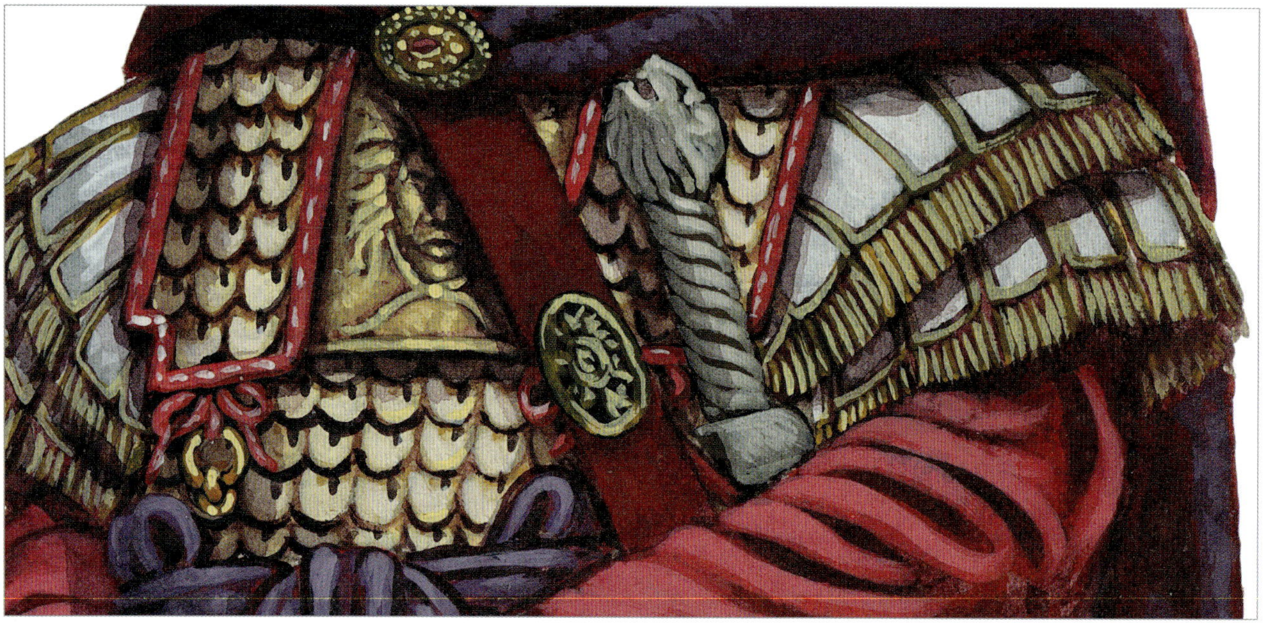

Plate IX

The Emperor Gaius Iulius Valerius Maximinus, "the Thracian"

Mounted on a sturdy black charger, the Emperor Maximinus makes ready to inspect the legions. He is a large man by ancient standards, but certainly not the colossus the sources make him out to be.

He wears a *tunica manicata russata* with purple decorations. His scale cuirass is modelled on those of the officers on the Ludovisi sarcophagus. Its design follows the classic muscle cuirass of Hellenistic fashion (which oddly does not appear on the sarcophagus). The Gorgon's head warding off harm is likewise a classical accoutrement and still in sculptural evidence in the 3rd century AD. The most famous depiction of such a *Gorgoneion* is probably that on Alexander the Great's cuirass in the Battle of Issos mosaic found at the Casa del Fauno in Pompeii (now on display at the National Archaeological Museum in Naples). The shoulder guards (*humeralia*) were laced to the front of the cuirass.

According to Hellenistic tradition, Maximinus has slung a purple officer's sash (*zona militaris*) around his cuirass. The fringed edges have been tucked underneath the scarf to the left and right of the so-called Hercules' knot (*nodus Herculis*) imitating the knot Hercules tied to secure the hide of the Nemean Lion around his chest. This is stressed by the fact that the ends of the general's sash on the Ludovisi sarcophagus terminate in stylised lions' paws. Maximus' panoply is completed by several rows of *pteryges* at shoulders and waist since the cuirass is too inflexible and short to provide protection for the upper arms, genitals, and thighs.

It is cold on the Rhine frontier and a long and arduous campaign is imminent. The old soldier therefore refuses to wear any imperial finery apart from the purple imperial *paludamentum*. The costs for this garment were ridiculously high, its dye being produced from several species of Mediterranean crustaceans the Romans collectively called *murex purpureus*. Maximinus wears woollen breeches, puttees, and the high red officers' *calcei mullei* boots indicating his elevated rank. In order to be seen clearly and to facilitate subsequent recognition by his troops, he wears no helmet. Since red hair was quite common in his Thracian homelands, we have reconstructed the Emperor with greying red hair and beard.

Maximinus' sidearm is a *spatha* with an ivory hilt, the pommel carved in the shape of a lion's head. In this we follow the depiction of the general's sword on the sarcophagus. The lion's pelt under his saddle blanket is copied from the same source: both the general's and the cavalry officer's horses have lions' skins as saddle blankets. This practice again has its origin in Hellenistic tradition – in the Issos mosaic Bucephalos is shown adorned with a leopard's hide edged in green.

S.Boriп'19

Plate X

Guardsman of the *Equites Singulares Augusti*

Standing beside his mount, a splendidly attired member of the Imperial horse guard awaits orders.

His equipment reflects the status of a crack formation in whose ranks the Emperor Maximinus himself once served with distinction. His elaborately decorated helmet is of Heddernheim type; helmets like these are worn by several Romans on the Ludovisi relief. The helmet was found at the Iron gates and is now in the collection of the Hungarian National Museum at Budapest. The mask was found at Zeugma (TR) and with its stylised hair decoration is a fairly typical example of the face masks of this type of helmet, several of which have been found at various sites. The horsehair crest has been added.

He wears body armour composed of bronze scales attached to a linen undergarment. Alternating scales have been silvered chessboard fashion for increased visual effect. Since this type of armour lacks flexibility, arms and thighs are protected by double rows of red leather *pteryges* adorned with fringes. In order to put on his cuirass, the trooper must unhinge the fastenings of the bronze chestplates, which were found at the fortress of Samum in Dacia (RO). They are decorated with busts of Minerva and mythical griffins. The cuirass was probably also fastened with laces or straps along the left side, which was protected by the shield. His red *tunica manicata* is decorated with purple applications, his breeches follow the common military fashion of the times. As a cavalryman, he wears spurs attached to his boots with red straps.

The decorative plates of his ring buckle belt mostly follow examples found at Dura (SYR). The baldric decorations, invoking the favour of the Gods, are from Zugmantel (D). His elaborate sword hilt follows examples found in Northern Europe. He could also be carrying a sidearm with an eagle head hilt, since swords of this type frequently appear on funerary stelae of guardsmen of the period. The scabbard has a central spine which was either carved out of the wood of the scabbard itself (cf. MIKS, 2007) or formed part of the metal lining. The perforated chape is again typical of Roman military fashion of the period. Many examples of these have been excavated all over the Empire.

The soldier's primary weapon is a lance which could be used for both thrusting and throwing. He might also have been equipped with several javelins carried in a quiver behind the saddle as depicted on a terracotta plaque found at Apulum in modern Romania. The inside of his shield has been painted according to a famous example found at Dura Europos.

The horse's harness has been dyed red. The braided headgear and bridle and the straps around the horse's neck follow the depiction of the horse of an unknown *eques singularis* on a third century AD grave stele in Rome[60]. The other metal fittings follow finds from various sites. They are slightly archaic in style but as such could well be the mark of an élite formation. The horned saddle has several leather straps attached, which could be used to secure the soldier's equipment on the march.

60 See plate XII

to have served five years in the legions and distinguished himself. The Praetorian cohorts did however lose the social prestige of their formerly entirely Italic background. This was aggravated by the fact that the soldiers from the frontiers often lacked the mentality and refinement necessary to make life in Rome bearable for everyone concerned. Clashes between guardsmen and the local populace occurred regularly and it is somewhat ironic that after Severus' reforms the Praetorians and their officers become more frequently embroiled in political intrigue than had previously been the case. On the other hand, large contingents of the guard were almost permanently in the field with the emperors. It would be a misconception to assume however that admission to the Praetorian cohorts was barred to Italians henceforth. COWAN states that sources suggest that Italians were still recruited into the cohorts, often having previously served in *legio II Parthica*.

A special unit which formed part of the Praetorian cohorts were the *frumentarii*, who acted as imperial messengers and performed the functions of an intelligence service[61]. These were supplemented by the *numerus* of *statores augusti*, who may have been a military police force formed from veterans[62], and the *evocati*, long-serving Praetorians who qualified for promotion owing to their experience or who served as military or technical advisors in the provinces or the capital itself.

The capital was also the base of the urban cohorts (*cohortes urbanae*, or *urbaniciani*), Rome's paramilitary police force recruited from Italians. They were commanded by the senatorial *praefectus urbi* and were responsible for the maintenance of public order and safety. Their numbers had also been augmented by Septimius Severus so that we may assume a cohort strength of 1,500 soldiers[63]. There were at least six *cohortes urbanae*, which were associated with the Praetorians on an organisational level, being numbered in the same sequence as the guard. Assuming that there were ten Praetorian cohorts, the first urban cohort was thus numbered *cohors XI urbana*. Apart from policing the capital, urban cohorts were stationed at Ostia, Puteoli, Carthage and Lugdunum in order to control the ports essential for the capital's grain supply, and to guard the Imperial mints. Apart from guard and police duties, the urban cohorts were also employed as a fighting force. *Cohors XIV urbana* is attested as having fought alongside *legio II Parthica* in Apamea in Syria[64].

The urban cohorts were supported in their duties by Rome's fire service and night watchmen, the *cohortes vigilum*, which were commanded by the equestrian *praefectus vigilum*. They consisted of seven cohorts, each of which was responsible for two of the city's fourteen districts. They were based in seven barracks (*stationes*) and fourteen fire stations (*excubitoria*) around the city.

The final unit which must be mentioned is the detachment of sailors on duty in the capital (*classiarii*). Soldiers from the Imperial fleets at Misenum and Ravenna were responsible for operating and maintaining the awnings at the Colosseum. They also operated as messengers between Rome and the naval bases.

ELLIOTT holds the view that Severus' massive augmentation of the Roman and Italic garrisons provided the emperor with a mobile reserve of roughly 21,500 troops which he could use to march from the capital to any part of the empire which happened to be under threat[65]. The garrison of Italy furthermore protected the Empire's core country against incursions from the Raetian territory beyond the Alps, these having revealed themselves to be a serious problem. However, these troops were not altogether immune to conspiracies and court intrigues; when it came to disputing the imperial purple they were not always reliable, as several emperors would be forced to learn.

61 BINGHAM, p.90.

62 LE BOHEC (1993), p. 24.

63 ELLIOTT, Paul, *Legions in Crisis. Transformation of the Roman Soldier AD 92-284*, 2014, p. 29.

64 Ibid., p. 29.

65 Ibid., p. 30.

The fleets

Since the main focus of this work lies on Maximinus' army, for the sake of completeness only a brief look shall be taken at the Roman navy of the period.

At the beginning of the third century AD Rome had at her disposal two main fleets, both of which were based in Italy: the *classis Ravennatis praetoria* based at Ravenna, and the *classis Misenatis praetoria* based at Misenum. Each fleet was commanded by an equestrian *praefectus classis praetoriae*. These two core fleets were supported by at least seven provincial fleets named after the provinces from which they operated. These too were commanded by prefects:

Classis Britannica
Classis Germanica
Classis Moesica and *Classis Pannonica* (Danube flees)
Classis Siriaca
Classis Alexandrina
Classis Pontica (stationed at Trebizond to patrol the Black Sea)

There also existed a small fleet on the Euphrates.

Apart from patrolling duties and providing logistic support for the land armies, the fleets took part in every military operation of the period. Especially on the Rhine and Danube frontiers the fleets played a crucial part in stemming the tide of barbarian incursions. The so-called Neupotz hoard from the 3rd century AD, a large amount of Roman household goods discovered near Germersheim in the Palatinate, may in fact have been lost in a clash between Roman vessels and Germanic raiders trying to make good their escape across the Rhine. In the middle of the third century a new and very serious enemy for the Roman navy arose in the form of the Goths, who invaded the Balkan provinces and Greece via the Black Sea, causing heavy damage before they could be repulsed. As a result of political upheaval and climatic changes which began to affect their homelands, Saxon and Jutish raiders began to make increasingly frequent appearances on the coasts of Gaul and Britain as the 3rd century progressed. In the second half of the century work was therefore begun on a string of fortresses and naval bases to protect these coasts from incursions (*litus Saxonicus*).

There is sufficient literature to provide information on the size, construction and armament of Roman warships; for reasons of space, these aspects must be ignored in this work. The Roman navy included both small and versatile craft suited to patrolling the rivers, and large five-bank galleys for patrolling the open sea (though ships commonly would keep close to the coast for safety reasons). Detachments (*vexillationes*) were commanded by naval centurions (*navarchae*), who – as was the case in the legions – held differing ranks in the hierarchy of the navy's centurions according to their responsibilities.

Both *classes praetoriae* (who despite their names did not enjoy the same prestige as the Praetorian cohorts) were assigned contingents of 10, 000 marines each (*milites classiarii*). These units were organised into cohorts, each cohort being commanded by a higher-ranking *centurio classiarius* who was senior to the centurions commanding the individual centuries.

In terms of organisation at least the larger battleships equalled a *centuria*. The captain was a *trierarchus* of centurion's rank. He commanded the oarsmen (*remiges*), sailors (*nautae*), and the vessel's contingent of marines. The nature of naval warfare made necessary a large number of specialists on board, among them helmsmen (*gubernatores*), galley masters responsible for striking the rhythm for the rowers (*hortatores*), carpenters (*fabri*), sailmakers (*velarii*), pursers (*dispensatores*), and artillerymen to man the ship's catapults (*ballistarii*). These specialists were either petty officers or *immunes*.

As said above, the honorary title of *praetoria* for both main fleets is misleading. Service in the navy was not held in particularly high esteem, being considered inferior to that in the legions. This can be attested by the social advancement felt by the soldiers recruited into the newly raised *legiones I* and *II Adiutrices* (author's plural) in AD 69[66]. As marines, they took pride in being admitted into the ranks of the legions. The navy recruited mainly freeborn men from peoples who were familiar with the trade and could look back on long seafaring traditions, e. g. Egyptians, Greeks, Phoenicians and Dalmatians. At least to a certain extent, the navy also seems to have been open to freedmen. In the third century, soldiers in the navy served for 26 years, which corresponds to service in the legions. The soldiers' pay more or less seems to have equalled that of the army[67].

66 The name *Adiutrix* literally means „helper" or "supporter", which seems peculiarly apt for a unit recruited from soldiers considered inferior in the Roman army's social hierarchy.

67 PITASSI, Michael, *The Roman Navy. Ships, Men and Warfare 350 BC – AD 475*, Barnsley 2012, p. 66D'AMATO, Raffaele, *Imperial Roman Naval Forces 31 BC – AD 500*, Oxford 2009, p. 14.

Two grave stelae of *Equites Singulares Augusti* from Rome

After Constantine's resounding victory over Maxentius at the Milvian Bridge (Saxa Rubra) in AD 312, the loser's hapless horse guard bore the brunt of Constantine's wrath: the barracks of the Equites Singulares Augusti *were torn down and the new basilica of San Giovanni in Laterano erected in their place. Constantine went as far as to raze the horse guard's necropole on the Via Labicana, thereby completing the* damnatio memoriae. *The gravestones were used to lay the foundations of the church of Santi Marcellino e Pietro. For us, this has turned out to be rather fortunate, since the recovered monuments provide us with a rich source of information on organisation, self-image, morale and appearance of this élite unit.*

Plate XI is the depiction of guardsman Ulpius Victorinus on his gravestone. SPEIDEL (*Kaiserreiter*, 1994, p. 289) dates the stele to the second half of the 3rd century AD owing to Victorinus's hairstyle. However, since we know that Maximinus's short military beard and hairstyle became iconic in the army, we may assume that the stele is from an earlier date, especially so since items of equipment point to this possibility.

Victorinus, who is holding his horse by its bridle, wears a long-sleeved tunic with a ring-buckle belt and long breeches ending in boots which are laced around the ankles. His fringed *sagum* cloak is held in place by a round fibula, the *balteus* seems to have two ornamental *phalerae* discs. The sheath of his *spatha* is lined with two metal ribs and terminated by a circular chape. The grooved rod next to the *spatha* remains a bit of a mystery – it could be a short javelin, or some form of gnarled staff.

Born in Pannonia, Victorinus the guardsman had served thirteen years with the standards when he died and three friends, two officers among them, had the stone erected to his memory. He holds a scroll in his hand, a hint at his citizenship, or the *honesta missio* so treacherously denied him by an untimely death? These scrolls are frequent on military funerary stelae, so and may simply point to the bearer's citizenship.

Plate XII shows an unknown guardsman from the 3rd century AD. We do not know his name since only the top half of his gravestone has survived. Like so many of his comrades, he chose to be commemorated together with his faithful charger, whom he holds by its braided bridle (bridles like this also appear on the Ludovisi sarcophagus). His horse chews impatiently on its bit. The trappings are designed to impress: the halter is decorated with metal discs, as are the leather straps running across chest and hindquarters.

Like Victorinus, the deceased guardsman wears dress uniform without armour. He has a long-sleeved tunic, and the sculptor has taken special care to accurately depict his ring-buckle belt, whose right end is tucked under the belt and terminates in two ivy-leaf-shaped metal pendants. Worthy of note is also the detailed workmanship depicting the disc-shaped chape of the *spatha*. Like Victorinus's, the man's *sagum* is held by a disc-shaped clasp. This *eques singularis* also proudly clasps a scroll, and shows off a peculiar round ring with a gemstone on his left hand. Its significance is not quite clear, but SPEIDEL (*Kaiserreiter*, 1994, p. 291) draws attention to Herodian's mentioning of Septimius Severus allowing the soldiers to wear golden rings, something which was considered the prerogative of the equestrian order. It may also be a personal gift from the emperor (another similar grave stele also shows a ring however), or simply a symbol of rank. It is possible that the *optiones* wore rings as a sign of rank.

Roman policy and strategy in Germania

It is a matter of controversy among scholars to what extent we may speak of any kind of geopolitical strategy pursued by the Roman Empire. American military historian Edward LUTTWAK postulated that there was indeed a consistent strategy regarding the northern frontier, which developed from the establishment of open and flexible frontiers in form of a *cordon sanitaire* screened by allied tribes into a rigid frontier defence and finally a defensive strategy in late antiquity which ultimately denied Rome the chance to regain the strategic initiative, whereas Michael SOMMER believes that varying political issues of the day, different emperors and their often conflicting foreign and domestic policies, and finally the Romans' restricted geographical knowledge did not permit such a grand strategy in LUTTWAK's sense of the word at all. SOMMER cannot make out any form of consistent and sustainable foreign strategy in the first and second centuries AD before Rome recoiled into a situation of "permanent crisis management" on its northern frontiers from the third century onwards[68]. It should be remembered however that until far into late antiquity the Romans were in the position to contain enemy invasions by mounting effective counteroffensives of their own. Maximinus Thrax's campaign into Germany proves that even beyond the era of imperial expansion, Roman armies were capable of operating deep in enemy territory.

First and foremost, the defeat in the Teutoburg Forest in 9 AD caused Rome to make profound changes regarding its policy in Germania. In the subsequent decades, Rome switched its strategy from expansion to consolidation, which – with the exception of the occupation of the *Agri Decumati* triangle between Rhine and Danube – remained mostly as such until the second century AD[69]. The construction of the *limes* in Germany from the second half of the first century onwards points to Rome's desire to firmly establish and define its northern frontiers. This policy of consolidation was continued under Hadrian, whose wall in northern Britain henceforth drew a clear line between Rome and *Barbaricum*. Large-scale incursions of tribal alliances into Gaul and Italy in the 2nd century AD generated a change of thinking and re-established the idea of imperial expansion on the northern frontier at least in theory.

After a prolonged period of expansion and consolidation, the reign of Antoninus Pius saw the Roman Empire confronted with a series of grave threats on different frontiers. The Emperor was forced to lead campaigns in Africa, Britain, Dacia and Germany. In Britain, the Romans pushed forward the frontier beyond Hadrian's Wall and built the Antonine Wall between the Firth of Forth and the Firth of Tyne. Designed to control and repel the warlike tribes of the Highlands, the Antonine Wall was abandoned after merely a century's occupation, and Rome once again withdrew behind the defences of Hadrian's Wall.

Beyond the Danube, political and social conditions were also in a state of transition. Migrations and military conflicts among the tribes caused the Germans living across the river, among them the Quadi, to seek refuge within the Roman Empire. Instead of seizing the chance to reduce the pressure on this part of the frontier by admitting them into the Empire, Antoninus declined. The Emperor instead placed his confidence in the realignment and strengthening of the *limes*, which was turned into a permanent frontier defence line fortified by a supplement of watch towers and forts garrisoned by auxiliary regiments.[70]

According to MOOSBAUER and REUTER/THIEL, the specific reasons for this strengthening of the frontier defences remain largely opaque as yet, but they were certainly caused by inner-Germanic conflicts beyond the Danube which either led to clashes with Roman troops in the region or were liable to do so in the near future.[71]

These clashes were not long in coming. Renewed migratory movements on the other side of the frontier, possibly by the Goths in modern Poland, increased the pressure on the Danube frontier[72]. Together with the Sarmatian Iazyges, Marcomanni and Quadi (based in present-day Bohemia) swept across the Danube defences and began to lay waste to the provinces beyond, causing considerable damage. Germanic warbands roamed as far as Northern Italy before the Emperor Marcus Aurelius drove them back across the river.

According to Herodian and Cassius Dio, the drawn-out and costly Marcomannic Wars caused Marcus Aurelius to contemplate the establishment of two new transdanubian provinces in modern Bohemia and Slovakia (*Marcomannia* and *Sarmatia*). These new provinces would have provided a convenient geographical connection with Dacia and acted as a buffer zone between the Empire and the Danubian tribes. It would also have enabled Rome to control the German tribes across the Rhine more effec-

68 SOMMER, p. 97.

69 In this context it must be observed that the *limes*, which screened off the area between Rhine and Danube (*Agri Decumates*) was not a construction designed to actively defend the frontier by creating a military obstacle; its garrison would not have been in the position to defend it. It was rather an instrument which channelled and controlled traffic in the frontier zone and was able to spot and slow down enemy incursions until reinforcements were available.

70 MOOSBAUER, Günther, *Die vergessene Römerschlacht. Der sensationelle Fund am Harzhorn*, München 2018, p. 7-12; REUTER, Marcus/THIEL, Andreas: *Der Limes. Auf den Spuren der Römer*, Darmstadt 2015, p. 35-37.

71 MOOSBAUER (2018), p. 13.

72 Ibid., p. 19 ff.

tively. Marcus Aurelius is even supposed to have considered the conquest of Germania to the sea. His death however brought all these plans to nought if indeed they had ever been concrete.

From Commodus to Alexander Severus – changes beyond the frontier

Even if the plan to establish new provinces beyond the Danube had been seriously made, Rome would hardly have been in the position to carry them out. The outbreak of the Antonine plague and the exhaustion of financial and military resources as a consequence of the prolonged fighting on the Danube left no option but to withdraw the legions from the territory beyond the river. Devastation and deaths among the tribes had likewise been so horrendous that the Rhine and Danube frontiers remained stable for almost half a century simply because of mutual exhaustion[73]. Only during the campaigns of Caracalla after 213 AD did the northern frontier again become a war zone.

While Alexander Severus was busy fighting the Persians in 233 AD, a large Germanic contingent smashed through the *limes* defences in a carefully coordinated attack, ransacked the frontier areas and advanced into Gaul. The Emperor broke off the Persian campaign and marched to the Rhine.

How had the military situation become so precarious? We know that towards the end of the 2nd century AD there began to occur profound changes which affected various spheres of life in free Germany. Archaeological finds attest to a cultural change beyond the Empire's borders, which among other things manifested itself in clothing and things of everyday life. Art and craft in Germany markedly improved in quality thanks to raids into Roman territory but also trade. This was supplemented by increasing cultural influences from southern Scandinavia, and possibly climatic changes which would have led to a critical food situation in at least some regions. All this however was eclipsed by demographic and political changes the consequences of which the Roman Empire was soon to encounter.

Burial finds in middle Germany point to the emergence of a new aristocratic élite which was materially much better off than its subjects. Forthwith these chieftains acted as commanders of large Germanic warbands which frequently threatened the Empire's frontier provinces. These circumstances were aggravated by a geopolitical shift of regional power hubs and settlement areas, which entailed a drifting south and unprecedented population density of the (culturally defined) Irmiones (or Herminones)[74]. One of these new settlement centres was the foreland of the Harz mountains, which had previously been inhabited mainly by the Rhine-Weser Germans. As a consequence of migratory movements, this area had come under the increasing influence of the Irmiones (referred to as *Elbgermanen* in German), who had nevertheless not completely given up their original settlement areas. Hans-Jörg NÜSSE has shown that when planning the campaign, Maximinus' generals could only concentrate on densely populated areas since only these would offer worthwhile targets and provide the army with the necessary provisions[75]. Under these circumstances the site of the Harzhorn battle is an indirect consequence of Roman staff work.

Contemporary German scholars presume that warbands of Irmiones were responsible for the recurring raids on the *limes* and the frontier regions beyond at this time[76]. Archaeologists have ascertained an increase in settlements of these peoples in southern Germany in the 3rd century AD. The name given to these new invaders in contemporary sources, *Alamanni* (meaning "all men", which etymologically points to a federation of tribes or, conversely, to a band of individuals from various backgrounds), is due largely to the Romans' embarrassment at being unable to identify these people's geographic origins and ethnic background (on the other hand, the names of the Rhine-Weser tribes whose territories the Roman army passed through are given in the sources). This insecurity as to the identity of the invaders is shared by modern scholars to a certain extent. While these developments were taking place in southern Germany, warbands coming from the western settlement areas of the Rhine-Weser tribes raided Roman territory across the lower Rhine from the mid-third century onwards. These warbands are referred to as *Franci* ("free ones") in Roman sources and like the Alamanni probably hailed from various tribes. According to contemporary research, neither Franks and Rhine-Weser tribes, nor Irmiones and Alamanni are ethnically identical groups[77]. It appears plausible to suppose that at this time a warrior's concrete tribal background became increasingly immaterial as charismatic chieftains promised plunder and glory to any man willing to pledge allegiance to them. Archaeological finds of Roman burial gifts in the graves of Germanic chieftains and in bogs seem to point in this direction.

Maximinus' campaign succeeded in once more restoring the old northern frontier for several decades. In the year 260 however the Alamanni exploited Rome's preoc-

73 LEHMANN, p. 98 f.

74 Cf. NÜSSE, Hans-Jörg, „Germanien im 3. Jahrhundert. Eine Zeit des Wandels", in PÖPPELMANN, Heike/DEPPMEYER, Korana/STEINMETZ, Wolf-Dieter (eds.), *Roms vergessener Feldzug.Die Schlacht am Harzhorn*, Darmstadt 2013, p. 126 ff.

75 Ibid., p. 130.

76 Ibid., p. 132. FUHRMANN, Jens / STEINMETZ, Wolf-Dieter,"Nach seiner Ankunft ließ er das ganze Land verheeren. Germanische Besiedlung entlang des römischen Marschweges", in PÖPPELMANN, Heike/DEPPMEYER, Korana/STEINMETZ; Wolf-Dieter (eds.), *Roms vergessener Feldzug.Die Schlacht am Harzhorn*, Darmstadt 2013, p. 140.

77 NÜSSE, p. 133.

cupation with the Persians and occupied the *Agri Decumates*. The *limes* was abandoned, Rhine and Danube once again formed the Empire's boundaries in the north.

The composition of Maximinus' army.

It is difficult to identify individual formations in Maximinus' army. The sources remain quite vague in this respect. Herodian emphasises the sheer size of the army, but names only a few specific units (VII, 2, 1 ff.). He takes care to stress the army's ethnic and military diversity by numbering the auxiliary units which had marched to the Rhine with Alexander Severus from the East. These were the (possibly mounted) Osrhoenian archers from north-eastern Mesopotamia, and the Moorish javelineers (Μαυρουσίων ᾽ακοντιστων [gen.]), who were particularly well-suited to tackling the German tribesmen (HA, *Duo Maximini*, XI). Numerous spear- and arrowheads have been recovered at the site of the Harzhorn battle. We may assume that the North African troops, who were organised in *numeri*, were at least in part mounted (the - heavily stylised – depiction of North African light cavalrymen is one of the most famous scenes on Trajan's Column). There were also Armenian archers and Parthian (or Persian?) troops who are not specifically defined, prisoners or possibly renegades from Alexander Severus' Persian campaign. It remains unclear whether these Parthian or Persian troops served as mounted archers or extra-heavy cavalry (*clibanarii*). Herodian mentions cataphracts in Maximinus' army when it marched to Italy (των καταφράκτων ἴλαι, *ton kataphrakton ilai*, "the regiments of cataphracts", VIII, 1, 3). Armoured cavalrymen on fully armoured horses (if the "cataphracts" rode armoured horses at all[78]) were designed for the desert plains of the Middle East but were hardly suitable for the rough, wooded and often boggy German terrain. Grave inscriptions for members of Oriental cataphract units (*numeri cataphractariorum*) from the 3rd century AD found at Stuttgart-Bad Cannstatt and Frankfurt-Heddernheim do however show that these soldiers served on the Empire's northern frontier. Regardless of this fact, they are no proof for the participation of extra-heavy cavalry in Maximinus' German campaign. The élite milliary *ala II Flavia*, the largest cavalry regiment based on the *limes*, will doubtlessly have taken part in the campaign.

Which other units did Maximinus' army comprise? According to the principle explained in the chapter on army organisation we may assume that the Rhine legions contributed detachments (*vexillationes*) for the campaign. Soldiers from *legiones I Minervia* from Bonn, *XXX Ulpia Victrix* from Xanten, *VIII Augusta* from Strasbourg and *XXII Primigenia* from Mainz will have taken part in the fighting; they will have been supported by auxiliary formations, among them very probably the *numeri exploratorum*, part-mounted scouts based in Cologne, Niederbieber, Heidelberg and Passau. These units, which are only attested in the Germanic provinces, will have reconnoitred the army's marching route and the settlements targeted for attack[79]. In this context, Thomas FISCHER has observed that Alexander Severus' army probably comprised a large number of legionary and auxiliary units which he had previously withdrawn from their garrisons along the Rhine[80]. This depletion of the Roman frontier garrisons had probably provoked the German attack in the first place. On the other hand, no legionary detachments seem to have been withdrawn from the eastern frontier.

The recovery of a Roman entrenching tool (*dolabra*) at the Harzhorn proves that legionaries from *legio IV Flavia Felix* based at Singidunum (Belgrade) on the Danube also took part in the campaign. Since the army was commanded by the Emperor in person, we may assume that several Praetorian cohorts and the *equites singulares Augusti* were also present. Two inscriptions from Cologne and Worms which unfortunately cannot be dated precisely suggest that *legio II Parthica* took part in the campaign. Its participation in Maximinus' Danube campaign and his siege of Aquileia (where it played a significant role in his downfall) is well-attested however. It seems reasonable to claim therefore that its soldiers also marched with him into hostile Germany[81].

78 Cf. WIEGELS, Rainer, „Die Reitergrabstele aus Stuttgart-Bad Cannstatt", in 358. The words *cataphractarius* and *clibanarius* are often used synonymously in contemporary literature although there is reason to assume that these may actually have been two different troop types. Depictions of *cataphractarii* on gravestones show armoured horsemen on unarmoured horses (κατάφρακτος, *kataphraktos* simply means "covered" or "armoured"), while *clibanarii* rode armoured horses (cf. Ammianus Marcellinus XVI, 10, 8); s. above.

79 WIEGELS, Rainer, „Reiter Roms an Germaniens Grenzen m frühen 3. Jh. n. Chr.", in PÖPPELMANN, Heike/DEPPMEYER, Korana/STEINMETZ, Wolf-Dieter (eds.), *Roms vergessener Feldzug. Die Schlacht am Harzhorn*, Darmstadt 2013, p. 235-241, p. 238 f.

80 FISCHER, Thomas, „Die Soldaten des Maximinus Thrax. Die Einheiten und ihre Bewaffnung", in PÖPPELMANN, Heike/DEPPMEYER, Korana/STEINMETZ, Wolf-Dieter (eds.), *Roms vergessener Feldzug. Die Schlacht am Harzhorn*, Darmstadt 2013, p.198-206, p. 199.

81 WIEGELS, „Reiter Roms...", p. 239.

Maximinus' German campaign

Which political and strategic aims was Maximinus pursuing as he led his army across the Rhine? As we have seen, the campaign was a welcome political means of securing his own position. The Emperor was keen to demonstrate vigour and skill to his soldiers, and to satisfy them by promising them glory and plunder. The enemy was to be made to understand that Rome was unwilling to tolerate further incursions into its territory. In other words, whoever threatened the Empire would find themselves facing massive retaliation.

Was the campaign thus simply a punitive expedition or did Maximinus pursue long-term objectives? First and foremost, the campaign indeed was a punitive raid designed to demonstrate to the Germanic tribes beyond the frontier that Rome was capable of launching massive and powerful expeditions deep into enemy territory.

The campaign itself is in many parts still a matter of conjecture, despite the Harzhorn battlefield and the marching camp at Hachelbich both having shed light on a number of issues. Herodian's account (VII, 2, 3 ff.) remains vague and follows literary convention in its formulaic style. The *Historia Augusta* also restricts its relation of events to a few general remarks, according to which the Roman army crossed the Rhine, laid waste to the countryside, plundered and torched enemy settlements, drove away livestock and made many prisoners[82] (HA, *Duo Maximini*, XII). The enemy mostly consisted of Irmiones, the Suebi and Hermunduri, but probably also of some groups of Chatti, who settled in an area roughly equalling modern Hesse (the word "Hesse" is actually derived from the word *Chatti*). The Germans retreated from the plains into the forests and marshes, where there were repeated fights and skirmishes. The sources give an epic battle in the bogs of Northern Germany as the climax of the campaign, which is at present impossible to locate, if indeed it ever took place since the accounts rely heavily on literary clichés. The emperor allegedly saved the day by personally intervening and charging the enemy at the head of his troops. Laden with booty, the victorious Roman army returned to the Rhine, where Maximinus was acclaimed "most supreme vanquisher of the Germans" (*Germanicus Maximus*) by his elated soldiers. Maximinus had pictures of his victorious deeds painted and ordered them to be put on display outside the Senate house in Rome.

Until recently, there has been some controversy among scholars regarding the range of the Roman expedition. This must be considered in the context of the distances given by the *Historia Augusta*, and what different generations of historians have made of these. Already in the 17th century Maximinus' claim of having ventured 300 to 400 Roman miles[83] into hostile territory (quoted by the *HA*) was dismissed as pure rhetoric. The Frenchman Saumais reduced this to 30 to 40 miles, which to him appeared more realistic, and edited the text accordingly. This would place the great battle a mere 50 miles away from the Rhine.

While Martin HOSE has altogether done away with the distances given by the *Historia Augusta* believing them to be a product of the author's imagination (he does not make a connection between the information given by the *HA* and the location of the Harzhorn battlefield)[84], Gustav Adolf LEHMANN attaches great importance to them. He argues that if one takes them as rough estimates, the distance given by the *HA* more or less corresponds to the Roman conception of the distance between Rhine and Elbe. Thus one may suppose that the objective of the Roman campaign was indeed the Elbe[85]. The Harzhorn battlefield, situated about 320 kilometres from Mainz is to be viewed in this context.

Herodian notes that Maximinus had planned to conquer all of Germania to the Okeanos (i. e. the North Sea and Baltic coasts) as a long-term objective (VII, 2, 9). It was never done. His subsequent campaign on the Danube and the ensuing civil war prevented the Emperor from returning to the northern frontier. It cannot be entirely ruled out that Maximinus intended to give new life to Marcus Aurelius' geostrategic plans, but this must remain guesswork until new findings can shed light on the Thracian's long-term strategy on the Rhine and Danube frontiers. At any rate, the conquest of new territory hardly appeared feasible in view of the pressure Rome's enemies were exacting on its various frontiers.

Maximinus led his troops across the ship bridge which the engineers had constructed across the Rhine at Mainz and marched north through central and northern Hesse. The army crossed the River Werra and turned east in order to march to the Elbe along the edge of the Harz mountains, as GESCHWINDE presumes[86]. A Roman marching camp recently discovered at Hachelbich in northern Thuringia has provided new information as to which route the army took to the Elbe.

Mario KÜßNER et al. have been able to gain the following insights regarding the Hachelbich marching camp: the camp was presumably large enough to house one legion, measuring ca. 23 ha. It was discovered during preparations for building a local bypass road and was positioned

82 The large number of prisoners is confirmed by a victory monument of Shapur I, which claims that numerous Germans served in the army of Gordian III (r. 238-244 AD; cf. LEHMANN, p. 102, footnote).

83 One Roman mile amounts to 1, 48 km, or 1 617 yards.

84 HOSE, Martin, „Ausgelöschte Geschichte. Der Feldzug des Maximinus Thrax in das Innere Germaniens 235/236 in der historischen Überlieferung", in PÖPPELMANN, Heike/DEPPMEYER, Korana/STEINMETZ, Wolf-Dieter (eds.), *Roms vergessener Feldzug. Die Schlacht am Harzhorn*, Darmstadt 2013, p. 111-115, p. 115.

85 LEHMANN, p. 103-104.

86 GESCHWINDE, Michael, „La batalla olvidada. La *expeditio germanica* del emperador Maximino el Tracio y los hallazgos arqueológicos de Harzhorn", in: *Desperta Ferro (Numero Especial XVII): La legión romana (V): La anarquía militar*, Madrid 2018-2019, p. 44-51, p. 47.

Plate XIII

Legionary of *Legio XXX Ulpia Victrix Pia Fidelis*, Harzhorn, c. 236 AD.

A legionary of the Thirtieth (garrisoned in Vetera/Xanten) makes ready for battle. He is pulling the leather cover from his shield before forming ranks. Marching has been rough, so the *capsarii* have not managed to tend to his light thigh wound sustained during a skirmish a few days back. Now he will have to stand his ground as well as he can.

Our soldier wears a bronze helmet excavated at Bodegraven (NL). The crest and cheekguards have been added. Underneath the *sagum* is the *lorica hamata* with chestplates, and a linen *subarmalis* with attached leather *pteryges*. His sword arm is protected by a *manica* of laminated iron strips. He wears woollen breeches and puttees (*fasciae crurales*), and woollen socks (*udones*) against the damp of the morning dew in the meadows. His belt is decorated with bronze lettering denoting his former legion: LEG III CYR, the Third Cyrenaican Legion. The belt strap passes through a loop under the letter Y. As a soldier of the Third under the Emperor Alexander Severus, he has fought a series of bloody engagements against the Persians in the East and will now do his utmost to prove himself under the new Emperor and return to the Rhine frontier covered with glory.

The legionary is armed with the standard Künzing type dagger suspended from a narrow baldric, and a *spatha*. He also carries a pair of slender long *lanceae* as depicted on two grave stelae from the period. They have been joined for marching with two leather thongs. On the leather shield cover (*tegimentum*) may be seen the *tabula ansata*, a tag identifying his unit sewn onto a strip of dark red leather. His unit identification, *Legio XXX Ulpia Victrix Pia Fidelis [Severiana?] Maximiniana*, is also painted on his shield, whose conjectural reconstruction is based on Roman monuments and the surviving Dura shields. The badges of the Thirtieth were the capricorn and Neptune, who appears in his chariot at the top of the shield. The depiction of the god in his chariot follows a mosaic from a 2nd century AD Roman villa in Zeugma (TR). Owing to their gracious appearance, horses were believed to have been created by the God of the Seas. To the left and right of the boss, Nereids worship their master. The boss itself, showing Mars amidst trophies of arms, was found at Kirkham (GB). At the bottom, the capricorn, a curious mixture of goat and sea monster, identifies the bearer's legion.

LEG II CYR
XVLP VIC P F SEV MAX
S.Borin '20

Plate XIV

Osrhoenian horse archer

At full gallop, a member of the crack Osrhoenian horse archers shoots his bow at Germanic warriors. He has come to the Rhine frontier with Alexander Severus and is now on campaign with Maximinus. The province of Syria Osrhoene, established under Septimius Severus, provided the Roman Empire with excellent horse archers, whose fighting technique hailed back to a long tradition in the Middle East. The strategic value of such troops was first made painfully aware to the Romans in the Empire's clashes with Parthia in the 1st century BC. Horse archers could also be found in the ranks of Palmyran and Persian armies. Mobility and speed enabled them to wear down the resistance especially of heavy enemy infantry so that they could eventually be ridden down and scattered by the *clibanarii*.

This soldier wears a conical bronze helmet commonly associated with troops from the East. A similar Persian helmet of ridge construction with a mail aventail and nosepiece was found at Dura (cf. plate XIX). His bronze lamellar cuirass of Hellenistic tradition with knotted sash follows several reliefs depicting Palmyran deities, some of which can be seen at the Louvre. The archer's elaborately decorated clothing has been reconstructed according to Hatrene, Parthian and Palmyran sources and underlines the soldier's élite status.

The horse archer employs a composite bow, a highly complex weapon whose efficiency relied on attached reinforcements of horn and sinew to increase its flexibility. The soldier wears an elaborately carved thumb ring on his left hand which allows him to rapidly and repeatedly draw the bow without injury. In his left hand he holds a spare arrow for speed, since he will not have to reach back into his quiver to reload. This technique is attested by a terracotta plaque of a Parthian horse archer now in the Antikensammlung, Berlin. The arrows have trilobate heads typical of Oriental weapons; examples have been recovered on the Harzhorn battlefield. When not in use, the bow is stored in a leather bowcase along with two spares on the left of the saddle. Often bowcase and quiver were combined, as contemporary depictions show. The horse furniture follows a relief of a Parthian horse archer now in the British Museum.

S. Borin '19

Plate XV

Moorish light horseman

Since Rome's conflict with Carthage in the 3rd century BC, North African light horse had fought both alongside Roman forces and against them. The nomadic Moors, living in the area between the Atlas mountains and present-day Algeria, specialised in hit-and run-tactics, conducting raids into Roman territory or remote oases and vanishing before their opponents had time to respond and hunt them down. The Moors also employed camels in a military context.

The sources mention élite Moorish light cavalry alongside the Osrhoenian horse archers in Maximinus' army. The reconstruction mainly follows a mosaic from Lepcis Magna (LBY), which shows javelin-armed local hunters on horseback. Their demeanour and clothing suggest that they are Moorish soldiers (cf. the tunic decorations). The soldier is mounted on a small but hardy horse of North African breed. The mosaic seems to call into question the common supposition that these horsemen rode without bridles (as for example Livy and Trajan's Column suggest). Being a skirmisher, this horseman does without armour.

The *Notitia Dignitatum* shows that Moorish cavalry were still a regular component of the late Roman army, unit names such as *Equites Mauri Alites* ("winged Moorish horse") confirming their role as light skirmishers.

S. Bogin '12

on an ancient trade and travel route through the valley of the Wipper river, which linked the valleys of the Weser and Werra rivers with the Thuringian basin. Following intensive excavations, the site was confirmed in 2014 as having been a temporary Roman camp. It formed an irregular rectangle with rounded corners with the typical ditch of Roman marching camps running for ca. 460 metres along the southern rampart. A gate with a protective ditch and rampart was positioned on the eastern side of the camp. Eight ovens provided the soldiers with their daily bread rations. The existence of these ovens proves that the camp was in use for not just a few nights, since the building and effective use of such ovens required several days', if not weeks' work. Finds inside the camp point to the camp's construction at the time of Maximinus' campaign. The skull of a calf recovered from one of the ditches (which the Romans had partly filled before departing) has shown that the area of the camp was still in use in the 5th or even 6th centuries. The animal was probably sacrificed in a religious ceremony. It is presumed that local German settlers knew the site and still made use of it, although not in a military context. Finds of bronze are comparatively rare; the Germans will have searched the camp for valuable materials once the Roman army had marched away.[87]

The Roman army continued its march through the eastern foothills of the Harz to the Elbe. After restoring the glory of Roman arms, the army, laden with plunder, began its return march along the northern foothills of the Harz in the direction of the Hessian basin. However, the enemy was not yet beaten. German tribesmen were preparing an ambush at the Harzhorn.[88]

The battle of the Harzhorn

Since a number of extensive, accessible and easily available works about the Harzhorn battle have been published recently, only a brief overview over the battle and its reconstruction with the help of contemporary battlefield archaeology will be provided here. The battlefield, which has been systematically excavated since 2008 after two treasure hunters found a Roman hippo sandal on the site in 2000, is situated on the north-western fringe of the Harz mountains in Germany; it extends over a distance of approximately two kilometres and is about 400 metres deep from north to south. The battlefield forms part of an ancient passageway running from the north-east to the south-west, which is still in use to this day. The Roman army chose this route on its return march, intending to reach its winter quarters via the Leine valley, the Hessian basin and the Wetterau hills. On this part of the way, a geographical obstacle was formed by the wooded ridge of the Harzhorn to the west, and the edge of the Harz mountains near the villages of Kalefeld and Northeim to the east. In those days, the killing ground of the Harzhorn battlefield was only around 350 metres across. The terrain, which forms the narrowest part of the way through the Harz mountains at this point, was rough and boggy in parts. The pass had been skilfully chosen by the German tribesmen for ambushing the Romans on their return march.[89]

The location of the more than 1, 500 Roman artefacts recovered from the site enables archaeologists to reconstruct the events, though theories vary. We choose to follow that of GESCHWINDE, LÖNNE and MEYER. At present the following course of events can be assumed[90]:

The Germans lay in wait as the Roman army, bogged down with plunder and captives, lumbered into the narrow defile formed by the hills to the west and the boggy terrain east of the pathway. According to archaeologists, the Roman column must have been roughly 3 km long. It must have been a dry autumn day, since the Romans were able to make use of their powerful composite bows, which were prone to disintegrating when exposed to water or damp. A military buff, Maximinus will have been warily eyeing the wooded hills to his right. It is possible that the Roman scouts had already got wind of an impending German attack. The Emperor and his generals however may have considered this merely an occupational hazard.

87 KÜßNER, Mario/SCHÜLER, Tim: „Truppen in Thüringen. Nordöstlichste römische Militäranlage entdeckt", in: *Archäologie in Deutschland* 3/2014, S. 6.; KÜßNER, Mario/WALTER, Diethard: „Ur- und frühgeschichtliche Besiedlung und archäologische Denkmalpflege im Kyffhäuserkreis", in: *Denkmaltopographie Bundesrepublik Deutschland. Kulturdenkmale in Thüringen, vol. 5. 1.: Kyffhäuserkreis, Überblicksdarstellungen,* Altenburg 2014, S. 32-69. More information was kindly provided by Dr. Küßner during several personal conversations.

88 GESCHWINDE (2018-19), ibid.

89 LEHMANN, p. 105 f.; MÄRTIN, Ralf-Peter, „Die Rache der Römer. Neues Schlachtfeld am Harz entdeckt", in *National Geographic Deutschland* 6/2010, p. 73 f.

90 The following account of events mostly follows GESCHWINDE (2018-19) and GESCHWINDE, Michael/LÖNNE, Petra/MEYER, Michael: „Eingefrorene Zeit. Das Harzhorn-Ereignis – Archäologie einer römisch-germanischen Konfrontation 235 n. Chr.", in: Wemhoff, Matthias/Rind, Michael M. (eds.): *Bewegte Zeiten. Archäologie in Deutschland* (Ausstellungskatalog), Berlin 2018, p. 283-293.

Maximinus's German campaign in 235/236 AD
(after GESCHWINDE 2018/19)

S.Borin '20

Plate XVI

Legionaries of *Legio I Minervia* attacked by Germanic warriors, Harzhorn, c. 236 AD.

We are witnessing the first moments of the German attack on the Roman marching column. Legionaries of *Legio I Minervia* have been caught off guard and are now frantically organising a line of defence.

Having hurled his *pilum* at the enemy, the legionary on the right has gained precious time to draw his *spatha* and receive the attackers at close quarters, a mode of fighting in which owing to his superior training he will most likely maintain the upper hand, if the Roman line holds. He has failed to kill his man, but has at least succeeded in disabling his opponent's shield, forcing him to face the Roman line without protection.

The legionary wears a splendid iron helmet decorated with bronze found at Frankfurt-Heddernheim, now in the collection of the Frankfurt Museum. It bears a depiction of the goddess Minerva on its cheekpiece. The crest has been added.

The reconstruction of the shield blazon is conjecture based on the Dura shields and pictorial evidence from the Arch of Galerius and the *Notitia Dignitatum*. The latter lists a unit of *Minervii* under the command of the *Magister Militum per Illyricum* (the unit may have evolved from a vexillation or was otherwise dispatched from its parent unit, possibly by Constantine during his struggle for power). The shield surface is depicted black with a yellow centre and a red rim. Shields on the Arch of Galerius and the Dura shields are emblazoned with protective deities, and unit badges. We have therefore reconstructed the shield (reproduced on the right) with a black surface and red leather binding. It has been painted with the legion's patron goddess Minerva bearing lance and *Palladium*, and with the legion's badge, the ram (*aries*). The legion's name and *epitheta* identify the bearer's unit: LEG I MIN P F MAX ANT (*Legio I Minervia Pia Fidelis Maximiniana Antoniniana*). The boss, showing a reclining Minerva surrounded by eagle, snakes, masks and *lunulae*, was once part of the Guttmann collection. The back of the shield could be painted rose red.

The veteran rallying his comrades in the foreground has campaigned with Caracalla in Germany, which is evident by his slightly outdated though richly ornamented equipment. His helmet is the famous Imperial Gallic type H helmet excavated from a gravel pit at Niedermörmter near Kalkar, Germany. He wears a long-sleeved iron mail corselet interwoven with a fine network of bronze chains for display which together with the single orichalcum chestplate was found at Bertoldsheim (D). The decorated hilt of his archaic ring pommel sword of Sarmatian design is based on a find from Mainz. The magnificent sheath binding was found at the Saalburg. The scabbard mountings of his dirk were found at Dura, as was the *phalera* disc decorating his baldric. It depicts Septimius Severus as the Sun God, possibly an heirloom from the soldier's father. The spear he is holding is painted in black and dark red to match the shield design. His simple bronze greaves are are of the type excavated at Künzing.

In the left background, a legionary has dropped his *sarcina* baggage pole and is hastily donning his bronze Niederbieber helmet. It is impossible to tell whether the crests were attached on the march in this specific instance, but the soldiers probably marched ready for immediate action. Over his woollen *tunica manicata* and a *subarmalis* with leather *pteryges* he wears a Newstead type cuirass. He carries a *semispatha* instead of a dagger, and a *spatha*. His *sarcina* includes a leather satchel, the rolled *sagum*, a field flask, a hatchet, a mess tin, and a casserole (*patera*). All this equipment is attached to the carrying pole (*furca*).

The German is wielding a spear whose decorated point was excavated on the Harzhorn battlefield. Dress and equipment mark him and the other warriors as men of superior rank in the hierarchy of the warband. His hairstyle and headband follow the depiction of a Marcomanni warrior on the 2nd century AD Portonaccio sarcophagus in Rome. Interestingly enough, beards appear to have been a mark of higher social rank among the Irmiones, since shaving knives are lacking among the grave finds of the warrior élite. His woollen kirtle, laced up on both sides, is based on a find from Thorsberg, as is his elaborately woven fringed cloak.The early crossbow fibula follows an example found in the grave of the "Gommern Chieftain" (s. below). He wears breeches and cross-gartered puttees according to contemporary Germanic fashion. Numerous bog finds have yielded laced shoes, among them those of the so-called "Damendorf Man" (Schleswig-Holstein, Germany). His *spatha* has been purchased from a Roman merchant and was found at Vimose (DK). A wooden *spatha* hilt was found at Thorsberg. *Baltei* excavated at Illerup and Vimose show that the Germans copied the Roman fashion of carrying the sword suspended from a decorated baldric. He carries a bone-tipped knife in a simple leather sheath as his secondary sidearm.

The second German is also of elevated social rank, possibly even a chieftain. This is recognisable by his moustache, dress and equipment. His cloak is a reconstruction of the cloak in which one of the Hunteberg bog bodies from the 3rd century AD was wrapped (Hunteberg, Lower Saxony). The rich blue of his tunic emphasises his wealth and social prestige. His tight breeks are laced at the inner thighs; such legwear was found at Thorsberg. The warrior has tied his long hair into a Suebian knot, of which one has survived on the skull of a bog body from Osterby (Schleswig-Holstein, Germany). His most valuable piece of equipment is his shield, whose depiction follows the reconstruction of the shield of the famous Gommern Chieftain. This Germanic warlord lived and died in the middle of the 3rd century AD and was buried in a wood-encased grave on the Gerstenberg hill near Gommern (Saxony-Anhalt, Germany). His grave yielded numerous precious deposits, among them many Roman artefacts. The most magnificent item however was his shield, which was decorated with two concentric circles of gilded ornaments and a boss made of a converted silver Roman drinking cup. The paintwork was applied according to Roman technique, and choosing Roman-manufactured colours.

The German calling on his fellow warriors for assistance wears a fringed and checkered red-dyed cloak based on the patterns of the cloaks of the previous two figures. It is held in place by a precious fibula, a discreet sign of prosperity. His kirtle is home-made but of good quality, the laced boots follow finds from Oberaltendorf (D) and Roswinkel (NL). His simple but sturdy *spatha* has been looted from a Roman auxiliary who perished in a skirmish in early summer, or is the result of much haggling with a merchant who happened to pass across the *limes* in more peaceful times than these. The discarded shield with its pointed conical boss follows depictions of German shields in Roman art in the 2nd and 3rd centuries AD.

Finds of contemporary Roman artefacts and weapons in Germany and Scandinavia serve to demonstrate that despite bloody military conflicts, a prosperous trade thrived between the Roman Empire and the endless lands of *Germania Magna*.

There was no real alternative route the army could have taken. The ensuing battle was to be series of individual engagements in different sectors of the battlefield.

As soon as the Roman advance guard and baggage train had entered the defile, the Germans struck. Up to now, they had been hiding in the woods several hundred metres away to the west to avoid detection by the Roman scouts and auxiliaries fanning out ahead of the main army. Storming down the heights of the Kahlberg and the Harzhorn, they assaulted the Roman marching column in several places at once. One group of Germans attacked the Roman advance guard as it was about to negotiate a steep ridge leading to a nearby spring. In accordance with their tactical role, the Romans were possibly expecting an attack and quickly closed ranks. The Romans stood and fought until a cavalry counter-attack scattered the attackers. However, these troops were in no position to come to the aid of their comrades engaged elsewhere along the line to the rear.

Another German warband attacked the baggage waggons in the middle of the marching column. The legionaries and baggage attendants however stood their ground and were able to drive the attackers off, using pickaxes to keep the Germans at a distance until Roman cavalry once again came to the rescue.

Further to the north however, the Romans were in dire straits. A massive German attack from the heights of the Harzhorn sliced the Roman column clean in two parts. The Roman troops in this sector abandoned the baggage and retired northwards to link up with the rearguard column, others made their way to the front of the column. The Germans meanwhile busied themselves with plundering the baggage vehicles, even attempting to drive them away so as to be able to search them at leisure. Chains excavated on the spot hint at German prisoners being freed by their fellow countrymen.

Up to now, the Roman rearguard column does not seem to have been engaged. When the soldiers heard the noise of the battle to the south and the horn signals calling for support, the legionaries dropped their field packs, removed the covers from their shields and donned their helmets. Led by Maximinus, the officers readied their men for action and prepared to counter-attack. Covered by the Osrhoenian archers, the infantry wheeled south and began to ascend the northern slope of the Harzhorn. A German attempt to turn the eastern Roman flank was repulsed with the aid of bolt-throwing catapults. Retreating to the south and west, the Germans were caught in front of the advancing Roman line and came within range of the Roman archery. The survivors fled south.

The Roman infantry had scaled the ridge of the Harzhorn and cleared the area with the help of the catapults and archers. Again using catapults on their eastern flank, the Romans drove the Germans away from the baggage vehicles in the valley at the foot of the Harzhorn and linked up with the advance guard. Roman auxiliaries set out in pursuit of the enemy retreating into the woods to the west. In their attempt to shake off the Roman pursuit, many Germans lost the booty they had made. Archaeologists have discovered a steady trickle of spoils between the remains of the baggage train in the valley and the hills to the west of the battlefield.

After some time, the auxiliaries called off the pursuit and returned to the main column. The Romans re-formed and recovered their dead and wounded. They then prepared to resume their march south. As the column began to move, many a legionary will have yearned for the comfort and security of the Rhine fortresses.

It is fortunate for modern scholars that the area of this ancient battlefield was never agriculturally cultivated. Especially with the help of metal detectors, archaeologists have succeeded in uncovering numerous Roman military artefacts preserved by the local lime marl and reconstructing the events that occurred. The hippo sandal unearthed in 2000 (a kind of non-permanent horseshoe attached to the hoofs of Roman pack animals to facilitate movement in rough terrain) marked the beginning of a large number of sensational finds which brought to life a battle between Romans and Germans. Since then, hundreds of catapult bolts, Oriental trilobite arrowheads (whose impact angle and resulting trajectory calculation allows for the locating of the Roman positions), javelin heads, *pila* shanks, cavalry lances (remains of their shafts permit radiocarbon dating), and the typical hobnails with which the soles of the *calcei*, the typical late Roman military boots, were studded, have been found. The latter provide ample information regarding Roman troop concentration and movements.

Other finds include tent pegs, the afore-mentioned entrenching tool, parts of horse trappings and bridles, a corn mill, metal mounts (the baggage wagon mentioned above crashed in the area German archaeologists have christened with the *Denglisch* word "Hotspot 5"), but only few pieces of military equipment, e. g. a bronze greave and a corroded fragment of Roman mail armour. On the northern slope of the Harzhorn the skeleton of a horse was discovered; radiocarbon dating revealed that the animal died between 230 and 240 AD. A precious few coins have also been unearthed (the most recent dating from 228 AD), as have a dagger sheath plate, a key to a chest, and a silver fibula. Excavations have also unearthed a set of chains, which suggests that the German attackers were able to free a number of their compatriots who had been unfortunate enough to be taken prisoner in previous engagements. The surviving evidence permits us to treat the Harzhorn as the site where in all probability there occurred a battle fought by the army of the Emperor Maximinus Thrax.

The high number of finds proves that the Harzhorn was not merely a skirmish involving a minor detachment; it was rather a full-scale battle involving all arms of a fully turned-out Roman army. The positioning of the finds, which remained undisturbed for one and a half millennia in the soil where they had been lost, allow us to reconstruct a hard-fought battle which the Romans were able to win thanks to superior armament and tactical flexibility.

The scarcity of finds which may be attributed to the German enemy stands in stark contrast to the vast number of Roman finds. Pride of place goes to a brass-decorated German spearhead. How may this be explained? Since the Romans were obviously interested in rapidly continuing their interrupted march southwest, they refrained from searching the hilly and wooded terrain for stray missiles and odd pieces of equipment. They will instead have recovered their casualties, carried out necessary repairs to the baggage train, and resumed their march. After the Romans had left, the tribesmen will have returned to gather their dead and collect lost items of equipment, and any equipment lost by the Romans which appeared worth the taking.

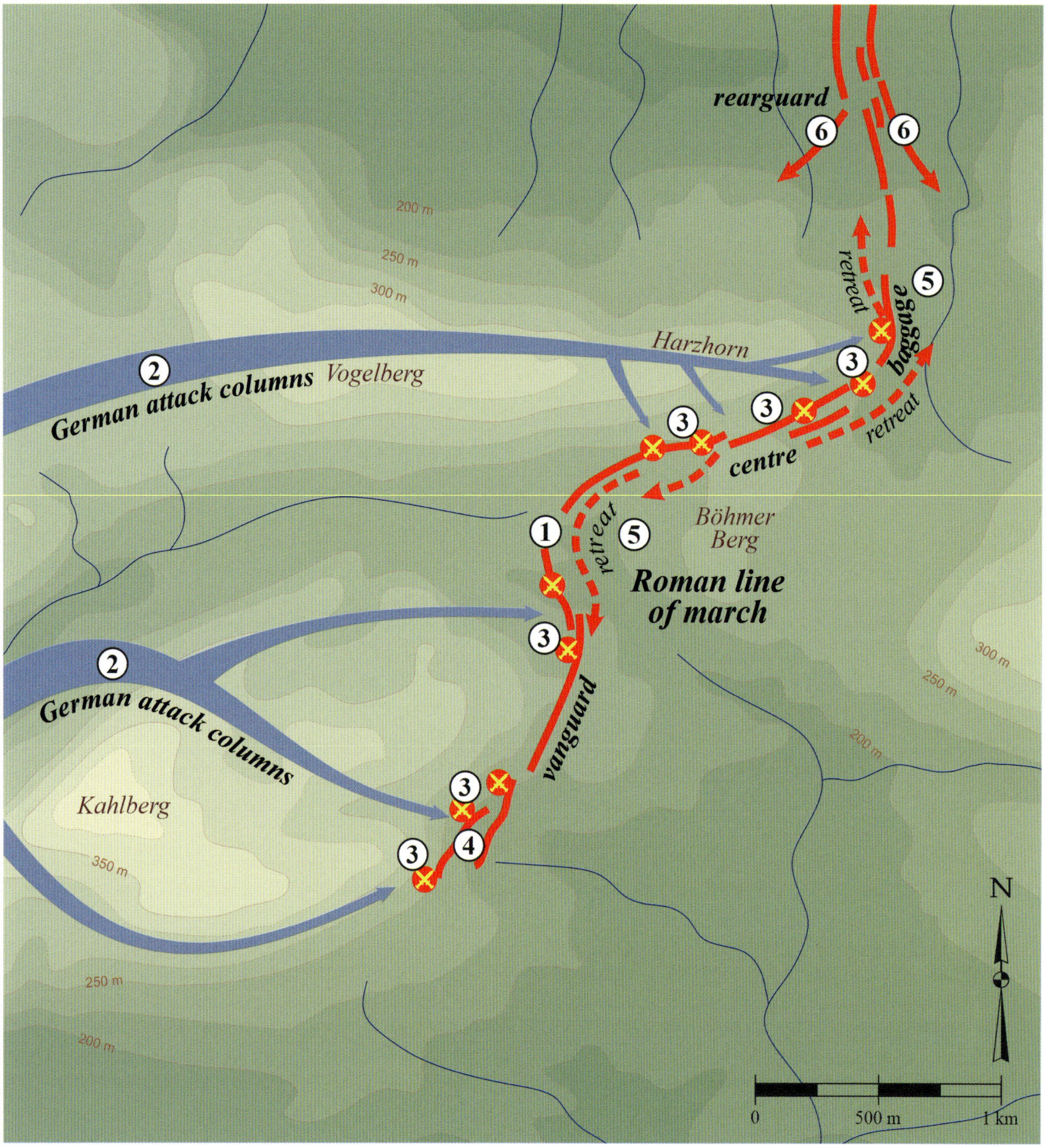

The Battle of the Harzhorn (Phase 1; after GESCHWINDE 2018/19)

1) The Roman marching column enters the Harzhorn defile. The trackway is dominated by wooded hills on both sides.
2) While the the Roman vanguard and baggage train are negotiating the way through the defile, columns of German warriors hidden in the forests on the hills to the west move to the attack.
3) The German attack simultaneously hits the Roman vanguard and flanks.
4) The Roman vanguard, which has been struggling down a ravine towards a spring, rallies and stands firm.
5) The German attacks on the baggage train and centre prove more successful. Roman troops guarding the baggage are unable to repel the attack from the heights of the Harzhorn and fall back towards the Roman rearguard which so far has not become engaged. Other Roman troops to the south are able to stand their ground and then retire in good order towards the troops fighting at the head of the column. The Roman column has now been split in two.
6) While the Germans now begin to plunder the baggage, free prisoners and attempt to drive away individual baggage wagons, the Roman rearguard deploys for action.

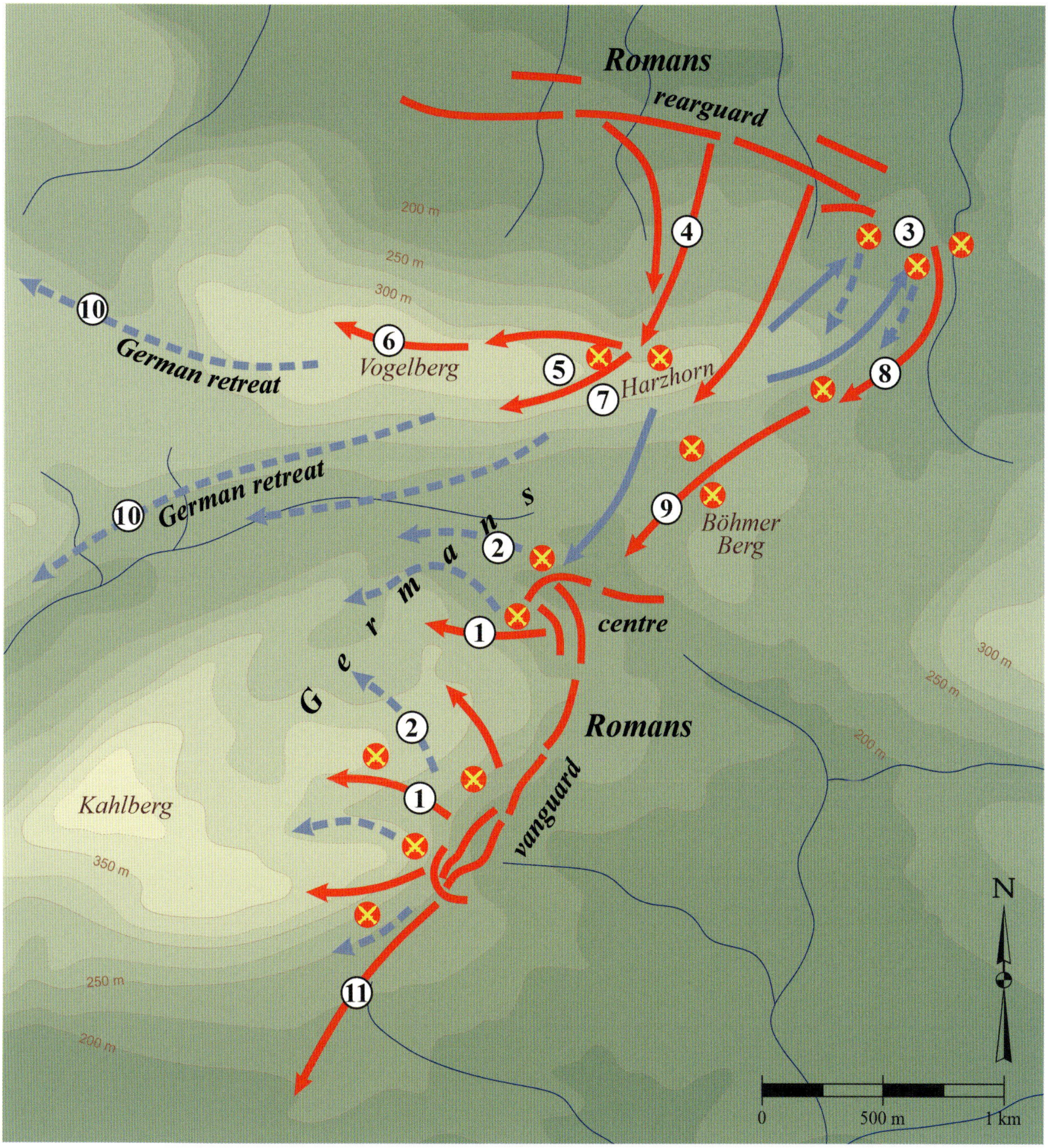

The Battle of the Harzhorn (Phase 2; after GESCHWINDE 2018/19)

1) Probably reinforced by troops from the centre of the column, the Roman vanguard counterattacks.
2) The Germans are forced to retire.
3) The deploying Roman troops of the rearguard use their catapults to repel a German attack on their left flank.
4) The Roman heavy infantry advances up the slopes of the Harzhorn. The Germans retreating from the left flank are hit by the arrows of the Osrhoenian archers coming up in support.
5) The Romans occupy the ridge and clear the hilltop of enemy troops.
6) Roman auxiliary troops begin the pursuit of the beaten enemy.
7) The Romans establish catapults on the ridge.
8) Covered by the catapults, the Romans advance into the pass.
9) The Romans succeed in making contact with the vanguard to the south.
10) The auxiliaries break off the pursuit. The remains of the German attackers retire into the deep woods with their booty.
11) The Romans reorganise their marching column and recommence their march south.

DRESS OF THE 3RD CENTURY ROMAN SOLDIER

Dress

Soldiers' tombstones and other sources of the first and second centuries AD depict legionaries and auxiliaries dressed in short-sleeved tunics and bare-legged, while cavalrymen in accordance with Celtic tradition wear mostly long-sleeved tunics and knee-length breeches (*feminalia*). In cold climates, *feminalia* also appear to have been worn by the infantry, especially by trumpeters, standard bearers and staff officers, as may be seen on Trajan's Column and the Adamclisi monument (RO). A further garment suitable for protecting oneself against rough weather was the *paenula*, a cloak of coarse wool tailored like a poncho which was open or slit at the front and fitted with a hood.

The second century AD seems to have ushered in a number of profound changes in Roman military dress. While short-sleeved tunics and bare legs appear to have remained frequent in warmer regions (the gravestone of Aurelius Alexianus, a soldier serving in Caracalla's army, shows the deceased in this familiar garb), Roman military dress in general began to follow new fashions and practical considerations. Many stelae and a few surviving frescoes and mosaics now show soldiers of all arms in a new manner of dress consisting of a long-sleeved tunic (*tunica dalmatica*, or *tunica manicata*), long, more or less close-fitting breeches with attached footlets (*bracae*), and closed laced hobnailed boots (*calcei*). As is suggested by the tunic's name, the origins of this new dress may probably be found in the Danube provinces. It is assumed that the soldiers recruited and stationed there adopted the regional dress suitable for local climatic conditions and spread it throughout the Empire in the course of the incessant troop movements and civil wars that determined the late second and third centuries. At any rate, the Praetorians and *equites singulares* stationed in Rome (many of which came from the Danube provinces) appear on their funerary monuments clad in the same "walking-out dress" as the auxiliaries of *cohors XX Palmyenorum* turned out for a religious ceremony on a fresco at Dura Europos in Syria.

Simon JAMES remarks that military tunics were tailored to be more close-fitting than their civilian counterparts and were thus tighter to wear[91]. The basic textile was wool, although other materials were also worn. In the past years, there has been much controversy and speculation regarding the colours of Roman military garments. Individual depictions and finds from Egypt and Syria, but also the items of clothing found in a bog in Thorsberg (Schleswig-Holstein, Germany) provide information about the Roman soldier's dress in this period. Some present-day popular scientific works feature illustrations of Roman soldiers clad in garish attire, the intensity of the colours resembling modern industrial dyes. Despite being based on contemporary images and other sources, these depictions ought perhaps to be treated with a fair amount of caution, since some illustrators tend to ignore the limitations which ancient dying methods, military economy and the soldiers' individual means set to military fashion. That said, it was perfectly feasible to achieve satisfying results by using herbal dyes such as madder (red), yellow weed (or weld, for yellow), indigo (blue) or woad (blue, yellow), some of which could be mixed to produce various hues. The more complicated and time-consuming the dye, the more expensive the garment became. It is probably not too wide of the mark to imagine Roman soldiers clad in tunics of red or a woolly off-white decorated with the coloured applications at shoulders, hems and sleeves which are typical of the time and can be found on archaeological finds and contemporary depictions (Dura Europos (SYR), Luxor, Fayum (EGY), et al.). Under campaign conditions, other regional textiles and garments more easily available will have been employed. On prolonged marches through different climate zones the soldiers probably often had to make do with whatever clothing was at hand. To what extent we may speak of the Roman soldier as wearing uniform in the modern sense is for good reason a matter of conjecture.

Another form of tunic was the *camisia*, a close-fitting garment which was made of linen, as was the *linea*, an under-tunic. The *Historia Augusta* relates Alexander Severus' predilection for white linen clothes, to which he gave priority over the imperial purple (HA, *Alexander Severus*, XL, 10). Many emperors of the second and third centuries, among them Caracalla and Tacitus (r. 275-76), took care to dress in simple garb and thus demonstrate their solidarity with the common soldier.

Although the military tunics of the third centuries were not as richly decorated as the garments of late antiquity, the applications fashionable at this time already point to a certain development in this direction. Hem, sleeves and neckline were decorated with stripes in contrasting colours (*clavi*), which were either applied to or woven into the garment's texture. Pairs of stripes running vertically across the shoulders from front to back hem were also popular (as on a tunic discovered among the Thorsberg finds). Often the *clavi* only extended over the shoulders and terminated in arrow-shaped decorations. Decorations in the form of crosses and sun wheels which were applied in pairs on the front of the tunic at thigh level were also frequent. It is impossible to ascertain whether different-coloured *clavi* in varying arrays served as rank distinctions; this appears fairly unlikely, even though the decorations on officers' garments would certainly have been more elaborate and made of more precious textiles than those of the men. In general, officers' clothes were

91 JAMES, Simon, *Excavations at Dura Europos 1928-1937, Final Report VII. The Arms and Armour and Other Military Equipment*, London 2004, p. 60.

Plate XVII

Grave stele of Aurelius Sabius, *legio II Traiana Fortis*

Sabius, who died aged 35, served with *legio II Traiana Fortis Germanica*, which was based at Nicopolis outside Alexandria, where the stele was found. He is shown armed but without helmet or armour. He wears a tunic and the *sagum* as well as boots. Despite the heat, he may also have worn tight-fitting breeches, but these would have been shown in paint, which has long since faded. Sabius wears the conventional ring buckle belt and his *spatha* suspended by a *balteus*. His oval shield lacks a visible boss, but this also would have been painted on. He is further armed with two slender lances tied together with a pair of leather thongs to facilitate transport. These weapons could be thrown or used in close combat. They appear to be too long to represent the javelins of the *lanciarii* however, and Sabius is not explicitly defined as a *lanciarius* in the inscription. The fact that daggers are missing on 3rd century military funerary monuments was once considered proof that these weapons had fallen out of use. Numerous archaeological finds confirm that this was far from the case however.

The gravestone of Aurelius Sudecentius of *legio XI Claudia Pia Fidelis*, found at Aquileia (I) and of slightly later date, shows the deceased in virtually identical pose and equipment. Apparently, twin lances supplemented the *pila* and *hastae* of the legionary infantry.

of better quality than those of their subordinates. A fresco found at Dura Europos shows Tribune Julius Terentius, commanding officer of *cohors XX Palmyrenorum*, wearing a white tunic with purple *clavi* [92].

The soldiers' breeches were either of wool or linen, but leather also seems to have been used, as is attested by a find from Valkenburg (NL). Like a toddler's romper suit or tights, these breeches had footlets attached and would have been held in position by leather or textile belts. For practical reasons, combat troops and cavalry will have worn breeches of natural dark woollen colours or dyes, or even leather (the Palmyrene auxiliaries of *cohors XX* wear dark breeches); the calves and feet were sometimes additionally protected against cold and damp by puttees or footwraps (*fasciae crurales, tibialia*). Officers and guardsmen may have worn white or red breeches at least on formal occasions. The above-mentioned tribune however wears the same dark grey legwear as his men. The *Historia Augusta* makes a point of mentioning Alexander Severus' special taste for fashion which had him wearing white breeches.

To counteract the cold and for extra protection, the men continued to wear the military scarf (*focale*); this also prevented the armour from chafing the neck. There is reason to assume that for identification reasons the soldier also wore a metal disc with his name and unit (*signaculum*) around his neck.

The *sagum*, a rectangular cloak of presumably Celtic origin measuring 1 x 2 metres, had been in use since Republican times. It also served as the soldier's blanket. In the third century the *sagum* seems to have replaced the *paenula* altogether, as the latter is no longer depicted on gravestones. The *sagum* was fastened at the right shoulder with a fibula, exposing the sword arm. These fibulae appeared in the form of so-called knee or hinged brooches, but more elaborate disc brooches were also common[93]. In fair weather, the *sagum* was flung back across the left shoulder, allowing the soldier ease of movement. Caracalla, whose actual name was Marcus Aurelius Severus Antoninus, received his nickname from the cloak he was fond of wearing and which became his hallmark, the *caracalla* (or *caracallus*), a long hooded cloak open at the front and without sleeves, which seems to have resembled the *paenula* and had its origins in Celtic or German culture. This garment also appears to have been in widespread use in the Roman army of the late second and early third centuries. Cassius Dio actually claims that the *caracallus* was the emperor's personal invention, while Herodian claims that the emperor sought to imitate the garb of the *leones* ("lions"), his German bodyguard (IV, 7, 3)[94]. In view of the fact that Caracalla always took great pains to demonstrate affinity with his soldiers by observing appearances such as simple food and dress, Herodian's notion appears the more plausible of the two. We must imagine the soldiers' s in natural woollen colours (the wool fat of the undyed cloak served as a natural rain repellent and protection against cold), while the officers wore red, blue or white cloaks with fringes in contrasting colours, perhaps according to rank. Julius Terentius' cloak, for example, is white with dark red fringes. Centurions, staff officers and the emperor still wore the heavy *paludamentum* at least on formal occasions, the emperor's being dyed purple. The Ludovisi sarcophagus depicts the general and his high-ranking officers wearing the traditional sash (*zona militaris*) knotted around their waists.

Apart from the items mentioned above, the Roman soldier had numerous other pieces of clothing at his disposal, among them socks (*udones*), gloves and caps (*pillei*), a number of which were discovered in a military context in Egypt. These caps consist of woollen triangles in contrasting colours sewn together to form a hemispherically-shaped headdress resembling modern baker's boy caps for children or the watch caps worn in contemporary armies. Some have ear flaps and small tassels and were presumably worn underneath the helmet. Sailors seem to have favoured the Greek *kausia*, a round hat with a narrow brim. The famous cylindrical *pilleus pannonicus*, the late Roman army's universal headwear, does not yet seem to have been worn. The broad straw hat so popular with modern re-enactors is not documented in this period.

Another distinctive feature of the Roman soldier of the Republic and early Principate, the hobnailed sandal (*caliga*), had fallen from use in the early third century AD. The soldiers at this time wore closed laced boots (*calcei*), which normally were cut from a single piece of leather and sewn up over the bridge of the foot (occasionally at the heel). These boots have been discovered by archaeologists in all former parts of the Roman Empire and are depicted on numerous military gravestones. They obviously formed part of a Roman soldier's standard equipment and were worn by soldiers of all arms. Pairs of eyelets were cut into the boots' upper leather above the bridge of the foot through which the laces passed. These laces formed an integral part of the footwear and were cut from the same piece of leather as the rest of the boot. They were done up around the ankle. The footlets of the soldiers' breeches remained visible, the *calceus* had no tongue; had the footlets not existed, the soldier would have had trouble tucking the legs of his breeches into the tops of his shoes. Just like their predecessors, the *calcei* had thick hobnailed soles. The *Historia Augusta* observes that it was customary to call a particularly tall and lanky individual *caliga Maximini*, "Maximinus' boot" (HA, *Duo Maximini*, XXVIII, 9). The giant Emperor must have had an impressive shoe size.

92 The purple colour of Terentius' *clavi* would have been died with a mixture of madder and woad; the imperial purple was the emperor's prerogative and was made from the gland secretion of a number of marine snail species universally named *murex purpureus* by the Romans. The cost of this dye was astronomical.

93 FISCHER, Thomas, *Die Armee der Caesaren. Archäologie und Geschichte*, Regensburg 2012, p. 336.

94 SUMNER, Graham, *Roman Military Dress*, Stroud 2009, p. 86 f.

Belt and baldric

In the early Principate, the approach of Roman soldiers was heralded by the crash of their hobnailed boots on flagstones, but above all by the rhythmic jingling of their studded aprons. Both legionaries and auxiliaries proudly present themselves on their gravestones wearing elaborately decorated crossed military belts (*cingula*) with broad aprons, from which are suspended sword (*gladius* or *spatha*) and dagger (*pugio*). Later the sword would be worn on a narrow baldric across the left shoulder (*balteus*). The apron, whose leather strips mounted with either round or rectangular metal discs or plates terminated in ivy-leaf pendants, served as rudimentary protection for the genitals (its effect was above all psychological) and helped to avoid embarrassment if the soldier did without a *subligaculum* (loincloth) and proceeded to sit down with his legs apart[95]. The apron had developed from the *cingulum*'s slit and decorated belt straps. The *cingulum* itself had become the distinguishing feature of the soldier's trade and object of fierce military pride. Its importance can be judged from the disgrace of having to stand in full view outside the *praetorium* without one's belt as a punishment, the laughing stock of the garrison with tunic flapping untidily and unsoldierly around one's calves.

The change in military fashion which began to manifest itself at the end of the second century AD brought with it a new form of military belt. Soldiers' tombstones of this period mostly present the deceased in their walking-out dress without armour or helmets, all however wear their belts and baldrics. The lavishly decorated belts described above have been replaced by so-called ring-buckle belts, which were of Sarmatian or Persian origin and probably spread throughout the Empire along with the other new items of military dress. These *cingula* were fairly broad affairs adorned with decorative stitching along the edges, whose ends were passed through a round or square-shaped buckle in front of the body and fixed on one or both sides with mushroom-shaped studs (presumably the belts had several holes to adjust width). The ends, some of which appear quite long, were adorned with decorated pendants (in the shape of drops, ivy leaves or *phalli* to ward off the evil eye) and hung down loosely or were tucked under the belt. Ring-buckle belts could also be decorated with metal applications. Charms like FELIX VTERE ("Use [the sword] with good fortune", or "Use as a fortunate one") were popular. Several inscriptions reading LEONI ([dedicated/presented] "to the lion") have survived. These might have belonged to members of Caracalla's German bodyguard, who were referred to as his Lions[96].

Occasionally soldiers depicted on military tombstones hold the pendants of their belts in their right hands in a demonstrative gesture as if proudly pointing to their military profession. Indeed the *cingulum* was still the symbol of the soldier's trade. The Christian martyr Marcellus, serving as a centurion in *legio VII Gemina*, unbuckled and threw away his belt as a gesture of defiance against the Emperors Diocletian and Licinius, thereby breaching his military oath[97].

The sword belt (*balteus*) was now worn across the right shoulder (of this more anon). This belt too was fairly broad (two examples found in Vimose (DK) have a breadth of 8cm), which prevented the belt painfully cutting into the wearer's shoulder. The baldric became more slender at hip level and was passed around the scabbard several times and held in place by a slide of metal or ivory attached to the front of the scabbard. The belt then broadened out again, passed over the wearer's right shoulder and was joined to the other end with a round disk (*phalera*) below the chest. The loose end was decorated either with a hinged decorated metal mount or with decorative stitching (one example found in Vimose sports the image of a dolphin for good luck)[98].Often the perforated disks and pendants were inscribed, e. g. two examples from Munich and Bonn bear the words OPTIME [frequently supplemented by MAXIME on other finds] CONSERVA NVMERVM OMNIVM MILITANTIVM (which roughly translates as "Supreme [and greatest] [*sc.* God Jupiter], protect all soldiers"). A mount found at Corbridge bears the (grammatically not entirely orthodox[99]) alternative inscription OMNIA VOS ("All of you")[100]. Other mounts of this type have been excavated at Corbridge and Strasbourg. The *phalerae* were often decorated by figures, e. g. eagles, the she-wolf and twins, imperial portraits, Hercules. Disks depicting the sun-wheel were also common. Like the *balteus*, the new form of military belt was probably of Sarmatian origin[101].

Belt and baldric were coloured in various natural shades from a light reddish brown to black. Pictorial sources, e. g. at Dura, indicate that many soldiers seem to have favoured red, a dye which was easy to produce and created a pleasing visual effect. The jingle of belt and baldric added to the proud military swagger of the wearer.

95 Cf. JUNKELMANN, Marcus, *Die Legionen des Augustus*, Munich[15] 2015, p. 212; SUMNER (2009), p. 191.

96 GRÄF, Julia, „Hingegen bereiteten ihm die Germanen keine Freude", in Archäologisches Landesmuseum Baden-Württemberg (ed.), *Caracalla. Kaiser, Tyrann, Feldherr*, Darmstadt/Mainz 2013, p. 80.

97 POLLARD, Nigel / BERRY, Joanne, *The Complete Roman Legions*, London 2012, p. 111.

98 Ernst KÜNZL sees these mounts as a continuation of the studded apron of the early Principate (2008, p. 105).

99 It is possible that *vos* is in fact a contraction of *vobis*, in which case the translation would be „May Jupiter preserve everything to you" (i. e. everything which is yours, or your due).

100 BISHOP, M. C./COULSTON, J. C. N., *Roman Military Equipment from the Punic Wars to the Fall of Rome*, Oxford[2] 2011, p. 162.

101 ELLIOTT (2014, p. 59) however presumes that the new fashion originated in the East.

The Antonine Revolution – new tactics, new equipment?

Silentium!	Silence in the ranks!
Mandata captate.	Observe your orders.
Non vos turbatis.	Do not be troubled.
Ordinem servate.	Stay in formation.
Bando sequute.	Follow the standard.
Nemo dimittat bandum et inimicos seque.	No one is to leave the standard in order to pursue the enemy.

Orders according to the *Strategikon* [102]

We have seen that the late second and third century AD ushered in significant changes in the organisation and appearance of the Roman Army. These changes also affected the soldiers' equipment and weapons. Pictorial sources and a large number of archaeological finds have made it possible for us to establish a clear-cut idea of how the men who followed the Soldier Emperors were armed and equipped. The climatic conditions along Rome's northern frontier, the *limes*, have preserved numerous metal artefacts, and the abundance of finds recovered from the desert fortress city of Dura Europos in Mesopotamia, which fell to Persian besiegers in AD 256, has provided a fairly reliable image of the arms and equipment of the Roman soldier in the first half of the third century AD. The similarity of equipment finds from various parts of the Empire points to a certain degree of standardisation as equipment of the legions and regular auxiliary formations became increasingly assimilated. It appears that the legions augmented their classic arsenal by adopting arms hitherto mainly associated with the auxiliaries as focus shifted from a difference in armament as a result of different tactical assignments of individual units to tactical versatility and flexibility in any given formation (though there were still specialist units specially trained in certain arms). This may have occurred in response to an overall change in the army's strategy.

As shall be explained, the arms and equipment of the Roman soldier began to undergo significant changes as the second century AD drew to a close. To which events exactly this change is attributable remains controversial. British scholars have coined the phrase *Antonine Revolution*, defining the phase in which these changes set in, namely the late second century AD. The word itself stresses the depth of change apparent, which is considered to be a significant tactical shift as the Roman Army encountered new enemies to whose fighting methods it was forced to adapt.

Let us take a brief look at the Imperial Roman Army's basic tactical concept. At the time of Maximinus Thrax' reign the Roman Army's fundamental tactical approaches had remained much the same as those of its earlier predecessors. Cohort tactics required the heavy infantry's role as the cornerstone of pitched battles while the cavalry guarded the flanks. When Vegetius wrote his *Epitoma Rei Militaris* in the fifth century AD, the model on which he based his (idealised) description of the Roman order of battle was probably the army of the third century AD. According to Vegetius, the first two lines consisted of heavy infantry, while archers and javelineers formed the third and fourth. The catapults were positioned behind the line. A portion of heavy infantry remained behind, forming a reserve. In his description of Septimius Severus' battle against Pescennius Niger at Issus in 194 AD, Cassius Dio mentions only three battle lines, namely heavy infantry, javelineers and slingers, and archers[103]. How many ranks deep the individual lines were remains unclear. STEPHENSON presumes that a battle line of the third century was generally three to four ranks deep (this could be doubled to receive cavalry (s. below)[104], STROBEL, quoting Arrian, favours a principle of four ranks based on the eight-man tent section (*contubernium*) forming the smallest training unit, with one *contubernium* forming two regular files, and one against cavalry[105]. The *Strategikon* may prove a help in this context: if we assume that a *centuria* numbered eighty soldiers, the legionaries may have formed ten ranks of eight, each eight-man file consisting of one *contubernium*. If the tactical situation required it, every second man would side-step and form a new four-deep file (space permitting) and thus double the extension of the battle line from ten files to twenty[106].

Catherine GILLIVER has observed that concrete written sources describing Roman battle deployments in the Imperial era are comparatively rare. None mentions the old-style classic *triplex acies*, the sophisticated checkered three-line deployment of the Republican legion based on manipular tactics. In contrast to Vegetius' account, the Imperial legions often actually seem to have deployed in only a single battle line of heavy infantry between four and eight deep, as explained above. GILLIVER attributes this to numerical and tactical superiority on the specific occasions, but also to training and high morale. Whether

102 *Maurice's Strategikon. Handbook of Byzantine Military Strategy* (transl. George Dennis), Philadelphia 1984, XII, 14, p. 145. The grammatical inaccuracies are due either to a gradual erosion of classic Latin, or to a copying error. The word bandum (βάνδον) is a word of Germanic origin and was not used in the 3rd century AD.

103 Cf. Arrian's description of the battle order against the Alans (see below).

104 Cf. STEPHENSON, Ian, *Roman Infantry Equipment. The Later Empire*, Stroud 1999, p. 113.

105 Cf. STROBEL, p. 276.

106 *Strategikon* XII, 16 (p. 145 f.). Maurice's Byzantine infantry actually stood up to sixteen ranks deep.

such tactics were the rule rather than the exception, especially when dealing with enemies with strong cavalry contingents, is very much a matter of debate.[107]

Once the army was fully deployed, the enemy was subjected to a hail of missiles. Light infantry, e. g. the élite *lanciarii*, might operate ahead of the main battle line, seeking weak spots in the enemy formation and attempting to disrupt cohesion. This phase was followed by the attack, Vegetius enumerating several strategies. The Roman infantry might choose a coordinated attack of the entire battle line (this is described by Dio), a means which required considerable training and discipline, or an assault in oblique order. Vegetius also mentions a simultaneous attack on both enemy flanks with the army's centre refused, or a concentrated wedge which sought to swiftly break into the enemy line. Immediately before closing in the legionaries equipped with the *pilum* hurled their javelins. What followed was a gory heaving and shoving with swords and polearms[108], the side which succeeded in breaking the enemy formation remaining victorious. The more adaptable and flexible manipular principle of earlier times seems to have gone out of fashion.

As a result of this, the soldiers in the front battle lines needed to be heavily armoured, especially in view of the missiles raining down on them from friend and foe alike. If the legion was in the defensive, the *fulcum* was formed, a static shield wall with the first rank kneeling behind their shields while the other two raised their shields and engaged the enemy through the gaps as the missiles from behind sought to break the momentum of the enemy attack.

Even though the details of Roman arms and equipment must be set aside at this stage, it can be accepted as a fact that the close of the second century AD the Roman legionary infantry began to adopt the cavalry longsword (*spatha*) as its main sidearm (without however completely abandoning the traditional *gladius* altogether, as we shall see). The legions also increasingly began to employ the auxiliary infantry's oval *clipeus* shield alongside the rectangular *scutum*. This change in armament was accompanied by the adoption of a new type of helmet with a deep neckguard which covered almost the soldier's entire head.

How are we to imagine the connection between tactics and this new type of equipment? First of all, it is vital to understand that despite the growing importance of the cavalry on the battlefields (in this time of hasty troop movements all over the Empire the Imperial field army as such was only just beginning to take shape), the legions remained the prime force in the Roman army capable of determining a battle's outcome. This did not change significantly until the Western Empire's final collapse. It would be a mistake to suppose an ongoing decline in the quality and morale of the heavy infantry. While the fighting potential of Parthian and Persian infantry was negligible, the Romans fought their cavalry with disciplined and steadfast foot soldiers. The sources indicate that up to the fall of the West it was the legions and their aggressive fighting spirit which decided a battle's outcome, as they did at the Harzhorn (235/6), Rhesaina (243) and – much later – at Strasbourg (357 AD). The fateful battle of Adrianople in 378 was lost only after the infantry collapsed in the face of physical exhaustion after hours of fighting in intolerable heat, and the unforeseen appearance of the Gothic cavalry.

New helmet designs, the moving of the longsword to the left side of the body (facilitating the action of drawing it), the introduction of new polearms and missile weapons, especially the thrusting spear in the legions, as well as the appearance of the oval shield in the ranks of the heavy infantry all appear to point to the fact that the Roman Army was facing new enemies, and that regardless of its traditionally offensive and aggressive tactics was forced to adapt to these new enemies' fighting techniques to deal with them effectively. Massive helmets reinforced with crossbars to protect the cranium[109] and sporting deep and wide neckguards hint at a new form of impact of enemy arms, mostly from above, which would obviously be attributable to cavalry. The infantry's adoption of the long *spatha*, a weapon designed for both thrusting and cutting, also suggests the need for a weapon to counteract both infantry and mounted troops. It is interesting to note that on the Ludovisi sarcophagus one of the legionaries depicted holds his shield above his head and proceeds to carve up a Germanic tribesman with a downward slash of his *spatha*. Clearly the *gladius* was considered of little use in certain combat situations. The legionary's effective weapon range thus extended[110], the introduction of the thrusting spear (*hasta*), which to a certain extent began to compete with the *pilum* as polearm of the legions, also seems to fit the bill of tactical modification.

What can we make of the *clipeus*? The rectangular *scutum* worked hand in glove with the *gladius*, the legionary ducking behind his large shield and lunging at an opponent's face and torso without exposing himself too much. The curve of the *scutum* allowed the soldier to protect most of his body effectively, only exposing his sword arm to his opponent's weapons. The *scutum* is however not

107 GILLIVER, Catherine M., „Battle", in:SABIN, Philip/VAN WEES, Hans/WHITBY, Michael (Hrsg.): *The Cambridge History of Greek and Roman Warfare, Vol. II: Rome from the late Republic to the late Empire, Part II: The Late Empire*, Cambridge 2007, p. 122-157, p. 130.

108 BISHOP presumes that the increasingly close formations of infantry led to the introduction of the longsword (*spatha*); BISHOP, M. C., *The Gladius. The Roman Short Sword*, Oxford 2016, p. 74.

109 This form of helmet reinforcement appears to have been hurriedly introduced during Trajan's Dacian campaigns to counteract the murderous Dacian *falx*, a heavy two-handed scythe-like weapon designed to be wielded from above.

110 BISHOP (2016), p. 74; ELLIOTT, Paul, *Legions in Crisis. Transformation of the Roman Soldier AD 192-284*, p. 71 ff.

Plate XVIII

Beneficiarius

This NCO finds himself on duty at the legionary base at Mainz on a cold winter's morning. He is a *beneficiarius proconsularis* in the service of the governor. While he may be performing administrative duties at headquarters, he might also be patrolling one of the roads of the Upper German province, manning one of the police stations (*stationes*) established for this purpose. Since daily routine service does not require the donning of armour, he merely wears his military *tunica manicata* over a woollen under-tunic, and saffron-coloured breeches. The tunic is decorated with coloured stripes at sleeves, hem and neckline. This type of military clothing is well attested by various contemporary finds, and pictorial evidence. A further precaution against the cold is his locally produced elaborate cloak, examples of which have been discovered in bogs at Thorsberg and Vehnemoor (D).

The *beneficiarius* is a veteran from the German provinces. His richly decorated military belt bears the inscription *LEONI* ("[awarded] to the lion"; cf. FISCHER 2012, p. 125), identifying him as a former member of the "Lions", Caracalla's once-famous German bodyguard. The belt may well have been a personal present from the Emperor himself. His bracelet serves as a further reminder of bygone eventful and surely more glorious days of service.

The *beneficiarii's* sign of rank was the special lance they carried on duty, several examples and depictions of which exist. One can be seen on the Cancellaria relief at Rome showing 1st century Praetorian guardsmen. The spearhead illustrated was excavated at Ehl in Alsace. As can be seen in the illustration, this distinctive form of spearhead could also be worn in form of metal mounts on belt straps and baldrics.

S. Borip '19

ideally suited to fighting with a long sword or a spear, since when cutting or slashing at an opponent with the *spatha* from above the high and rectangular edge of the shield can prove an encumbrance and lead to bruising the sword arm. The spear can also be wielded more effectively overarm if the edge of the shield is curved.

How may the introduction of a longer sword be explained if we consider the confined space of two interlocked blocks of infantry in combat as described by Vegetius and Dio? It is to be presumed that the augmentation and modification of the legions' arsenal can be attributed to what was considered to be the tactical necessity of coming to terms with new enemies. If equipment was modified to counteract an increased threat from mounted enemies without completely abandoning the established approach to infantry combat the parallel existence of old and new kinds of weapons could be convincingly explained. As yet, this is conjecture however.

If one supposes that the Antonine Revolution occurred to counteract new enemies, the question poses itself who these enemies actually were. In the course of the second century AD Rome's armies found themselves increasingly faced with enemies whose military doctrine relied mainly upon mounted troops[111]. In the east the Parthians and their Persian successors with their heavily armoured cataphracts continued to pose a threat, while along the Rhine and Danube Sarmatian and Alamannic cavalry increasingly began to determine events on the battlefield. On the North African frontier, Berber tribesmen on horseback raided Roman settlements.

The traditional fighting methods of the Roman infantry are well known both to the military enthusiast and the historian. The legionaries would begin combat by hurling their javelins at the enemy and then charge to close quarters with their *gladii*, exploiting the confusion and mayhem their *pila* had caused among the enemy. The soldiers would cut and thrust with their short swords and to punch their shield bosses at their opponents to knock them off balance. This aggressive and offensive approach is counterbalanced by a defensive strategy which some scholars consider fairly typical of changing tactics in the third century AD:

In 135 AD the governor of Cappadocia, Lucius Flavius Arrianus, was forced to take the field with the XIIth and XVth legions to repel an incursion by the Alani, a people of Sarmatian stock. In his account of the Roman order of battle (Έκταξις κατά Άλανϖν, *Ektaxis kata Alanon*), Arrian provides the reader with a fairly detailed description of Roman infantry fighting a defensive action against cavalry. His account, which is both a theoretical and occasionally idealizing treatise, is not always entirely precise, but events may have occurred as follows:

The Romans deployed eight ranks deep, the first levelling *pila* or spears to prevent the enemy from penetrating the Roman line, since horses will not charge a solid bristling wall of spears[112]. The second, third and fourth ranks used their spears to thrust overarm at the horses and riders and to dispatch any enemy horsemen who succeeded in penetrating the shield wall, the fourth rank throwing its *pila* should the need arise. The last four ranks consisted of legionaries possibly armed with *lanceae*, designed both to thrust and to employ as missiles to keep the enemy at a distance. A ninth rank consisted of archers, who were supported by the catapults at the rear. The flanks were protected by auxiliary infantry and several cavalry formations. A cavalry reserve was positioned in the rear between the archers and the catapults.

The Romans were to start the battle with a barrage of missiles. If the first rank with couched spears aimed to hold the Alani horsemen at bay, the use of the spear or *pilum* from behind a line of rectangular *scuta* must have proved difficult. Oval shields have the advantage of providing sound defence for the bearer (and, to a certain degree, his right-hand neighbour) while enabling the soldier to wield his spear more effectively[113].

Arrian's legionaries succeeded in driving off the attack of the Alani. His tactics relied on holding back the cavalry and sending half of it in pursuit while the other followed at a distance to contain any sudden counter-attack and extend the pursuit. If the enemy were routed, the light missile troops were to join in the pursuit with the heavy legionary infantry following in formation as a precaution against further enemy attack[114]. Similar tactics seem to have been implemented at the Harzhorn, when auxiliary infantry and cavalry pursued the fleeing German tribesmen back into the forests towards the west while the legions remained static.

If however Roman infantry were forced to retain this passive role against a more obstinate enemy denying them the opportunity to break out of the deadlock and resume the initiative (tactics at which, for example, Parthian horse archers excelled), things could take a marked turn for the worse. This was the fate of one of Alexander Severus's three army columns at Ctesiphon in 233 AD, when the Roman infantry was surrounded and slaughtered at leisure by hit-and-run Persian horse archers which did not allow them to apply the close-quarter fighting techniques

111 ELLIOTT (2014), p. 77.

112 In the course of his preparations preceding his proposed Asian campaign, Caracalla allegedly equipped 16, 000 infantry with Macedonian *sarissai*, turning them into *phalangarii*. In view of the formidable Parthian cavalry, this appears a tactically sound move. I am indebted to Dr. Werner Zitzmann for raising my awareness towards this aspect.

113 MACDOWALL, Simon, „The Roman Army in Transition. Legions of Marcus Aurelius", in: *Ancient Warfare* VII/6, pp. 12-16, p.15.

114 GILLIVER, S. 139.

they were accustomed to. The more educated officers on the Emperor's staff will have remembered accounts of Crassus' last stand against the Parthians 280 years earlier.

As regards the role of legionary light troops, a new branch seems to have established itself in the course of the third century AD, namely the corps of *lanciarii* armed with javelins. Lanciarius Aurelius Mucianus of the élite *legio II Parthica* is depicted on his gravestone at Apamea holding a quiver storing a handful of comparatively short javelins. Although scholars are sure that the legions had always fielded light-armed troops, the *lanciarii* appear to have constituted a novelty. COWAN places them either behind the main line of battle, from where they would pepper the enemy with missiles, or in gaps between the heavy infantry from which they would conduct sudden sorties to wreak havoc among their opponents, which they seem to have done in the battle of Nisibis (217 AD)[115]. Since such a flexible role on the battlefield required courage, initiative, and drive, these picked men were considered élite troops. Relying on a passage from Cassius Dio narrating an episode from the reign of Commodus, COWAN gives the number of these troops as probably 500 per legion[116]. This is cohort strength, but we know little about the internal organisation of the *lanciarii* and their integration into their parent unit's structure.

Rome's armies in the defensive – although Arrian's account was written almost a century before the period concerned, it does nevertheless provide a sound idea of how the legions fought defensive actions, a situation they were increasingly finding themselves in as the third century progressed. The establishment of the *lanciarii* was obviously deemed a necessary measure to add tactical flexibility in the face of new challenges on the battlefield. The augmentation of the legionary arsenal and changes in equipment may also be attributed to this fact, yet this does not mean that time-tested and sound tactics were automatically abandoned. Changes in the Roman army's armament and equipment occurred gradually and lasted long periods of time.

The Roman cavalry does not at first appear to have been affected to the same degree by tactical reorientation as the infantry. It remained its duty to patrol the frontiers in peacetime and together with the infantry garrisons to contain incursions penetrating into the Empire's territory, or to delay the enemy until the legions could be moved in to deal with any more substantial threat. This fact serves to explain the presence of numerous cavalry regiments on the Rhine and Danube defences, the *limes*, since horsemen were able to swiftly reach any area of crisis and react with more tactical flexibility to enemy movements. In times of war cavalrymen served as dispatch riders and scouts, and protected the army on the march. Cavalry supported the infantry in battle by securing its flanks, skirmishing and engaging enemy horsemen, and by pursuing a beaten foe. A majority of Roman horsemen both in the *alae* and the *cohortes equitatae* were thus medium cavalry equipped with helmets, shields and body armour, and armed with lances, swords and javelins. Apart from in the *clibanarii* regiments, horses were not commonly armoured. There was a large number of specialist units, among them the *contarii* armed with lances ca. 4 metres long whose length required both hands to wield them effectively (the *contus* was of Iranian origin), Moorish light horse (*Mauri*), mounted archers (*equites sagitarii*), among them probably the élite Osrhoeni in Maximinus' army, and a few regiments of heavily armed cataphracts (*cataphractarii* and the more heavily armoured *clibanarii*), which can be ascertained from the time of Trajan but only seem to have started to appear in larger numbers from the third century onwards, a reaction to more aggressive Persian . JUNKELMANN counts the Mauri and the Osrhoeni as part of the Imperial field army of the early third century[117]. As we have seen, they were always to be found in the ranks of the Emperor's army whenever he was forced to beat back enemy incursions on various frontiers of the Empire.

Most contemporary scholars have meanwhile abandoned the notion that Gallienus (r. 253-268) can be credited with the creation of an independent mobile cavalry reserve at Imperial disposal which many have considered the precursor of the late Imperial mobile field armies. Gallienus's horsemen were probably simply part of a mixed Imperial force originally created by Septimius Severus' reinforcement of the Italian garrison, which was intended as a central reserve and which continued to exist in various forms as different Emperors were forced to fight the never-ending conflicts of the third century. The famous *Equites Dalmatae* and *Equites Illyricani* mentioned by the sources in this context have so far not been clearly defined. JUNKELMANN and SOUTHERN suggest that these crack horsemen were in fact not themselves Illyrians or Dalmatians but soldiers from regiments garrisoning the Danube frontier. These experienced and battle-hardened veterans were consequently considered something of an élite.

115 COWAN (2003), p. 24 ff; COWAN (2007), p. 63

116 COWAN (2003), p. 25.

117 JUNKELMANN, Marcus, *Die Reiter Roms*, vol. 2, *Reitweise und Militärischer Einsatz*, Mainz 1991, p. 76.

Plate XIX

Cataphractarius

This reconstruction of an armoured lancer from a *numerus cataphractariorum* is based on the fact that grave stelae depicting soldiers of these units invariably show them riding unarmoured horses. The grave stele of Aurelius Saluda and his brother Regrethus of the *ala nova firma cataphractaria* was found in Stuttgart-Bad Cannstatt, other stelae of *cataphractarii* were excavated at Worms (D) and Lyon (F).

The cavalryman wears a helmet of Ostrov type, now in the collection of the Musée d'Art Classique at Mougins (F); another specimen can be found at the Museum of History and Archaeology in Constanta (RO). It is possible that helmets of this type were derived from the Dacian and Sarmatian types in evidence in pictorial sources from the Trajanic period. These helmets in turn may have been modelled on the classical Thracian helmets resembling pointed Phrygian caps. The scale aventail of the helmet, erroneously reconstructed at a later date, has been replaced by mail bound with red leather.

He wears a coat of mail (*lorica hamata*) over a padded linen *subarmalis*, both items slit at the side to facilitate riding The elaborate chest plate adorned with various small busts was found at Ritopek and is now on display at Belgrade (SRB). His arms and legs are protected by laminated defences. These are frequently found in pictorial sources, and some examples have been excavated at various military sites. A pair of magnificent greaves, excavated at Straubing (D) are worn to protect the rider's knees and shins. They are adorned with busts of deities and depictions of dolphins, a sign of good fortune. The massive lance (*contus*) is wielded in both hands, so the rider's equipment lacks a shield. Belt and baldric are based on finds and are in accordance with contemporary military fashion.

The *cataphractarius* uses the typical Roman horned saddle which was modelled on Celtic saddles. The horse's splendid chamfrom and peytral are based on examples found at Straubing (D) and Carnuntum/Deutsch-Altenburg (A). Both examples depict the abduction of Ganymede by Zeus in the guise of an eagle, a popular motive which is repeated on various other finds.

Plate XX

Legionary standard bearer of First Cohort

The *signifer* carries a standard as depicted on the Ludovisi Sarcophagus. The twin hand decoration is unusual and may point to a First Cohort's double century. The shaft is adorned with six silvered *phalerae* and has a handle both to plant the standard in the ground and to remove it. To prevent damage, the shaft has a bronze buttspike.

The standard bearer holds one of the subaltern *principales* ranks. His equipment points to his elevated status. His conspicuous helmet was found at Heddernheim (D). The visor is attached to the bowl with a hinge at the brow and a strap running around the neckguard. Some scholars believe that the wearer's face was protected by a heart-shaped mask, but evidence is lacking in this case. His rigid bronze scale cuirass is supplemented by three rows of fringed *pteryges* at shoulders and waist. His sidearms consist of a heavy Künzing type dagger, and a *spatha* with an elaborate bone hilt of Niederbieber-Vimose type. The fittings of his *balteus* were excavated at Dura. His military belt surely deserves pride of place, being embellished with fittings in the shape of Greek letters spelling the owner's name: MNHMΩN (Mnemon).

COH I

ARMS AND EQUIPMENT

Helmets

The Roman soldier of the third century was magnificent to behold, his equipment combining practicality and splendour. Numerous finds from all over the Empire have enabled archaeologists to create a reliable image of what the soldiers of the Emperor Maximinus looked like, and how they were equipped and armed. The limited size of this publication does not allow for an archaeological analysis in depth of the examples of equipment addressed. Nevertheless, an attempt shall be made to place individual arms and pieces of equipment in their evolutionary and military context. Since the change of the army's equipment already began in the second century, examples of the equipment of this period have been included.

Especially helmets from this time are determined by the notion of combining military prowess with pragmatic functionality. There is a comparatively large number of different types worn either by infantry or cavalry, or both. While some types were clearly designed to offer a maximum of protection and little else, the resplendent masked helmets of the cavalry and the conical helmets of the Levantine archers were intended not merely for protection but also for display, and, as we shall see, psychological effect.

The third century marked the end of the development of the iconical infantry helmet of Weisenau type (classified by RUSSELL ROBINSON as either Imperial Gallic or Imperial Italic). The splendid late 2nd century infantry helmet formerly owned by a soldier of the XXXth Legion which was discovered at Niedermörmter on the Lower Rhine (Imperial Italic type H) can be defined as both the climax and conclusion of the constant development of this helmet type. It is now on display at the Rheinisches Landesmuseum in Bonn. The elaborate and lavishly decorated helmet has large shell-shaped earguards as well as a low and particularly broad, flaring neckguard designed to protect not just the nape but also the wearer's shoulders. It also sports a comparatively large peak. The Niedermörmter helmet was clearly made to offer a maximum degree of protection against weapon effect directed from above, i. e. from missiles or enemy cavalry.

The above helmet type was superseded by a new category, which RUSSELL ROBINSON originally assumed was worn only by the cavalry. He consequently classified these helmets as Imperial Cavalry Types D, E and F. Various stelae nevertheless clearly show infantrymen wearing this helmet, which may originally have been adopted from the cavalry[118]. These helmets (which can only be basically described here) cover the entire head. The deep and broad neck protector descends right onto the wearer's shoulders. The large cheek guards cover the ears and occasionally overlap in front of the chin. Horizontal extensions flaring out at the bottom of the cheekguards run from the chin to the neckguard and were obviously intended to protect the throat and collarbones by deflecting downward cuts and thrusts. Helmets of this type literally sit like saddles on the wearer's shoulders and only leave a heart- or T-shaped cut-out exposing the eyes, nose and mouth. Instead of two separate hinged cheekguards, some helmets sported one-piece mask-like visors covering forehead, cheeks, chin and ears, which were attached to the helmet with the aid of a hinge or hook above the forehead and straps or thongs passing around the neckguard. These helmets, classified by German scholars as Heddernheim and Rainau-Buch types, exist in a large number of variants. Some are made entirely of bronze, some are of iron with bronze applications, while others are silvered, tinned or bronzed. Many have studded-on or embossed crossed reinforcements to protect the skull, some have mounts or brackets to accommodate plumes or crests. All examples would have had large pointed peaks protruding to protect the face. Remains of helmets of this type have been excavated at the Harzhorn.

Helmets constructed in this manner gave protection especially against blows and missiles from above, but sources show that there were drawbacks. Legionary Sextus Julius Africanus recorded his comrades' complaints, claiming that the helmet was of little use against against slingshots and impaired vision and hearing. It also prevented free movement of the wearer's head[119]. The soldiers were thus unable to dodge enemy weapons and missiles, hear orders clearly, and to move their heads in order to monitor events in their immediate surroundings. Experiments conducted by re-enactors and experimental archaeologists with helmets of the Niederbieber type have confirmed the soldiers' reservations. While cavalrymen were probably able to wear the helmet without any serious impediment since they would have fought enemy horsemen on the same level as themselves or enemy infantrymen, which would have required looking downwards, the low and broad neckguard would have made it difficult for a foot soldier to duck behind his shield and look upwards, since the helmet sat almost immediately on the wearer's shoulders. As a consequence, the soldier would have been best off standing upright behind a (preferably oval) shield, an aspect which may serve to further explain a shift in the Roman infantry's fighting technique and tactics[120].

A gravestone discovered near the Roman fortress of Housesteads on Hadrian's Wall depicts the deceased soldier, a Syrian archer from the First Cohort of Hamians

118 The military tombstones of Ares (London), Aurelius Avitianus (Brigetio/Szöny (H)), and of trumpeter Aurelius Surus (Istanbul (TR)) may serve as evidence; cf. ELLIOTT (2014), p. 81.

119 ELLIOT (2014), p. 81.

120 Cf. STROBEL, p. 277.

(from modern Homs), with a conical helmet similar to the ones worn by the exotic-looking archers in their flowing robes on Trajan's Column[121]. These have been identified as Syrians or Arabs owing to the fact that conical helmets were equipment clearly associated with the military culture and equipment of this region. Two examples of this helmet type from the third century AD have survived. One is a bronze specimen found at Dakovo (HR) with a rectangular browpiece depicting three deities, and a slightly lower neckguard. The other helmet (excavated at Intercisa (H)) is also made of non-ferrous metal, and like the Dakovo helmet tapers into a point of pearl- or ring-shaped design. Holes punched into the back edge point to the attachment of a mail neckguard. Holes on both sides indicate the attachment of cheekguards. Two inscriptions signify that the helmet was worn by cavalrymen, thus showing that this type of helmet was worn by infantry and cavalry. It appears reasonable to assume that Maximinus' élite Osrhoenian archers also wore ornate helmets of this type.

On the left-had side of the Ludovisi sarcophagus a Persian surrenders to a high-ranking Roman officer. The Roman is wearing a stylised Attic helmet whose bowl is adorned with embossed feathers and decorated with a crest in the shape of an eagle's head. A pseudo-Attic helmet of Ostrov type on display at the Mougins Museum of Classical Art in southern France seems to fit the bill. The browband and the cheek pieces are decorated with depictions of various gods (victories, Mars, Minerva). The reconstructed scale neckguard is probably an error, mail being more likely. As for the helmet's remarkable, distinctly un-Roman form, RUSSELL ROBINSON presumes Sarmatian influence[122]. A gravestone from the third century AD foundat Salò near Brescia and belonging to an *eques singularis* shows a *calo* handing a similar helmet to his master[123].

A well-known fresco excavated in the synagogue at Dura Europos which depicts the battle of Eben-Ezer between Philistines and Israelites, shows mail- or scale-armoured foot soldiers equipped with shields wearing a peculiar kind of coif apparently made of the same material as their body armour. Soldiers in an illustration of the so-called Vergilius Vaticanus manuscript from the fourth century AD are equipped with similar hoods, obviously of mail. These garments have caused numerous illustrators and re-enactors to reconstruct Roman soldiers of the third century wearing a mail coif or an odd form of scale hood in place of a helmet. The interpretation of the sources in this manner must be treated with caution however. First of all, there is no hard evidence that any such armour was in use by either the Roman or the Persian army of the time, since other archaeological and literary evidence is lacking. Other problems are of a more practical nature: even if worn with some form of padding, a mail coif worn on its own offers no real protection against blows or missiles. The face is left completely unprotected (unless covered with a mask, for which there is no evidence). A sword cut or blow with a Persian mace directed from above would instantly shatter such a coif and render its wearer *hors de combat*. There is no space between the mail and the wearer's skull to contain the force of the blow. Such a coif might merely offer some protection against spent arrows or glancing blows. A coif or hood constructed of scales would be extremely complex in the making and involve some technical problems: scales would of necessity have to be quite small and would taper in circles towards the top of the skull without being able to cover it completely since a circular hole would have to be left at the top. This could only be covered by a circular or slightly concave disk, but the fresco does not show this. Of course the density of the tapering layers on top of the wearer's skull would offer a degree of protection, but it remains doubtful if such a coif would be able to maintain its protective quality after a hit (in contrast to a metal helmet). The head is one of the key targets in combat, since a hit will immediately incapacitate the soldier. Mediaeval mail coifs were therefore invariably worn with closed helmets or bassinets. The mail hoods of Renaissance and 17th-century Polish and Ottoman cavalrymen were reinforced by a semi-spherical bowl to protect the skull from enemy blows. It is of course quite possible that in Roman times mail hoods were worn under the conical helmets described above, or that these helmets had attached mail aventails to protect the wearer's neck, cheeks, and face, as a Sassanid specimen found under Tower 19 at Dura seems to indicate[124]. Such a construction would render cheek pieces obsolete and facilitate ventilation, even though we must assume that this variant would also have been worn with some sort of padding. A blow to the head would otherwise have driven the hood's metal rings into the wearer's face and ear with painful and potentially fatal consequences.

Like the infantry, the cavalry will have worn the Niederbieber and Rainau-Buch types described above, especially the horsemen of the *cohortes equitatae* whose financial resources were limited. The Roman Army of this era however also sported magnificent masked helmets, among these the splendid specimens from the well-known Straubing hoard (categorised by RUSSELL ROBINSON as Cavalry Sports Types E and F). Scholars formerly assumed such helmets to have been specifically designed for the

121 HAYNES, suspicious of the ethnically defined dress features commonly associated with the Levantine archers, argues that the Housesteads stone in fact shows a hunting deity, not an archer (p. 292 ff.).

122 RUSSELL ROBINSON, Henry, *The Armour of Imperial Rome*, New York 1975, p. 134 f.

123 Eagle-shaped crests were also common on other types of Roman helmets, for instance various examples of the Heddernheim type (cf. D'AMATO, Raffaele/NEGIN, Andrey, *Decorated Roman Armour. From the Age of the Kings to the Death of Justinian the Great*, Barnsley 2017, p. 172).

124 For a reconstruction s. STEPHENSON (2001), plate 11, and D'AMATO/Nevgin (2017), plate 17. Cf. also plate XXXIV.

Plate XXI

Three pictures of helmets from the Ludovisi Sarcophagus

The majority of Roman soldiers depicted on the Ludovisi sarcophagus wear so-called Attic helmets with rounded skulls, visor-shaped peaks and small neckguards adhering to the curve of the bearer's nape. The cheekguards have been reduced to expose the wearers' faces. In this, the sculptor follows classic artistic convention, and opinions as to what extent these sculptures actually depict the contemporary reality vary considerably. Although the full depiction of the soldiers' faces follows an aesthetic tradition of the depiction of heroism common to a large number of ancient sculptures from Classical Greece to the Roman Empire, and despite the fact that the helmets shown are strictly speaking not in keeping with archaeological evidence, it cannot be denied that the sculptor did include a specific number of features peculiar to 3rd century Roman helmets.

The Roman officer capturing a Persian (**1**) wears an Attic helmet decorated with feathers and surmounted by a protome in the shape of an eagle's head. The eagle, Jove's sacred bird, was worshipped in the form of depictions on military standards; displayed on weapons and armour, its totemic effect protected the wearer and struck terror in the hearts of the enemy. Numerous 3rd century helmets found at various sites feature eagle decorations, e. g. two examples from Theilenhofen and Heddernheim have eagle-shaped protomes, while a helmet found at Ostrov (now on display at Mougins; cf. plate XIX) and a specimen from Vechten (NL) both have crests in the shape of eagles' heads.

The foot soldier to the left of the general (his proximity to the general suggests that he may be a praetorian) also wears an Attic helmet, which however is slightly more simply decorated than that of the officer (**2**). Again, a number of similarities with archaeological finds is apparent. The soldier's helmet crest has been made to resemble a lion, while the skull is also adorned with a lion in profile. KÜNZL (2010, p. 89) points to the cavalry helmet excavated at Theilenhofen, the sides of which are decorated with depictions of lions. Possibly, such decorations also adorned the helmets of the infantry.

The officer on foot raising his shield to protect his comrade from a sabre cut from a Persian cavalryman (**3**) wears a helmet which differs from other examples on the frieze in that it sports a deep and prominent peak resembling so-called Etrusco-Corinthian examples which developed from the classic Corinthian helmet worn by Greek hoplites. When not immediately required, the helmet, which afforded limited visibility and impeded hearing, was worn pushed back so as to reveal the wearer's face. Thus eventually developed a completely new helmet, whose long peak became a rudiment of the Corinthian helmet's long cheekguards. Ironically, the Etrusco-Corinthian helmet acquired a new set of cheekguards, which were attached according to Italic and Celtic tradition.

The crest of the officer's helmet sports a protome (unfortunately damaged) and decorations to the skull, identified by KÜNZL (2010, S. 87 f.) by Triton, sea lions and sea serpents. A flowing horsehair crest is attached. A bipartite 'cavalry sports' helmet excavated at Frankfurt-Heddernheim (cf. Plate XX) sports a peak surprisingly similar to that of the helmet depicted on the sarcophagus. The peak of the Heddernheim example is decorated with a stylised face resembling the eyeholes and nosepiece of classic hoplite headgear and later Etrusco-Corinthian pieces. Like the Ludovisi example, the Heddernheim helmet features a protome depicting an animal, in this case an eagle's head. A crest may have been attached.

The three above examples serve to show that artistic convention notwithstanding, the Ludovisi sarcophagus is a valuable source regarding the decoration and splendour of 3rd century Roman military equipment.

1

2

3

Plate XXII

Masked „female" helmet of „Oriental" type from the Straubing hoard

The Straubing hoard, discovered by chance near a late Roman *villa rustica* in 1950, comprised among highly decorated armour for horses and riders as well as numerous other precious objects seven helmet masks, of which three seem to depict women. Their elaborate hairstyle, piled locks forming a triangular peak, and their facial features have led scholars to define them as orientals. In recent years, several attempts have been made anew to categorise the huge variety of Roman headpieces. While RUSSELL ROBINSON (1975, p. 124), who introduced the Amazon theory, categorised the helmet as Imperial Cavalry sports type E, FISCHER (2012) assigns an individual category to the Straubing and Eining finds of this type of mask. D'AMATO/NEGIN (2017, p. 213) simply refer to them as "Helmets with Amazon masks". FISCHER (2012) places the hiding of the Straubing hoard in the context of the Alamanni incursions and the fall of the Raetian *limes* in the third century AD.

The helmets thus may have belonged to the cavalrymen of *Cohors I Flavia Canathenorum sagittariorum milliaria* based at Straubing (*Sorviodurum*) at this time. This unit of archers was originally recruited from Syrians, but it is far from certain whether the cohort was indeed part-mounted. The high level of craftsmanship involved also raises the question whether the troopers of the lowly *cohortes* were able to afford these pieces at all.

Like RUSSELL ROBINSON, D'AMATO/NEGIN (*ibid.*) believe the helmet masks to collectively depict Amazons since three virtually identical masks of the same type found together exclude the possibility of individualisation in the sense of the *mater castrorum* helmets. Since four "male" masks were also found, one might suppose that the "female" masks were in the possession of a troop which formed the "Amazon" team at the *hippika gymnasia*, while another squadron was pitted against them acting as their Greek opponents in an *amazonomachia* (αμαζωνομαχία, "Amazon battle") as described in Virgil's *Aenid* et al.

JUNKELMANN (1996, p. 47) disputes this interpretation however, claiming that the male "Greek" helmets in fact represent an earlier development of the masked helmet and were thus not originally designed to form the counterpiece of the female "Amazon" helmet. He also believes that the somewhat luxurious appearance of these "female" masks (if female they are) does not correspond to the classic depiction of these warlike women in ancient pictorial sources.

The Straubing helmets are now in the collection of the Gäubodenmuseum in Straubing, Bavaria. We choose to reconstruct one of these helmets with the face silvered, although according to Professor Günther Moosbauer, curator of the Gäubodenmuseum, there is no evidence that they ever were. However, many reconstructions show these masks treated in this manner for a more pleasing visual effect (as many others were), so we are giving it the benefit of the doubt. . The mouth is open to facilitate breathing. The helmet of the same type excavated at Eining (*Abusina*) has a blue stone set in its forehead and possesses a tube at the apex to receive a crest.

Plate XXIII

This simple yet elegant bronze cavalry helmet from the early third century AD was excavated at Vechten (NL). While the front part extends upwards into a slender triangular diadem, the apex of the back part is surmounted by an eagle's head echoed by other contemporary helmets of various types. While BISHOP/COULSTON (2006, p. 178) believe the piece to have possibly been supplemented by a face mask, there is no real evidence for this. The height of the diadem is reminiscent of the high curly hairstyles of the "oriental" masked helmets found at Straubing and Eining (D), while the apex resembles the "Phrygian bonnet" of the helmet recently excavated at Crosby Garrett (GB).

Plate XXIV

Partly reconstructed helmet of Heddernheim type (categorised by Russell Robinson as *Imperial Cavalry Type H*) from Nijmwegen (NL). It was probably produced in the late 2nd to early 3rd century AD. Like the example from Frankfurt-Heddernheim, this helmet is composed of both iron and bronze. A further helmet of identical type also excavated at Nijmwegen like the Frankfurt example possesses a brow panel decorated with stylised hair and a panel at the nape reaching down onto the neckguard decorated with a box frieze and bronze scales.

The cheekpiece has been largely reconstructed. While the rhomboid bronze plate below the hinge is an original part, the star-shaped ear ornament follows the Heddernheim helmet. The Heddernheim piece also has the figure of a god etched into its right cheekpiece. We choose to follow this also, the depicted deity having been adopted from a contemporary cheekpiece fragment excavated at Deutsch-Altenburg/Carnuntum (A). While the Frankfurt and the other Nijmwegen specimen both lack peaks (which undoubtedly existed), this helmet has retained its triangular peak, which is decorated with a ribbon of embossed pearls. The bronze ribs running down the skull at the front and the sides have been reconstructed. Like the Frankfurt-Heddernheim helmet, this example also possesses a bronze crest-holder resembling a poppy seed vessel. Due to the large number of seeds every individual plant possesses, the poppy to the Romans signified good fortune, wealth, and health. The bronze half moons (*lunulae*) attached to the neckguard were likewise designed to ward off harm. The helmet was carried by means of a bronze loop attached to the neckguard. Unlike the cheekguards of the Niederbieber helmets, the Heddernheim helmets' cheekguards do not always seem to have overlapped at the chin.

Plate XXV

Pseudo-Attic bronze helmet excavated during a ploughing contest inside the *vicus* (civilian settlement) area at the *limes* fortress of Theilenhofen (Iciniacum) in 1974. It was the prized possession of several generations of cavalry troopers from *Cohors III Bracaraugustanorum*: Aliquandus from Nonus' squadron, Atto from Paterclus' (or Paterclius') squadron, and Flavianus from Atauluanus' squadron. The piece is decorated with depictions of eagles, standards, lions, Victories, Gorgons' heads, and a raised crest imitating feathers. Holes in this crest presumably served to accomodate a crest of horsehair or feathers. The helmet was originally tinned. KÜNZL (2008, pp. 97-99) claims it may have been lost during the incursions of the Alamanni in 234 AD.

cavalry sports displays of Roman mounted troops (Ἱππικα Γυμνάσια, *hippika gymnasia*), but recent works have cast doubt on this interpretation, claiming that in fact these helmets were also worn in combat[125]. It remains unclear how common they were however. Experiments involving masked helmets have shown that they do not seriously impair breathing or hearing while offering valuable protection for the face. Marcus JUNKELMANN has convincingly shown that masked helmets were well-suited to combat conditions[126]. What is more, the psychological effect of an encounter with cavalrymen thus attired must have been considerable. Other arguments include the notion that the decorative effect of a masked helmet on parade would hardly have borne any relationship to the considerable expense of its manufacture. We may presume that these splendid pieces of equipment woud mostly have been owned by troopers of the guard regiments, and of the more prestigious *alae*.

The helmets themselves consist of either two (mask, bowl) or three parts (bowl, visor, facemask) and were commonly richly decorated with images of gods, mythical beasts, wreaths, or embossed hair. Some have features resembling portraits of female members of the imperial family in accordance with the official propagandistic *mater castrorum* ("mother of the camps") role assigned to these women[127], while other "female" helmets have faces of oriental appearance ("Amazons"), or Gorgon faces. Male, "Greek" masks are also in evidence, some resembling portraits of Alexander the Great. The *hippika gymnasia*, intended not just for display but also as combat exercise, were performed by two teams, attired for instance as Greeks and Amazons (something seemingly suggested by the "Amazon shield" excavated at Dura). Possibly helmet designs differed according to squadron, which would have allowed an identification of the two teams apart from, say, the colour of their tunics. If the use of masked helmets in combat by regular cavalry appears plausible, we may say that the heavily armoured *clibanarii* almost certainly employed them right from the start. Later sources compare *clibanarii* to iron statues. An attacking troop of these horsemen with their glittering expressionless faces, covered in steel and bronze from head to toe, must have terrified the enemy.

125 TRAVIS, John and Hilary, *Roman Helmets*, Stroud 2014, p. 93. DIXON, Karen/STEPHENSON, Ian, *Roman Cavalry Equipment*, Stroud 2003, pp. 21-24.

126 Cf. D'AMATO/NEGIN (2017), p. 155 ff. JUNKELMANN, Marcus, *Reiter wie Statuen aus Erz*, Mainz 1996, p. 44, ff.

127 Marcus Aurelius' wife Faustina was the first to be awarded the title of *mater castrorum*, thus forming a counterpoint to the traditional image of the Roman woman as mere safekeeper of the household. The awardance of this title is indicative of a shift of political principles towards the Imperial family's dynastic legitimacy and military support. Cf. M. SPEIDEL, "Faustina – *mater castrorum*. Ein Beitrag zur Religionsgeschichte", published in *Tyche. Beiträge zur Alten Geschichte, Papyrologie und Epigraphik* 27 (2012) (*https://tyche-journal.at/tyche/index.php/tyche/article/view/42/html_24, 11.5.17.*

Another masked helmet type from the third century AD is an example found at Heddernheim (Cavalry Sports Type G). It resembles the old pseudo-Corinthian type with a lomg peak displaying an embossed face, the bowl surmounted by an integrated crest terminating in an eagle's head (cf. plate XX). The visor, which was attached to the bowl with a hinge above the forehead, was decorated by embossed locks and sideburns. Eyes, nose and mouth remained uncovered. The visor was secured with a strap passing around the nape above the narrow neckguard. The face was possibly protected by a heart- or t-shaped mask which woud have been inserted into the visor. An officer is depicted on the Ludovisi sarcophagus wearing a similar helmet, which proves that such ornate pieces were actually worn in combat. Since the Heddernheim helmet is of very elaborate construction and lavishly decorated with bronze, it might also have belonged to an officer. Bowls and visors which may be associated with this type have been excavated at Vaskapu, Brigetio/Szöny (both H), and at the Iron Gates (RO).

The last helmet type to be introduced is the so-called pseudo-Attic type (Cavalry Sports Helmet Type I; this type was probably also worn in combat). These helmets have large cheek pieces covering the ears, fairly high browbands, and narrow neckguards. Most finds of this type are magnificently embellished with large integrated multiple crests in the form of animals or deities, and embossed decorations on cheekguards and bowls. Slightly earlier examples from the Antonine period have been excavated on several sites, among them Nawa (SYR). An impressive specimen found at Rusovce (SLK) has a crown-shaped browband surmounted by an eagle. The probably most famous example of this type was discovered at Theilenhofen, formerly Icinacium on the Raetian *limes* defences. Decried (to my lasting delight) by a disgusted Peter Connolly as "the epitome of Roman bad taste"[128], the helmet has a massive crenelated browband, two side crests in the form of prostrate lions, and a large integrated central crest designed to represent feathers, terminating above the wearer's forehead in a protome of an eagle spreading its wings. A crest of feathers or horsehair could be attached. The cheekguards were also decorated by embossed eagle images. It is perhaps a surprise that such a magnificent helmet was in fact not worn by an officer but by an ordinary trooper, and of a lowly *cohors equitata* at that. Icinacium was garrisoned by the Lusitanians of *cohors III Bracaraugustanorum*. Variants of this type (Cavalry Sports Types H and I) were excavated at Worthing, Guisborough (UK), Chalon (F), and Tel Oum Hauran (SYR). Some have cheekguards, while others have visor masks, as finds from Worthing and Rodez indicate. These visors left eyes, nose and mouth exposed and were fastened to the bowl with hinges and straps.

128 CONNOLLY, Peter, *Greece and Rome at War*, London 1981, p. 237.

Body armour

The *subarmalis*

Several written sources mention a padded garment intended to be worn under the soldier's armour. This *subarmalis* (*SHA* VI, 11), the Grecized word being *thoracomachus* (*De Rebus Bellicis* XV), was designed to increase the protective quality of the armour by further arresting and containing the effect of enemy weapons, since blows or thrusts to metal armour which failed to penetrate could still cause severe bruising and internal injuries. It also served to protect the wearer's clothing from fraying and soiling, e. g. from the grit and rust particles caused by the abrasion of the rings of a *lorica hamata*. In cold climates it helped to keep the soldier warm. It can confidently be said that the *pteryges*, the fabric or leather strips visible at Roman soldiers' shoulders and thighs in so many pictorial sources, were attached not to the wearers' armour but to the *subarmalis*.

The *subarmalis* was constructed either of several layers of fabric, e. g. linen, wool or felt, or was a quilted garment made by stuffing padding material between two outer layers of cloth, or leather and adding vertical, horizontal or diamond-shaped stitching. Some archaeologists believe that pictorial sources actually show the *subarmalis* being worn without armour (COWAN for example lists a fairly crude gravestone from Croy Hill on the Antonine Wall, but in this specific case the evidence appears slightly thin[129]). This is not at all improbable if one considers that the wearing of padded fabric armour was common practice in mediaeval European, Byzantine (where it was called βαμβάκιον, *bambákion*), and Islamic armies. In warm climates, and if the tactical situation required speed and mobility, e. g. when scouting or skirmishing, the *subarmalis* alone could be worn as body armour, providing the wearer with a minimum of protection without sacrificing agility. Rain however could prove an inconvenience, since the garment would swiftly become heavy with water and weigh down on the unfortunate wearer. Drying would probably require a considerable amount of time.

Body armour

Among the Harzhorn finds are a number of different forms of Roman body armour. Fragments of mail, scale and segmented cuirasses have been excavated.

The mail coat (*lorica hamata*) was worn both by the legions and auxiliary infantry and cavalry formations. This type of armour was employed by the Roman army without interruption from the Republic (when it had been adopted from the Celts) right into the late Empire, owing its popularity to the protection it was able to offer to the soldier's body and limbs without seriously impeding mobility. According to a soldier's gravestone excavated at Brigetio/Szöny (H), the mail coat (which was still cut like a modern t-shirt or pullover) in the third century AD reached down to a hand's breadth above the wearer's knees. The soldiers wore their belts over their armour to take some of its weight away from the shoulders. Cavalry mail coats could be slit at front and back to facilitate mounting and to prevent the coat from slipping up when the soldier was in the saddle. Sleeves commonly reached to above the elbows, but coats with long sleeves also existed. According to STEPHENSON, individual rings of different finds are on average 7mm in diameter and 1mm thick[130]. The mail coat consisted of rings which were joined by riveted rings, each ring being joined to four others. A coat found at Bertoldsheim (D) is composed of square-shaped patches of iron rings joined together by bronze rings, which produced a rather pleasing checkered effect.

The infantry standard bearer on the Ludovisi sarcophagus wears a coat of mail painstakingly depicted by the sculptor. Mail coats of the third century no longer seem to have had the u-shaped doubling reinforcements or capes covering the wearer's shoulders (*humeralia*) which were worn during the Republic and the early Principate. These were designed to give additional protection against weapon effects from above (e. g. missiles or cavalry) and covered the neckhole necessary to slip the coat on. This neckhole was narrowed in the third century, slipping the coat over one's head being facilitated by one or a pair of decorated chestplates of rectangular or trapezoid shape, of which examples have been found at Bertoldsheim (in this case with the mail still attached), Brigetio, Ritopek (SRB), and Enns (A). These plates were rounded at the top to accommodate the wearer's neck and were fastened with a system of pins, hooks and eyes after putting the armour on. It used to be assumed that these elaborately decorated plates (decorations include geometric patterns as well as images of deities and animals) were the prerogative of parade armour but this notion has recently been largely abandoned.[131]

Due to its schematic depiction on Trajan's column and the column of Marcus Aurelius (to name these two triumphal monuments as examples), segmented armour[132] has commonly been associated with the legions and the Praetorians, but it cannot be entirely ruled out that this type of body armour was also worn by the auxiliaries. Finds at auxiliary bases seem to point towards this possibility. Segmented armour of this type was a genuinely Roman invention. The earliest examples were excavated on the supposed site of the Varus disaster at Kalkriese, proving that it was already in use in the early Principate. The *lorica segmentata* was modified over the years and came in several versions. Finds from Eining, Zugmantel (D) and Carnuntum/Deutsch-Altenburg (A) show that in the third

129 COWAN (2003), p. 59. The legionary on the left, to which Cowan refers, may actually be depicted wearing body armour with three rows of *pteryges*.

130 STEPHENSON (1999), p. 34.

131 FISCHER (2012), p. 165; STEPHENSON (ibid.), p. 32 ff.

132 The term *lorica segmentata* is a modern neologism.

century AD the Newstead type (after a find on Hadrian's Wall) was commonly worn. Compared to its predecessor, the Corbridge cuirass (also named after an example found on Hadrian's Wall), the Newstead type was more robust and of simpler construction. In contrast to the Corbridge type A, which had eight, the Newstead cuirass only possessed six torso rings; it also had fewer hinges on the shoulder sections, and its simpler system of fastening the cuirass with hooks and toggles made the armour less prone to breaking. A relief from the third century discovered at Alba Iulia (RO) actually shows a *lorica segmentata* with only three torso segments, but so far there has been no further archaeological evidence for this construction. Thomas FISCHER has proved that the *lorica segmentata* was still in use at the time of the Emperor Maximinus Thrax[133]; Ross COWAN points to finds excavated at León (E) and Carlisle (UK), which suggest that in contrast to common assumptions, *lorica segmentata* was in fact still in use in the Roman Army of late antiquity[134]. The *lorica segmentata* offered better protection to the torso from direct hits, but it did not cover the lower abdomen and thighs (which is why it was never employed by the cavalry), it was more difficult to maintain (in contrast to segmented armour, constant abrasion of the rings of a *lorica hamata* automatically prevented rust, and rings were easy to replace), and its complex construction made it more susceptible to damage. This is why the *lorica segmentata* was never able to fully replace mail as the Roman soldier's main body armour.

The Ludovisi sarcophagus shows several soldiers, among them the general himself, wearing scale corselets (*lorica squamata* or *plumata*, "feathered"). This type of body armour was employed by both cavalry and infantry. Scale corselets, whose origins may be traced to the Middle East, combined the benefit of easy production with pleasing visual effect. Scales of various metals and sizes from different epochs have been excavated all over the Empire. Elements of scale armour from the third century AD have been found at Dura (SYR), Musov (CZ), Manching, Straubing (D), and Carpow (UK). In the latter case the scales were still attached to fragments of the garment to which they had been attached.

Scale armour is relatively easy and cheap to manufacture, and production time is comparatively low. Its protective qualities are fairly high, since (admittedly depending on the angle and force of impact) missiles as well as spear and sword thrusts which would puncture a coat of mail will glance off the surface of the corselet. However, depending on the manner of its manufacture, a scale corselet may impair the wearer's mobility and fail to effectively protect parts of the body which mail would cover. Its maintenance is more complex than that of mail, since individual scales may be lost more easily and are more difficult to replace than rings of a mail coat. This is due to the rows of scales being threaded onto one or several strings or wires and sown onto a garment for support. If a string snapped or was cut and individual scales were lost, it could happen that one entire row had to be threaded all over again.

Scales of Roman armour vary considerably in size; small specimens measure 1,5 x 1,3 cms, but larger, longer examples also exist, some resembling feathers with embossed quills (hence the name *lorica plumata*). The longish and narrow scales found at Newstead have an overall length of approximately 4 cms. Scales could be square in shape, triangular and tapered, some had semicircular edges. Some soldiers chose to have alternate rows of bronze scales tinned or silvered, or even every second scale in a row, which produced a splendid visual effect.

There are several variants regarding construction, and not all can be addressed here. The reader is refered to the extensive works of RUSSELL-ROBINSON, STEPHENSON (1999) and TRAVIS at this point[135]. The following examples must suffice: overlapping scales could be threaded onto one thread or wire using holes at the upper end and then sown to an undergarment. The advantage this method offered was that the corselet retained a certain degree of flexibility, allowed the incorporation of short sleeves and could be put on in a similar manner to the mail coat (cf. the depiction of the Emperor's *equites singulares* on the Arch of Galerius at Thessalonica). However, if a thrust from below hit the wearer at an oblique angle which allowed it to simply lift one row of scales, it could inflict serious injury[136].

Fragments of scale armour discovered at Musov, Aalen and Mainz reveal how Roman armourers sought to counteract this hazard. These corselets were made using scales which were attached with wire to the four surrounding scales. Such corselets offered better protection but allowed for less ease of movement. This aspect leads us to the question of how such corselets were employed, and how they were put on and fastened.

It is no mean feat to construct a rigid scale corselet of the type described above while still maintaining the wearer's capacity to move freely. Pictorial sources however show sleeved scale corselets. A relief which dates from slightly later than the period in question, presumably originally part of the Arch of Diocletian, actually shows a foot soldier wearing a scale corselet with long sleeves. TRAVIS and STEPHENSON both believe that separate sleeves were attached to the rigid corselet by means of straps, the gaps being covered by the *pteryges* of the *subarmalis* (if any was worn. The scales were after all sewn to an undergarment). If sleeves were not worn, *pteryges* either

133 FISCHER, ibid., p. 168-169.

134 COWAN, Ross, *Roman Legionary AD 284-337. The age of Diocletian and Constantine the Great*, Oxford 2015, p. 44.

135 Cf. bibliography.

136 This fact is another aspect which would dismiss the notion of scale hoods being worn instead of helmets.

of fabric or of leather (often dyed in bright or contrasting colours) helped to protect the shoulders and upper arms. These were frequently supplemented by *manicae* (see below). Rigid scale corselets of the Musov type only protected the torso. The groin and thighs were likewise protected by *pteryges* and, in the case of the cavalry, with laminated thigh guards of a construction resembling that of the *manicae*.

Like the *lorica hamata*, scale corselets could possess either one or a pair of chestplates which enabled the wearer to slip on the cuirass and which gave additional protection to the throat region. Numerous examples have been excavated at various sites, among them Vienna, Ritopek and Orgovany (H); all are lavishly decorated with embossed pattern and images. Scale corselets were probably open on the left side of the body (the one protected by the soldier's shield) and laced or buckled up. This is as yet a matter of scholarly debate.

The panoply of the extra-heavy *clibanarii* represents a peculiarity, since it combined several types of armour. A graffito of a charging *clibanarius* at Dura, drawn by an expert hand and often reproduced in works on the topic, shows the (probably Parthian or Persian) rider wearing a segmented helmet with a mail aventail extending to the front and covering the entire face save the eyes (Roman *clibanarii* will also have worn masked helmets). The limbs are covered by segmented armour. The rider wears a mail corselet reinforced around the abdomen by two rows of steel or bronze plates. The accuracy of the depiction is confirmed by later descriptions of *clibanarii* (Julian the Apostate, *Panegyric honouring the Emperor Constantius, Oratio Prima*, 37C-38A).

The soldiers of the Emperor Maximinus also made use of other forms of body armour, e. g. the iron or bronze muscled cuirass (*lorica musculata*), whose complex and expensive manufacture probably restricted its use to officers, and, probably, so-called hybrid armour composed of several elements, for instance mail or scale shirts fitted with *lorica segmentata* shoulder and chest plates (as found in Rusovce (SLK)). Unfortunately, such armour is not attested for the specific period in question. It must be added that there is no archaeological evidence whatsoever for the leather armour so frequently seen in recent reconstructions.

Vambraces and greaves

Laminated vambraces to protect the sword arm (*manicae)* were adopted by the Roman army from gladiatorial armour. They were probably quite commonly employed. Depictions of legionaries wearing these *manicae* may be found on the metopes of the famous Trajanic Adamclisi monument in Romania. Legionary Valerius Sabinus had himself depicted on his gravestone at Mainz wearing such a piece of equipment[137]. More pictorial evidence can be found on a relief at Alba Iulia (RO) dating from the late 2nd or early 3rd century AD. The *manica* excavated at Carlisle is from the Hadrianic period. It can thus safely be assumed that the infantrymen of Maximinus Thrax employed *manicae* to protect their exposed sword arms, as did the *clibanarii* and *cataphractarii* "heavies" and their brethren in the *contarii* cavalry regiments, since the long and unwieldy *contus* had to be negotiated with both hands and did not permit the use of a shield. The soldiers' thighs were protected by segmented strap-on thigh guards of similar construction. A specimen found at Zugmantel (D) probably belonged to a cavalryman.

Original finds of greaves (*ocreae*) are comparatively rare. In contrast to the popular concept that during the Principate greaves were the prerogative of the centurions as a mark of rank, greaves formed an indispensable part of the equipment of both infantry and cavalry. Examples have been excavated at the Harzhorn and at Künzing, the lining of a greave was found at Dura. The Exodus fresco from the Dura synagogue shows troops equipped with greaves. While the Künzing examples are simple and functional and only cover the shins, other finds (e. g. from Regensburg-Kumpfmühl, Oberstimm (D), Hebron (ISR) and Slavonski Brod (HR)) are of a type also covering the knees and ankles. The knee pieces are joined to the greaves with hinges. The latter types are lavishly decorated with images of masks, mythical beasts and deities and are believed to have been worn by the cavalry. Both greave types were attached to the leg with chains or straps.

Gorgets

A soldier's throat was a potentially lethal target. Although the helmets of this era with their massive flanged cheekguards gave considerable protection to the wearer's face and neck, the *focale* scarf above the body armour's chest plates afforded only flimsy protection against enemy weapons. The soldier's gravestone from Brigetio/Szöny previously referred to depicts what appears to be a triangular gorget covering the throat, the upper chest and parts of the shoulders. It remains a matter of debate as to how this piece of equipment, if a gorget it actually is, was constructed. STEPHENSON suggests a leather cape the size of a 17th-century lace collar to which scales were attached, and which could be fastened at the back. Such a piece of equipment would resemble a gorget from the 4th century BC (!) found at Derveni (GR). Such a gorget may also have been made of mail, or plate. The relief from Alba Iulia mentioned above shows the soldier attired with a lorica segmentata wearing a kind of cape with attached scales covering the shoulders and fastened with a pair of chestplates. It is unclear how common such pieces of equipment actually were.

137 Cf. BISHOP/COULSTON (2012), p. 98 ff.; DIXON/STEPHENSON, p. 56.

Weapons

Swords

In accordance with the historical term *Antonine Revolution*, German archaeologist Ernst Künzl has coined the phrase of an "armament revolution" regarding this era[138]. This definition is indicative in many respects, especially if we consider the weapon which had become the hallmark of the Roman art of war, the infantry short sword. The *gladius hispaniensis*, adopted by the Roman army from Celtiberian tribes in the 3rd century BC[139], formed the basis of Roman tactics and fighting technique until well into the 3rd century AD. It was the legions' standard sidearm, while the auxiliaries in accordance with their predominantly northern and central European ethnic origins, preferred the Celtic longsword (*spatha*). The *gladius* underwent a series of changes and modifications, from the Mainz type of the late Republic and early Principate with its tapered blade to the Pompeii type popular in the Imperial high period with parallel sides and triangular point. Ideal both for slashing and thrusting, it was as versatile as it was effective. Even its sturdy round or ovoid pommel could be used to deliver debilitating punches[140].

In spite of its virtues, the *gladius* declined in popularity as the third century AD wore on. In the second century AD, another variant had found its way into the Roman arsenal, the so-called *Ringknaufschwert* (ring pommel sword). This type, of which numerous examples have been found inside and outside the Empire, had its origins in the Black Sea region. The Romans probably adopted the ring pommel sword from the Sarmatians. True to its name, the ring pommel sword has a round or oval metal ring-shaped pommel and narrow hilt. Swords of this type are between 50 and 80 cm in length. The pommels and hilts of excavated specimens are frequently richly decorated with damascened and encrusted ornaments[141]. These weapons will still have been quite common in the army of Maximinus Thrax, a fact which can be attested by contemporary finds from Eining and Künzing[142].

The days of the *gladius* were numbered however. The longsword of the cavalry and auxiliary infantry, the *spatha* with its longer range, was making an appearance in the ranks of the legions and was to replace the *gladius* as the standard sidearm of the late Roman army in due course. The tactical reasons for this prominent change have been outlined above. Scholars distinguish between two basic *spatha* types, the Straubing/Nydam type with a slightly tapered blade ca. 65-80 cm in length and with a breadth of around 4, 4, cm[143], while the Lauriacum/Hromowka type with its length of ca. 56-67 cm is slightly shorter. The latter type has a blade with parallel sides which is between 6 and 7 cm broad, and possesses a triangular point. Numerous excavated examples of both types have inlaid metal decorations depicting deities or standards set into the blade close to the hilt (e. g. two examples from South Shields (UK) and Ovre Stabu (N)). One or several grooves in the blade are common features. Pommels are spherical or ovoid and like the hemispherical or oblong-shaped hilts are made of bone, ivory, or wood. Grips made of bone are either cylindrical or slightly bulbous in shape and frequently have horizontal or spiralling grooves (cf. finds from Zugmantel, Bad Cannstatt, Butzbach, Niederbieber). Wooden grips form parts of Danish bog finds (Nydam, Vimose). Gravestones of the Praetorian Guard at Rome from the second half of the 3rd century AD frequently show deceased guardsmen carrying *spathae* with eagle-headed pommels similar to the ones carried by the statues of the Tetrarchs now in Venice. The axes of the eagle heads are either at right angles or parallel with the blade. It is quite likely that these weapons were personal gifts from Emperors and were thus proudly displayed by the soldiers as a mark of their loyalty and valour. The young general on the Ludovisi sarcophagus carries a *spatha* with a pommel in the shape of a lion's head indicating his personal bravery. High-ranking officers sometimes carried the *parazonium*, an officer's dagger of Hellenistic origin which according to its name was commonly thrust under the officer's sash wound around the waist of the cuirass and knotted at the front. Remains of statues of Emperors often feature *parazonia* as part of the military dress uniform.

The *spatha* was now carried on the left side of the body, which made it easier to draw. The sheath (*vagina*) also underwent a series of changes. The practice of attaching the sheath to the belt or baldric by means of a set of rings was replaced by the practice of winding the baldric around the sheath and securing it with a clasp located at the front of the sheath. These clasps were of metal, ivory or bone construction and often came in the shape of animals (the dolphin as a bringer of good fortune was popular), or mythical beasts. Perforated chapes of metal or bone were no longer merely triangular but often trapezoid (as excavated in Corbridge and Colchester (UK)) or crescent-shaped (Caerleon (UK)). Contemporary pictorial sources however most commonly depict cylindrical, i.. e. round chapes, of which examples have been found in Cologne, Niederbieber, and Kaiseraugst. These examples are decorated with niello vine ornaments or geometrical patterns. The sheath itself was constructed of two

138 KÜNZL, Ernst, *Unter den Goldenen Adlern. Der Waffenschmuck des Römischen Imperiums*, Regensburg/Mainz 2008, p. 93.

139 BISHOP presumes that Publius Cornelius Scipio Africanus was responsible for the introduction of the *gladius* Hispaniensis but concedes that current archaeology is as yet unable to resolve this question definitely. M. C. BISHOP, *The Gladius. The Roman Short Sword*, Oxford 2016, p. 10.

140 Ibid., p. 18.

141 KÜNZL (2008), p. 104.

142 BISHOP/COULSTON (2012), p. 157.

143 Ibid., p. 155 ff.

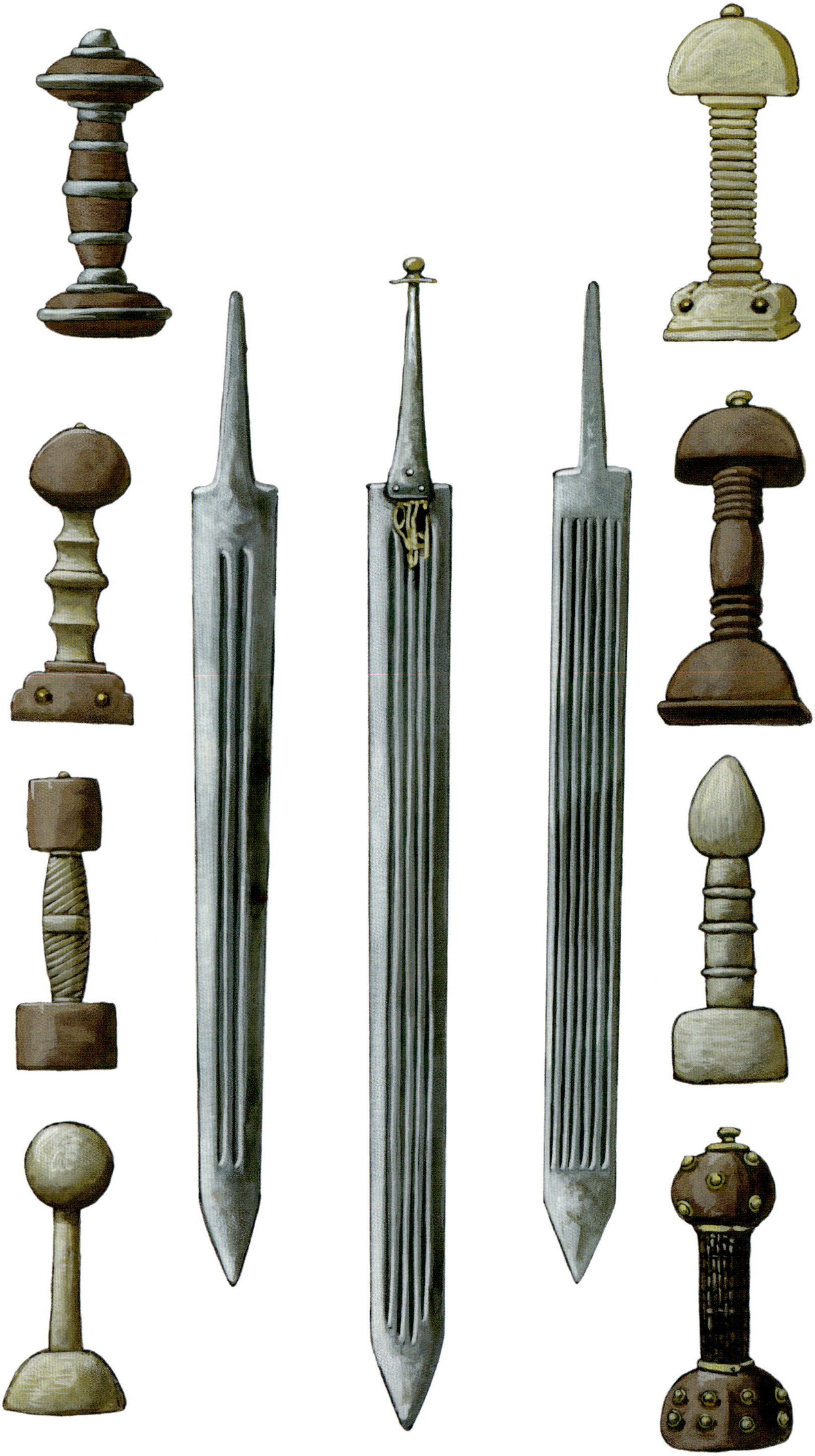

wooden halves sheathed in leather and often edged with metal binding terminating in the chape. Midribs of metal and other forms of edge binding were also common[144].

The introduction of the *spatha* did not however entail the complete abolition of shorter blades. Apart from the military dagger (s. below), another short sidearm, the so-called *semispatha*, continued in use. This weapon, literally "half longsword", continues to puzzle scholars. The name appears in Vegetius' later work on military theory (*Epitoma Rei Militaris* II, 15), which claims that the heavily armed infantry of the front ranks were armed both with *spathae* and *semispathae*. Several weapons found at Künzing may fit the bill. Blades are up to 40 cmin length (*gladius* blade lengths measuring between 40 and 70 cm). Other finds are from Augst (CH), Wehringen and Köngen. It remains difficult to clearly define these weapons as *semispathae* however, as they may also be large daggers. KÜNZL has suggested that these weapons may in fact be broken *spathae* which were converted into short swords by the armourers[145]. If the *semispathae* were indeed a different weapon altogether, they will have been carried instead of a dagger and used whenever the circumstances rendered the *spatha* useless, e. g. in the confined space of front-line combat.

144 MIKS, *Studien zur römischen Schwertbewaffnung der Kaiserzeit* (2007), quoted in FISCHER (2012), p. 179.

145 KÜNZL (2008), p. 103.

The dagger

Like the *gladius*, the military dagger (*pugio*) had its origins in the Iberian peninsula and since the 1st century BC formed an integral part of Roman military equipment. It was carried attached to an individual belt in gunslinger fashion at first, later it was fastened to the one remaining military belt while the sword was carried on a baldric. In the early Principate the dagger seems to have enjoyed particular favour with the legionaries and foot auxiliaries (cavalrymen are not depicted carrying them) as a means to display both military pride and personal wealth. Finds show that the soldiers set great store by richly decorated dagger sheaths, often silvered, with a variety of embossed, enamelled, damascened or inlaid ornaments. The blades themselves became increasingly slender and elegant (Vindonissa/Windisch (CH) type). A last resort in bloody hand-to-hand combat or brawl, the dagger was also a versatile everyday tool as well as sign of its owner's military profession.[146][147]

Plate XXVI

Spathae

The plate shows examples of (partly reconstructed) *spathae* hilts and blades of Lauriacum-Hromóvka type, comprising finds from Illerup (DK), Vimose (DK), De Meern (NL), Gušća (HR), Stuttgart-Bad Cannstatt, Zugmantel, Rainau-Buch, and Niederbieber (D)[146]. As ever, pommel, handgrip and handguard could be of either wood, bone or ivory. Pommels and handguards were occasionally coated in metal.

In the course of the later 2nd century AD, the manufacturing of the *spatha* underwent a number of changes. Analysis of preserved *spatha* blades demonstrates what a long and complex affair the making of a Roman long sword was. Put simply, iron or steel rods were first intertwined, folded and welded together in numerous and time-consuming steps, thus creating the strong and flexible core of the weapon. In a second step, the steel edges were added. [147]

This new production method seems to have introduced *spathae* whose blades were furrowed with several grooves. This new type, whose blades are stouter than those of the comparatively slender Straubing/Nydam category, have been typefied as Lauriacum/Hromóvka type after excavation sites both inside and outside the Empire's boundaries. The furrows (often erroneously referred to as "blood channels"), of which up to six could occur, gave the blade additional stability and flexibility while reducing its overall weight. So-called "pattern welding", which gave blades an individual appearance according to the amount of carbon contained in the rods employed to weld the core, added to the appeal such weapons exercised on the soldiers who used them. This could be increased by non-ferrous images of warrior gods, Victories, and standards inlaid below the handguard (cf. BISHOP [2020], BISHOP/COULSTON [2011]), obviously intended not just for display but to increase the weapon's impact on the Empire's enemies.

The left blade illustrated follows a find from Croatia, while the middle one is from the voluminous Illerup/Ådal bog hoard (MIKS [2007]). A warrior god image serves as a blade ornament, the grip tang has been attached with rivets and is still surmounted by a disk shaped rivet decorated with a hemispherical knob which would have sat on top of the pommel. Interestingly, *semispathae* of similar construction have been excavated at Köngen and Künzing (D) (BISHOP [2020], p. 58, after MIKS [2007]). The blade on the right was found at Vimose (DK).

146 Illustrations are partly based on BISHOP/COULSTON (2011), COWAN (2003), and MIKS (2007). In this commentary, we follow mainly BISHOP (2020).

147 BISHOP 2020, p. 23 ff., 26.

Plate XXVII

3rd century AD Roman daggers of Künzing type (not to scale) from various sites.

The absence of daggers on the big triumphal monuments of the 2nd century AD led to the supposition that they had fallen out of use by this time. That this was in fact not the case is attested by finds from the 3rd century in Mainz and Künzing. These weapons are markedly different from their precursors however in that they are broader and of much simpler manufacture, hilts being frequently of organic material instead of the previous metal. They are completely devoid of the elegance and grace of earlier examples. Some dagger blades from this period are as broad as swords (one dagger found in London is 8cm in breadth) and their length of up 30 cm leaves no doubt whatsoever as to their primary employment as combat weapons. Double-edged blades are parallel or tapered. Remains of sheaths are simple metal frames, some of which still have the traditional four-ring suspension system. This functional simplicity stands in somewhat stark contrast to Herodian's account of the Emperor Septimius Severus stripping the Praetorians of their cherished ornamented daggers (II, 13, 10).

It remains slightly unclear how the dagger was carried in the 3rd century. While FISCHER assumes daggers were fastened to the belt with thongs passing through rings attached to the sheaths, STEPHENSON believes they were worn suspended from a baldric worn across the left shoulder[148]. The dagger remained in use well into late antiquity.

Spears and javelins

Although the *pilum*, the classic javelin associated with the legions, was supplemented by a number of polearms during this period, pictorial sources as well as finds at the Harzhorn and the Saalburg show that it continued to be in use. Both tanged and socketed *pila* were employed by the legionary infantry and the Praetorians, as gravestones show these soldiers (and, oddly, even a lone *eques singularis*!) armed with *pila*. The javelins depicted are heavy affairs, some having two ball-shaped leaden weights for increased penetrating force attached below the ferrule (the gravestone of Quintus Proculus, soldier of *Cohors III Urbana*, actually shows three). Some *pila* of the third century seem to lack the ferrule, the iron shank protruding immediately from the weights and lacking the well-known pyramid-shaped triangular point. Some shafts appear to be wound about with cord in their entire length, as depicted for example on the gravestone of Praetorian guardsman Septimius Valerinus (the winding of the shaft with cord was usual restricted to the top of the shaft to ensure a firm grip). Other shafts of sculpted *pila* have narrow grooves at regular intervals, some in spiralled form, suggesting that they were painted in contrasting colours (cf. the gravestones of the Praetorian guardsmen Vitalis and Marcus Aurelius Mucianus). Such painting is well-attested for later periods. The *pilum* of a *beneficiarius*

148 STEPHENSON (1999), p. 78.

whose gravestone was found at Apamea (SYR) shows what appears to be ornamental ribbons tied to the lower of the double weights (if it is a *pilum* at all, that is).

Vegetius states that the *pilum* was ca. 1, 63 metres long (*Epitoma Rei Militaris*, II, 15). As a missile, the *pilum* with its small pyramidal point was designed to penetrate an opponent's shield and kill or wound the man sheltering behind it. It could also be employed as a spear at close quarters. This versatility may be the reason why in spite of the introduction of spears in the legions the *pilum* did not fall out of use but continued to exist in variants (*spiculum*, *verutum*) right until the end of the Empire.

A gravestone of a legionary of *legio II Traiana Fortis* from the period in question shows the soldier holding two man-high spears with triangular heads lashed together with thongs. Another gravestone of a legionary of the Eleventh Claudian Legion also shows the deceased with a pair of spears, suggesting that at least one of them was intended for throwing. Are these spears a different type of javelin (*lanceae*), as suggested by COWAN[149], are they thrusting spears, or a weapon designed for both purposes? Other stelae show soldiers armed with only one spear, probably for thrusting at close quarters (*hasta*). It remains difficult to ascertain the exact length of such thrusting spears, since gravestones tend to show these weapons modified to fit the size of the stone, thus not being of any value regarding the spears' actual length. No finds of spears with intact shafts attached have as yet been found within the Empire's frontiers. STEPHENSON, using finds from Danish bogs at Nydam and Illerup as evidence, presumes that a spear that was to prove effective in keeping an enemy at bay while still being easy to wield must have been around 2, 50 metres in length[150]. Like the *pilum*, the *hasta* had an iron or bronze butt spike to ram the weapon into the earth when not in use, or as a last resort if the spear broke. An enemy already trampled underfoot in a melée could be swiftly dispatched with the buttspike without it becoming necessary to reverse the weapon first. Several buttspikes have been found at Roman sites, e. g. the *limes*.

Socketed spearheads from the third century have survived in comparatively large numbers and come in a variety of shapes, often making it virtually impossible to assign them to a certain specific weapon form. Some spearheads are more than 20 cm in length, others are barely half as long. The heads vary in shape: some are leaf-shaped, others are triangular or rhombical. Cross-sections of blades can be either triangular or rhombic. If the *pila* were indeed painted, we may suppose that spears were too.

It remains impossible at present to ascertain how many soldiers in the *centuria* were armed with the *hasta*, and how many retained the *pilum*, and to what extent this distinction existed at all. If one takes into account the tactics explained above, it is possible that the front-rankers

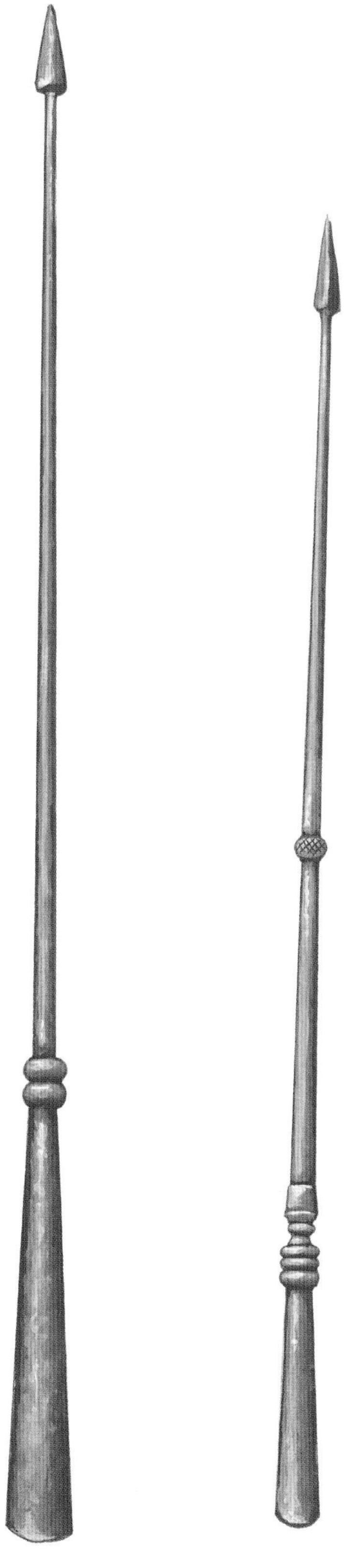

Plate XXVIII

Two *pila* shanks excavated at the Harzhorn battlefield.

149 COWAN (2015), p. 9.

150 STEPHENSON (1999), p. 55.

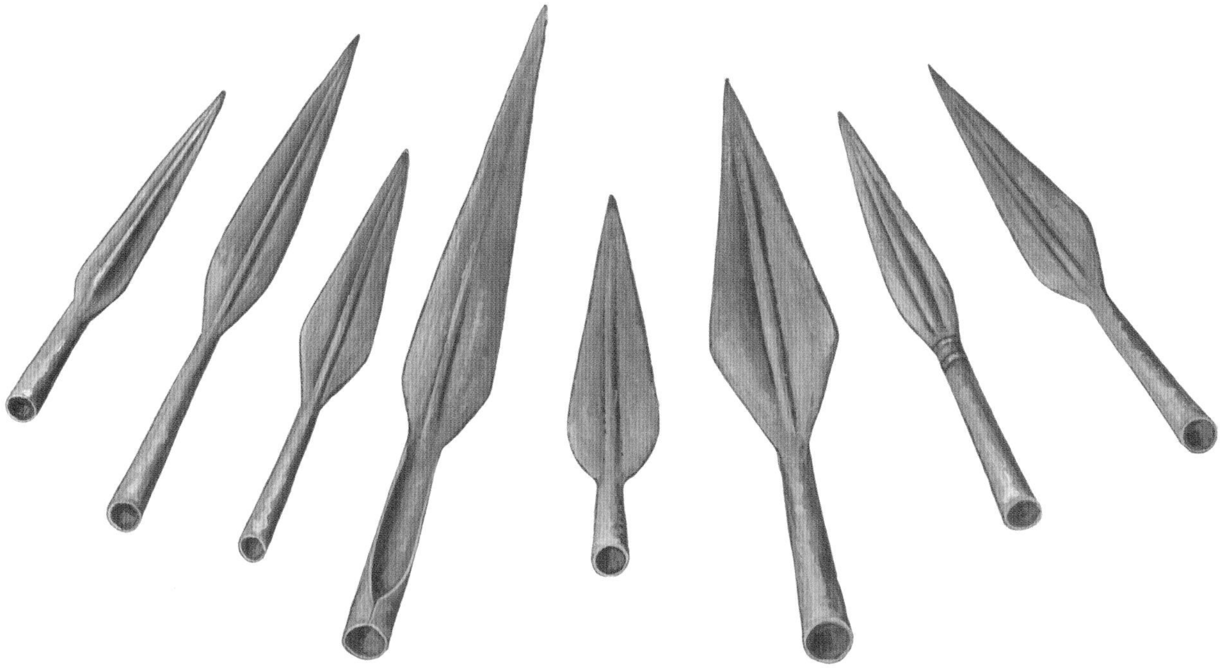

Plate XXIX

Roman spearheads and javelin heads from the Harzhorn battlefield and various other sites, third century AD.

carried the *hasta* in order to repel or keep cavalry at a distance and to fight infantry at close quarters, while the other soldiers used their *pila* to contain any attack on the formation; for the time being, this must remain mere speculation however.

The Roman regular cavalry also carried a thrusting spear (which could also be thrown), and javelins. A relief of a native caravan guard from Palmyra proves that the local camel-mounted *dromedarii* also carried lances. In the case of the *dromedarii*, these were supplemented by bows and javelins. The heavily-armed horsemen of the numeri *cataphractariorum*, the *clibanarii* and the *contarii* wielded the two-handed heavy *contus*[151].

Two grave stelae of *lanciarii* of *legio II Parthica* were excavated at Apamea and Palmyra. Legionaries Aurelius Mucianus and Septimius Viator are depicted carrying small oval shields (which have presumably been scaled down for artistic convention) and bundles of five short javelins each (*lanceae subarmales* or *iacula*), Mucianus storing his in what appears to be a quiver. Heads of javelins like this have been excavated in Northern Britain and, in large numbers, at the Harzhorn. These spearheads can be classified as belonging to javelins since their comparatively narrow sockets (13mm) would have been designed for short and slender shafts measuring about about 1, 5 metres[152]. The tips of the javelinheads excavated at the Harzhorn are 2cm long. All finds have four-cornered cross-sections, which can be square or rhombic. Javelins like this were employed by infantry and cavalry alike. Mounted troops carried the javelins in a quiver attached to the saddle, a fact which is attested by Josephus in his account of the Jewish War, and a terracotta statuette from Alba Iulia depicting a horseman from the late second century AD. Infantry *lanciarii* will have carried their javelins in a quiver worn on their backs like a rucksack, the only really feasible solution given the dished form of the oval shield (s. below). To carry any number of these javelins in the hand negotiating the shield would have been extremely risky, since firm control of the shield was vital; if the shield was dished (earlier *clipei* were flat), this method of carrying javelins was impossible due to the length of these weapons.

151 DIXON/STEPHENSON, p. 71 ff.

152 GESCHWINDE, Michael/LÖNNE, Petra, „Relikte einer Schlacht. Die Funde vom Harzhorn", in: PÖPPELMANN, Heike/DEPPMEYER, Korana/STEINMETZ, Wolf-Dieter (eds.), *Roms vergessener Feldzug. Die Schlacht am Harzhorn*, Darmstadt 2013, p. 272-284, p. 274. Vegetius (II, 15) gives the length of javelins as 1, 03 m. S. also STEPHENSON (1999), p. 55.

Shields

The shield was the main defence of the ancient warrior. It served to contain or at least modify the effects of enemy weapons so that the soldier's armour could arrest their impact and thus avoid serious harm. The shield could also be used as a weapon by attempting to push the enemy backwards or knock him off balance with a punch of the shield boss. We commonly associate Roman legionaries and Praetorians with the curved rectangular or cut-down oval shields of the early and middle Principate (*scuta*), while the auxiliaries carried flat oval, rectangular or hexagonal shields. Grave stelae like those of Gaius Valerius Crispus from Wiesbaden and Trajan's Column seem to ascertain this standardization of equipment. This, however, is not altogether tenable. The base of a column found in the *praetorium* of the legionary fortress in Mainz depicts a soldier with an oval shield and javelins long considered to be an auxiliary infantryman; modern scholars are less certain, claiming that the soldier may also have been a legionary skirmisher, an *antesignanus* (literally "man ahead of the standards", i. e. the main body of heavy infantry[153]). The gravestone of Castricius Victor of *legio II Adiutrix*, a unit originally recruited from marines, shows Victor equipped with an oval shield (though admittedly this might have been a relic of his marine equipment). The unit distinction *cohors scutata* in the auxiliary infantry regiments indicates that at least some infantry regiments were equipped with *scuta*, the term *scutata* pointing to what seems to have been an exception.

While Trajan's Column still shows legionaries and Praetorians consistently equipped with richly decorated *scuta*, an examination of the Column of Marcus Aurelius, the (restored) base of the Column of Antoninus and the Arch of Septimius Severus will render different results. These triumphal monuments show legionaries and Praetorians (if they may be recognised as such) equipped with oval shields. All the soldiers on the Ludovisi sarcophagus carry oval shields. Many, though not all, grave stelae of the third century depict soldiers carrying oval shields. The gradual withdrawal of the rectangular *scutum* in favour of the oval shield is confirmed in later pictorial sources such as the Arch of Galerius at Thessalonica as well as the Arches of Diocletian and Constantine, and mosaics in the Villa Casale (Piazza Armerina, Sicily) and Ravenna. The *Notitia Dignitatum*, the final turnout of Rome's armies in the twilight of the Empire, shows round shield emblems, which indicate oval and round shields used by both infantry and cavalry.

An attempt to explain the causes for this change in military equipment must rely on the Roman Army's late 2nd century's tactical shift. Tactics which focused more on defence required different equipment. The introduction of the longsword and the thrusting spear rendered the use of the *scutum* increasingly impractical, and in the wake of defensive tactics involving shield walls such as the *fulcum* oval shields were more suitable since they enabled the soldier to provide cover to his left-hand neighbour's unprotected right side, which – the efficiency of the ancient *testudo* notwithstanding – the curved *scutum* could not as easily provide, while leaving spaces to thrust at the enemy with spears and swords.

The spectacular finds in the ruins of the Roman fortress of Dura Europos in Syria have given scholars far-reaching insight into the construction and appearance of 3rd century Roman shields. Excavations carried out between 1928 and 1937 brought to light examples of no less than four different shield types, many of them still complete, 21 shield bosses and six metal shield grips (all finds belonging to an approximate total of fifty shields[154]). The Dura shields remain the sole examples of preserved genuine Roman shield decoration to date.

Among the finds were four tall leather shields resembling mediaeval pavises pierced with wooden rods for stability, the alternating rods and leather surface forming a v-shaped pattern. Scholars have presumed that these shields were employed as targets at the archery butts, or served as mobile shields for archers. Their construction and shape resembles shields of Persian manufacture, examples of which are known from the time of the Greek and Persian wars as belonging to the equipment of the *sparabara* infantry units. Since they do not conform to traditional and typical Roman military equipment standards, they shall be ignored in this work. More or less the same can be said of two oval shields of plywood construction, now lost, which lacked bosses and were presumably carried with the help of straps, as may be deduced from four drillholes forming a rectangle. They may have been strapped to the forearm or upper arm and formed part of the equipment of either horse archers, *contarii* or the *dromedarii*, making it possible for the soldiers to control the reins and operate their bows or *contus* lances[155]. The grave stele of Aurelius Bitus, a trumpeter serving with *legio II Adiutrix*, shows him carrying what may be a small curved rectangular shield lacking a boss which allowed him to play his *cornu* using both hands, which seems to confirm that such shields were indeed carried by Roman soldiers at the time.

The majority of the shields excavated at Dura were oval in shape and designed to accommodate a central metal shield boss (*umbo*). Altogether, a total of thirteen shields of this type were found. These dished shields with a total depth of 10 cm between the edge and the shield centre were about 1 metre in height and 90 cm across. In contrast to the elaborate multi-layered plywood construction of preserved *scuta*, the oval shields were constructed of planks of poplar wood glued together vertically. It is worth

153 Cf. TRAVIS, John and Hilary, *Roman Shields. Historical Development and Reconstruction*, Stroud 2014, p. 126.

154 JAMES (2004), p. 159.

155 TRAVIS (2014), p. 66, JAMES (2004), p. 163.

Plate XXX

„Amazon shield" from Dura Europos

The shield is decorated with concentric floral and other patterns around the (reconstructed) boss. Against a red background, an *amazonomachia*, a battle between Greeks and mounted Amazons, is taking place. While some of the Greeks are engaged, others hold their weapons at the ready or stand at ease. They are attired with crested Attic helmets, long-sleeved tunics, cloaks, muscled cuirasses and boots, and carry round shields. Some appear to be wearing tight-fitting breeches. Short-sleeved over-tunics (or *pteryges?*) are also in evidence. The Amazons, at least two of which are employing the "Parthian shot" with their short composite bows, are dressed merely in belted tunics. Some of the figures have name tags in Greek (e. g. the Greek at 9 o'clock: ΔΗΜΟΦΩΝ [Demophon]; probably the son of Theseus of Athens. He took part in the Trojan War together with his brother Akamas. At 2 o'clock we see a man named ΙΠΠΟΤΗ[Σ] [Hippotes], possibly a Trojan nobleman). Greek was *lingua franca* in the Eastern provinces of the Empire. The shield (1, 17 x 0, 97 m) was excavated from embankment N of Tower 24 at Dura. Due to the elaborate paintwork, JAMES (2010, p. 166), who gave the shield its distinctive name, presumes that this was no shield designed for everyday use, let alone for combat. He suggests that it was employed by the "Amazon" team of a cavalry regiment at the *hippika gymnasia*.

Tafel XXXI

Partially reconstructed „Homeric“ shield from Dura Europos

Like the "Amazon shield", this shield (measuring 1,18 x 0,95 m) was found together with a third example inside the walls of the fortress at embankment N near Tower 24 (JAMES (2010), p. 178). At the time of excavation at least two of the right outward planks and at least four of those on the left side were missing. JAMES presumes that the horizontal iron grip which ran across the entire breadth of the shield was forcibly removed at some point, resulting in the destruction of the planking. The original position of the missing grip is echoed by a rectangular horizontal gap running towards the centre in the middle of the shield. The shield was never fitted with a boss (it has been added in the reconstruction) – the holes for the rivets are missing (*ibid.*, p. 178). The edge of the shield has holes for stitching a rawhide edging into place.

Again, the shield's main decoration depicts scenes from the Trojan War. Since the shield's condition does not permit conclusions concerning the decoration of the area of the missing planks, the reconstruction leaves these parts bare; the balance of the shield design's horizontal composition however suggests that only a few figures, if any, are missing.

The preserved painting of the shield has suffered considerably over the years. It shows two episodes from the fall of Troy. The lower scene depicts the arrival of the Trojan Horse outside the walls of the city. Sinon, perched on its back, seeks to dispel the suspicions of the king and his entourage, who have ventured outside the gate, just visible behind the female figure between Priam and the horse. Other Trojans look on from the safety of the walls.

At top, there is massacre and mayhem. The victorious Greeks, forming impermeable ranks, are shown slaughtering the hapless inhabitants of Troy. There is no escape, the soldiers are standing astride piles of bodies, among them women and children. Again the Greeks wear muscle cuirasses, crested helmets, and cloaks. In the centre there is an altar. A Trojan kneels before it as a Greek warrior prepares to strike the lethal blow. Since in the bottom painting all male Trojans wear Phrygian bonnets, we are probably witnessing the death of King Priam, killed by Achilles' son Neoptolemos at the altar of Zeus. The female figure at left may represent Cassandra.

The shield shows literary episodes universally popular among the inhabitants of the Roman Empire, and the soldiers were no exception. While the modern viewer may find the craftsmanship of a local Syrian painter hard to resist, the depiction of the remorseless brutality of ancient warfare is driven home in a manner which leaves us in no doubts as to what the inhabitants of Dura might have expected when the Persians appeared outside their gates.

Plate XXXII

Rectangular *scutum* from Dura

Of all the Roman shields excavated at Dura, this is surely the most widely known. The curved semicylindrical *scutum* (1,06 x 0,86 cm) was found in Tower 19 of the fortress and is evidence for the continued existence of the classic legionary *scutum* of the early Empire. It is the only surviving complete example of this shield type. In contrast to the convex oval shields excavated on the same site, which are composed of planks glued together, this shield is of the same plywood construction which already characterised the Republican *scutum* found at Fayoum (EGY) in 1900. The boss has been added. It is missing on the original shield, though one rivet was still found embedded inside the shield's surface. This is constructed of three layers of plane wood strips and is altogether only 6 mm thick, which more or less rules out the possibility of it being a shield intended for use in combat. The edges of the shield are sewn with rawhide. The surface was covered with rawhide dyed red and magnificently painted as shown. Around the boss there are rectangular concentric patterns of floral ornaments lined with an undulating edge. The corners are decorated with stylised lily-shaped darts. At centre an eagle with a laurel wreath in its beak and spread wings hovers above a globe. It is flanked by two victories making as if to crown it with further laurels. The bottom of the shield is decorated with a lion between two starbursts. The lion was the badge of *Legio IIII Flavia*, detachments of which served with Maximinus in Germany. It was based at Singidunum/Belgrade. Unfortunately, there is no evidence for it operating on the Syrian frontier at this time. This is also true for *Legio XIII Gemina*, stationed at Apulum/Alba Iulia (RO), whose emblem was also the lion.

noting that the planks are between 3 and 5 mm thinner at the edges than they are at the shield's centre, where they are between 7 and 9 mm thick. The wood was probably treated with water or steam to provide flexibility before being cut, glued together and inserted into a concave mold to give it its final shape[156]. Finally two holes were cut into the centre to provide the horizontal hand grip, which was later covered by the hemispherical metal boss. The upper hole was semicircular, the lower either semicircular or trapezoid in shape. The shield was reinforced by a metal cross brace semicircular in profile (examples of which have been found at Dura and Öhringen) riveted to the inner surface, which ran across the grip and the entire breadth of the shield (at right angles to the grain of the planks). The gravestone of Aurelius Iustinus, soldier of *legio II Italica*, shows the deceased carrying his dished shield casually slung over his left shoulder, giving a clear view of the cross brace. Iustinus carries his shield slung with the help of a braided rope. Some shields of this type (among them the so-called "Amazon shield"; s. below) have a single ring attached in the upper left quarter of the inside surface, presumably to accomodate a strap or rope with which to sling or carry it when not in use (the other end probably being slung around the grip).

The shield's wooden surface was covered with fabric or transparent rawhide or sinew, to which glue was applied to achieve adhesion. This was in turn covered with leather or gesso, which served as a basis for painting. While earlier shields had received a lining of bronze riveted to the edges, these shields were edged with rawhide, which was attached by sewing, the twisted yarn passing through holes drilled into the shield's edge at intervals of approximately 2 cm[157].

The three rectangular *scuta* excavated at Dura have achieved far more fame than the oval shields described above. One of these, now at Yale, has survived almost intact. It is in fact not entirely rectangular, the upper and lower edges being slightly convex. In contrast to most of the other examples, the shield itself was not found in the context of the sappers' war in the tunnels beneath the fortress walls but in Tower 19, where it had probably been stored for maintenance work[158]. The boss had been removed. Measurements are 1.05 times 0, 85 m, the shield being constructed of three layers of wooden strips 1, 5 to 3 cm across, the two outer layers having been applied horizontally, the inner vertically. The shield is surprisingly thin, measuring only 6mm. The aperture for the boss is circular with a horizontal grip. The *scutum* was reinforced by a quadrangular wooden frame attached to the inner surface, a fifth brace running horizontally above the grip, which was wound about with leather[159]. The shield's surface and edges was of a construction similar to the oval examples. It is unclear whether the soldiers defending Dura Europos against the Persians were regularly equipped with oval shields, even though the relatively high number of specimens found seems to suggest this. It appears reasonable to suppose however that while some units carried oval shields, others still continued to use the *scutum*, at least as long as these remained servicable. The 3rd century relief from Alba Iulia mentioned previously shows a soldier carrying the classic rectangular *scutum*. Ares, a legionary serving at Nicopolis outside Alexandria is also shown on his grave stele with a rectangular shield. It can thus be said with confidence that at the time of the Emperor Maximinus, the *scutum* was still being employed by the Roman Army. To what extent, is a different matter.

Altogether 21 shield bosses (*umbones*) were excavated at Dura Europos, seven of which were of iron, the others being of copper alloy. The majority of pieces is round, while some are oval, measuring 18 to 21 cm in diameter. Some examples are star-shaped. One example, now lost, had a quadrangular flange and may have belonged to a *scutum*, while the rest were intended for oval shields. All bosses possess between four and six symmetrically spaced rivet holes The bosses are universally hemispherical in shape, only one sporting a button-shaped ornament on its apex (Cat. No. 608). Decoration is mostly simple, ornaments consisting mostly of concentric circles. Finds from other parts of the Empire show that shield bosses could in fact be richly decorated, a famous example being a *scutum* boss from the 2nd century AD excavated at South Shields (UK). The hemispherical boss is made of bronze and decorated with an eagle and laurel wreath. The square flange is divided into square fields depicting deities, allegorical images of the seasons, standards and a bull (probably a legionary badge) in niello work. A similar piece round in shape was excavated at Szàzhalombatta (H). Other finds identified as shield bosses have been placed in the context of the *hippika gymnasia* (both identification and purpose are now frequently disputed). These show mythical beasts and characters, e. g. one well-known example from Carnuntum/Deutsch-Altenburg (A) depicts Ganymede being abducted by Zeus in eagle form. Another example from Blerick (NL) has the shape of a Gorgon's head surrounded by a laurel wreath.

Let us now turn to the painting of the shields. Some of the Dura shields are in fact so magnificently painted that scholars were inclined to identify them as parts of the soldiers' parade equipment. The ornaments have nothing in common with the decorations we are familiar with from Trajan's Column. While this monument depicts legionaries and Praetorians carrying shields decorated with (among other things) laurel wreaths, winged lightning bolts, *lunulae* (crescent moons) and starbursts, the shields of the auxiliaries sport a multitude of different blazons. Some scholars believe that the stone masons at work on the column

156 Ibid., p. 65.

157 JAMES (2004), p. 161.

158 TRAVIS, (ibid.), p. 68.

159 JAMES (2004), p. 183.

had at their disposal a catalogue depicting the individual shield designs of the units involved in a given incident in order to identify them in the respective panels, while others believe that the blazons shown are simply products of the sculptors' imagination. It can be assumed nevertheless that every unit possessed an individual shield design, since Tacitus (*Histories*, III, 23) mentions an act of particular daring during the second battle of Cremona in 69 AD, in which two legionaries used shields from an enemy unit to hide their identity in a successful attempt to knock out an enemy catapult.

In the 3rd century AD the above-mentioned designs, if they were ever fixed, do not seem to have been universally continued. They can no longer be ascertained in pictorial sources. We must take into account that even in the early Principate there were shield designs (gleaned from other sources) which do not appear on Trajan's Column. The painting of the Dura shields is impressive in its obsession with detail and the perfection of its execution at least on some examples. The Yale *scutum* (beloved by military artists) is painted bright red, the square hole for the boss being surrounded by concentric squares in dark grey, yellow and black. The outer square is bordered with white and yellow meandering ornaments with white lily-shaped corner decorations pointing outwards. The yellow square is decorated with oblong floral as well as wavy- and wreath-shaped ornaments with stars and sunwheels in the corners. The boss itself would have been framed by two white borders. The upper quarter of the shield shows in its centre an eagle ascending with spread wings. The sacred bird of Jupiter is bearing a laurel wreath in its beak as a sign of military triumph. The eagle is flanked by two winged Victories also bearing laurel wreaths. The lower quarter of the shield shows a lion flinked by two starbursts, possibly a legionary emblem (for example of *legio IV Flavia Firma*). Similar heraldic designs may be found, for instance, on the Arch of Galerius (Hercules, the patron deity of the *Herculiani* legion) and at Piazza Armerina (boar; the charging boar was the badge of *legio XX Valeria Victrix*). We may thus suppose that at this time the soldiers'shields were painted with depictions of their units' badges or patron deities (*genii*). A series of coins issued by Emperor Gallienus which shows diverse legionary heraldic animals surrounded by aureoles points to the continuing sacred veneration of these *genii legionu*m.

One of the three painted oval shields (which was presumably still in the state of construction since the boss was missing) depicts on a medium blue ground a frontal image of a military deity with a black lance, pale yellow cloak and a white shield bordered in red. The figure wears a hat-shaped auburn helmet, the head surrounded by a yellow halo[160]. The god wears yellow armour adorned with two red stripes across the chest, and a dark blue undergarment. This shield blazon is unique and has nothing in common with other examples found *in situ*.

The other two oval shields are similar to one another and to the *scutum* in that both are painted red and are decorated with complex concentric floral patterns around the shield boss. Both shields are painted with scenes from the Trojan War. While one shield shows a battle involving Amazons (*amazonomachía*) whirling around the central boss, the other shows the fall of Troy with the arrival of the Trojan horse below, while above the city is being pillaged and its population slaughtered. The polychrome figures have been painted with great care and are identified by names written in Greek.

While the back of the *scutum* is comparatively simple, the blue inside of the Amazon shield has heart-shaped ornaments painted in white, sky blue and red interspersed with suns and stars arranged in spokes meeting at the centre. This magnificent example proves that the soldiers were also fond of decorating the insides of their shields.

Examination of the shields has revealed that they were painted with the so-called encaustic method, which is familiar from North African mummy portraits. Pigments are dissolved in wax and applied to the surface. JAMES (2004) remarks that this method was employed to make the shields more resistant to damp and water[161]. Other shields were painted with water colours or colours produced on an egg-white or casein basis. Pigments include indigo, vermilion, coal and a russet-shaded umbra[162].

Roughly contemporary shield decorations from other sources are much simpler in design. The oval shields of the soldiers depicted on the base of the Column of Antoninus Pius are decorated with cruciform botanic ornaments, a similar cross formée blazon decorates the round buckler of a statuette depicting a Numidian light cavalryman now in the British Museum. It is commonly assumed that shields were also painted with the unit's name and number. On the Column of Marcus Aurelius, the depiction of the so-called "rain miracle" (attested by Cassius Dio), a sudden torrent of rain which saved a Roman army surrounded by the Quadi from dying of thirst, shows Roman soldiers equipped with oval shields decorated with cruciform blazons. The legion involved, *XII Fulminata*, was said to have had Christians within its ranks, whose prayers saved the army from certain death. Despite this incident, Marcus Aurelius was no friend of the Christian faith and it is very unlikely that the soldiers' shield decorations have anything to do with the Christian religious symbol. It would have been unthinkable for a proud Roman legion to sport a torture instrument for slaves and highwaymen on its shields. A gravestone of legionary Flavius Tryphon of the Second Parthian Legion found at Apamea (SYR) shows the deceased with an oval shield quartered by a cruciform

160 The helmet is strikingly similar to the hat worn by the right-hand deity depicted on a fresco showing the sacrificial ceremony of *cohors XX Palmyrenorum* at Dura.

161 JAMES (2004), p. 164.

162 Ibid.

Plate XXXIII

Extra-heavy cataphract, or *clibanarius*

This cavalryman is on duty on the Empire's eastern border, and expects to fight his likewise heavily armoured Persian counterparts. It was these men that Ammianus was later to call living statues "carved by the hand of Praxiteles" (XVI, 10, 8).

The masked helmet of female "Amazon" type has distinctly oriental features but like the chestplates was excavated at Straubing, Germany. He wears a scale cuirass over a padded *subarmalis*. His arms are protected by laminated plates, which are depicted in the famous 3rd century graffito of a *clibanarius* found at Dura. His thighs are covered by scale armour (in this we follow JAMES's (2010) reconstruction). He wears a tightly knotted scarf (*focale*). His greaves were found at Eining (D).

His primary weapon is the heavy armour-piercing two-handed lance (*contus*), supplemented by a *spatha*. The baldric is stitched with the decorative image of a dolphin, designed to ward off harm. An example of such a baldric was discovered in a bog at Vimose (DK).

The horse armour is one of the sets excavated at the Roman fortress of Dura Europos, stormed by the Persians after a siege in the year 256 AD. In this case, the rows of bronze scales have been silvered to enhance the optic effect. The chamfrom was excavated at Straubing, the neck armour is reconstructed according to the graffito mentioned above.

Stefano Borin

design. This cruciform design is possibly merely what is left of the shield surface being divided into four sections with different designs or images applied with paint onto the stone surface[163]. The discrepancy between the magnificent Dura shields and other pictorial sources defies a simple explanation and will probably only be solved satisfactorily by finds yet to occur.

Archers and slingers

A large number of trilobate arrowheads were excavated on the Harzhorn battlefield. This type of arrowhead has its origins in the east, yet is only one of the many forms of arrowhead employed by the Roman army. The considerable number of the trilobate arrowheads excavated at the Harzhorn has led to the conclusion that they were missiles fired by the élte Osrhoenian archers (*sagittarii*) in Maximinus' army.

Although we may suppose that most soldiers of the Roman army would at least have received some basic archery training[164], it was left to specialist units to bring this weapon to bear effectively in action. The majority of these regiments, many of which were mounted, stemmed from the Empires eastern provinces, where the bow had long since been a traditional weapon. Thus we meet Palmyrenes, Canathenes, Commagenes, Hamians, Ituraeans, Osrhoenes and Arabs serving the Emperor as archers even in the remotest provinces of the Empire.

The Roman army's standard bow was of composite construction, a complex weapon system which required considerable skill, strength and experience to operate effectively. The manufacture of the bow took a large amount of time. It owed its unrivalled tensioning forces and range to its various components which combined to give it its effectiveness. Its core was made of hardwood which was additionally braced by glueing strips of horn to the bow's belly. The weapon's flexibility was increased by gluing layers of sinew onto the outside. This procedure of combining the various components with the help of glue was extremely time-consuming. The bow ends, or ears, were reinforced by horn or bone antlers which also received the string. Thus manufacturing a single composite bow could take several years. Bone and horn limb reinforcements have been excavated at various military sites, among them Caerleon (UK), Ehingen, Rainau-Buch and Frankfurt (D).

When unstrung, the bow was stored in a leather bowcase (*gorytos*), since the glue which held it together was sensitive to damp. To string the bow, the archer would brace his weapon on the ground and bend it using his knee. Unstrung, the bow took the form of a crescent in a reverse angle to its shape when strung. In order to retain its flexibility, the bow was strung only for action and practice. STEPHENSON assumes an effective range of between 50 and 150 metres with a maximum range of ca. 200 metres[165]. The range and effectiveness of the bow relied on a number of factors however, e. g. the archer's experience, practice, skill, height and strength as well as the quality of the bow's manufacture, rate of fire, traction, and whether the archer was mounted or not.

It is a matter of debate which method Roman archers favoured to draw the bow. A pictorial source from Dura depicting a mounted archer and a thumb ring found at Vindolanda suggest that the string was drawn and retained with the thumb, but it would be wrong to deduce that this was common practice[166]. Archers were equipped with leather or even metal bracers to prevent the rebounding bowstring from puncturing the skin of the left arm. Quivers were worn either slung across the back or suspended from the archer's waistbelt. Mounted archers attached their quivers and bowcases to the saddle.

While trilobate arrowheads were particularly effective against lightly armoured or unarmoured opponents like the Germans or Dacians, Roman archers used quadrangular arrowheads with higher penetration against armoured opponents, some of which have been have been excavated at the Saalburg (D). Leaf-shaped arrowheads (also found at the Harzhorn) and fire arrowheads capable of accomodating flammable material (as found at Straubing) were also used. Arrowheads were either socketed or spiked to the arrow's shaft and secured with glue or sinew. The arrow's fletching was likewise attached with glue, as examples found at Dura confirm. If the shaft was made of reed, the arrowhead was first attached to a socket of firmer wood which was then affixed to the shaft with sinew and glue. This was done to avoid the shaft splitting on impact, thus reducing the arrow's penetrative power.[167]

In contrast to the Varus battlefield at Kalkriese, no slingshot bullets have been found at the Harzhorn as yet. This is all the more surprising since the sling was as simple a weapon as it was effective, and it was employed throughout the ancient world. Slingers (*funditores*) were first employed by the Roman army in the Punic wars, and although legionaries were required to know how to handle the weapon, the army recruited specialists, mostly from the Balearic Islands whose inhabitants were renowned slingers, since this weapon too required a considerable amount of skill and practice. These auxiliaries normally possessed a set of different slings which they chose from according to range. Slings fired either round pebbles or specially made clay or leaden slingshot, often

163 Shields of this type from the 5th – 6th centuries were found at Fayoum (EGY).

164 MEYER, Michael/MOOSBAUER, Günther, „Osrhoener, Mauren und Germanen. Bogenschützen und Speerschleuderer", In: PÖPPELMANN, Heike/DEPPMEYER, Korana/STEINMETZ, Wolf-Dieter, Roms vergessener Feldzug. Die Schlacht am Harzhorn, Darmstadt 2013, pp. 223-226, p. 225.

165 STEPHENSON (1999), p. 81.

166 Ibid.

167 Ibid., p. 154.

inscribed with obscene insults. In many ways, slingshot were a more effective weapon than arrows, since they are hardly recognisable in flight and do not need to penetrate an enemy's armour to dispatch him (cf. Vegetius I, 16). Sling bullets possess the ability to stun or cause severe internal injuries, being especially dangerous to the head, causing severe concussion, fractures or even death without penetrating the helmet (cf. the complaint of legionary Sextus Africanus mentioned above). Stone sling bullets, presumably from the 3rd century AD, have been found at Buciumi (RO). Surprisingly so far, units of slingers have not been ascertained for this era.

Horse furniture

The cavalrymen's arms and equipment have been dealt with in previous chapters, so let us now briefly focus on the horses.

At this time, the Roman cavalry still employed the four-horned saddle adopted from the Celts in the 1st century BC. Parts of the leatherwork of these saddles have been found at Valkenburg (NL) and Vindolanda, as well as two complete sets of bronze horns (excavated at Newstead). These horns served to provide the rider with stability at a time in which stirrups were as yet unknown. Whether these saddles possessed an inner wooden frame, a saddletree, remains the object of much academic debating[168]. In contrast to Peter CONNOLLY, Marcus JUNKELMANN believes that the Celtic saddle was a flexible affair which thanks to the rider's weight enabled the four horns to wrap around his thighs and buttocks, thus giving him a firm hold (stirrups were as yet unknown). Leather or fabric straps hung from the saddle's four corners, either for display or to attach items of the cavalryman's equipment, e. g. his flask, rolled cloak, a bag holding fodder, shield, quivers for javelins or arrows in the case of the *equites sagittarii*. Chest strap, crupper and girth straps were also attached to the saddle itself. Several studded leather straps running roughly parallel from the saddle around the horse's hindquarters and beneath the tail can be seen on the stelae of two *equites singulares Augusti* of the 3rd century discovered at Saló near Rome and in Rome's Via Labicana. The depicted mounts also have ten narrow metal-studded straps passing around their necks. The bridles appear to be braided leather straps. Harnesses were the natural colour of leather according to age but may also have been dyed red for show.

Pictorial sources and finds confirm that Roman military horse furniture of the 3rd century AD was richly decorated with metal and organic ornaments. Metal studdings in alternating colours were supplemented by bells and pendants in the shape of ivy leaves, phalli or *lunulae* to ward off harm and the evil eye. Coloured melon beads were also popular. Pendants and the strap-dividing *phalerae* were frequently of open-work design and often decorated with pearl- or vine-shaped ornaments. The Roman cavalry used ring snaffles adopted from their Celtic adversaries (examples of these have been excavated at numerous sites), but also lever bridles (with or without hackamores). A complete example of the latter was excavated at Augsburg[169].

While the majority of the regular Roman cavalry seem to have shunned horse armour, chamfroms were popular. These were employed both for the *hippika gymnasia* and in combat. Several examples have survived, among them a few from the era in question. Chamfroms could be made either of metal or leather. A leather example from from the late 1st/early 2nd century AD found at Newstead on Hadrian's Wall covers the entire front of the horse's head and possesses triangular flaps protecting the animal's ears. It lacks the familiar perforated hemispherical eye protectors, but these may have originally existed and since been lost. Possibly they were removed when the chamfrom was discarded. The chamfrom was further decorated with studs forming vine- and leaf-shaped patterns. Below the circular eyeholes was attached a *tabula ansata* tag carrying the owner's name. A circular patch between the eyeholes would have originally held some form of ornamental fitting.

Metal chamfroms come in a variety of forms. There are examples designed to cover the entire head, while others consist merely of two eye-protectors joined by a decorated hexagonal bridge roughly covering the horse's blaze. Chamfroms of the former type have been excavated at Eining, Straubing (D), and Gherla (RO). The three plates of non-ferrous metal are joined by hinges and have perforated hemispherical eye-protectors. All of them are lavishly decorated with embossed images of animals and deities of war (Hercules, Mars, Minerva, Dioskuri, dolphins, eagles, lions). The side pieces of the Straubing chamfroms have stylised boar's tusks embossed. The tripartite examples resembling goggles are frequently composed of bronze and iron; examples have been found at Straubing, Eining, and Gilau (RO). They too are richly decorated, the eye-protectors sometimes taking the form of busts of deities. Another example found at Carnuntum (A) sports a bust depicting Ganymede[170].

In the context of so-called parade panoplies and equipment several medallions depicting gods (Minerva, Ganymede) have come down to us whose function remains unclear. In modern reconstructions they either feature as shield bosses or peytrals[171].

168 Cf. FISCHER (2012), JUNKELMANN, Marcus, *Die Reiter Roms*, vol. 3, *Zubehör, Reitweise, Bewaffnung*, Mainz 1992, p. 34 ff.

169 KEMKES, Martin/SCHEUERBRAND, Jörg, *Zwischen Patrouille und Parade. Die römische Reiterei am Limes*, Stuttgart 1997, p. 40 f.

170 KÜNZL (2008), p. 120; DIXON/STEPHENSON, p. 112 f.

171 Cf. JUNKELMANN (1996), p. 86-87.

Tafel XXXIV

Dromedarius of *Cohors XX Palmyrenorum*

A camel rider of *cohors XX Palmyrenorum*, to the soldiers of which we owe so much of our knowledge about the Roman military at this time, is on patrol in the surrounding countryside of his garrison town Dura Europos. He has seen service under Maximinus and remembers him from the time when he was serving as the *dux ripae* in charge of the Euphrates defences.

The one-humped dromedary was employed as a beast of burden by the peoples of the Middle East and North Africa since the 12th century BC, and also served them in wartime. Camel troops were to be found in Persian, Hellenistic, Parthian, Arabian, Jewish and even Carthaginian forces. Having encountered them during the wars against the Hellenistic successor kingdoms, the Romans raised regular units of *dromedarii* only at the beginning of the 2nd century AD, when Trajan's conquest of Arabia Petraea prompted him to form previously allied contingents into *ala I Ulpia Dromedariorum Palmyrenorum*, henceforth stationed at Palmyra to guard the frontier with the Parthian Empire. The 5th century AD *Notitia Dignitatum* lists several regiments of *dromedarii* stationed in North Africa and the Middle East under the command of the *Dux Palaestinae* and the *Dux Thebaidos* respectively, and other local auxiliary units probably had smaller contingents at their disposal for escort and patrol duties.

Since no enemy action appears likely (the peace along the Persian frontier is brittle at the best of times), the *dromedarius* relies only on his *subarmalis* for protection. Thus attired, his duty is to protect military supply caravans and provide security along the trade routes criss-crossing the deserts of Mesopotamia. He will also keep a watchful eye on the horizon, since there is the constant risk of a Persian raid or an ambush by bandits.

A duty roster preserved at Dura informs us of the fact that there were no specific sections of , in the cohort. The troopers were attached to the infantry. Since the cohort recruited itself mainly from locals, most soldiers will have been familiar with camels from infancy.

Since a number of pictorial sources have come down to us in the form of reliefs and mosaics from the region, it is fairly easy to reconstruct ancient camel riders, although no specific depiction of a Roman *dromedarius* exists as such. As is often the case today, dromedaries seem to have had high saddlebows to prevent accidents when the animal rose or lay down. Sources show animal pelts and blankets serving as padding, the relatively simple bridles are adorned with bells and tufts. All in all, not much has changed.

To protect his head from the sweltering sun, the *dromedarius* has donned a headscarf. His mail coat has been wrapped up and stowed away in a linen bag attached to the saddle. His modern state of the art Persian ridge helmet hangs from the saddlebow. This specimen was found beneath the ruins of Tower 19 at Dura and may possibly represent an anachronism, since the fortress only fell around twenty years after Maximinus's reign. Nevertheless, similar conical yet differently constructed helmets had been in use in the region for centuries so we are giving it the benefit of the doubt. The helmet in question was assembled from several plates joined by a central ridge and had a nosepiece and a mail coif. This type of helmet was to influence helmets worn by the Roman army of late antiquity.

The *dromedarius* wears a military tunic and breeches; these are worn both by a caravan guard on a relief from Palmyra, and soldiers of the cohort as depicted on the famous fresco at Dura. The puttees are taken from a hunt mosaic from North Africa.

Apart from carrying several days' rations and plenty of water, the soldier is armed with a lance (attested by the afore-mentioned relief), and a *spatha*. For long-range fighting and skirmishing he carries a powerful composite bow in a bowcase, and a quiver of javelins. We do not know anything about the shield blazon of the Twentieth Cohort of Palmyrenes despite the Dura shield finds. The depiction of the Persian light god Mithras, universally popular throughout Rome's armies, is therefore merely conjecture.

COHXXPAL

We have seen that apart from chamfroms horse armour did not form part of the standard equipment of the Roman mounted soldier, since this was not in accordance with his function as a medium cavalryman. Only the heavy *clibanarii* rode barded horses. What this armour looked like exactly can be seen from the afore-mentioned graffito of a Parthian or Persian *clibanarius* at Dura. Excavations at Dura promptly brought to light no less than three sets of horse armour from the 3rd century AD, two of which are virtually intact. The first barding (measuring 1,22 x 1,69 m) is constructed from overlapping bronze scales (35 x 25 mm) sewn onto a fabric padding. A broad strip of red leather runs from withers to crupper, leaving a large circular hole lined with red leather to accommodate the saddle. The horse's tail was protected by a protruding triangle of scales on a red leather base. The armour consisted of 31 rows of scales on each side and protected the horse's flanks, withers, croupe and hindquarters, but not its chest. The second complete set (1, 48 x 1, 10 m), which is of similar construction, only has 19 rows of iron scales (60 x 45 mm) but has two extensions which can be joined in front of the horse's chest[172]. If one takes the above-mentioned graffito as an idea of what these horsemen looked like, the barding was supplemented with scale armour for the horse's neck, and a chamfrom.

Two trapezoid-shaped sets of rawhide lamellar armour were found at Dura. Their measurements and peculiar shape has led DIXON and STPHENSON to presume that these are two halves of a horse's neck armour worn together with the metal barding[173].

In the context of these archaeological finds it makes sense to briefly focus on the problems that arise when it comes to the question of what these heavy cavalrymen were called. The words *cataphractarius* and *clibanarius* and their specific meanings are still a matter of controversy among scholars and authors. It is by no means clear how many heavily armoured cavalry units of Persian or Parthian type the Roman army had at its disposal in the mid-3rd century AD.

So-called *cataphractarii* were part of the Roman forces at least since the middle of the 2nd century AD. According to Cassius Dio, Marcus Aurelius received and sent 5, 500 armoured horse to Britain as part of a treaty with the Sarmatians in AD 175. The first regular regiment of this arm can be ascertained in the form of *Ala Gallorum et Pannoniorum Catafractaria*. HA mentions the cataphracts as forming part of Alexander Severus' army, and according to Herodian *cataphractarii* followed Maximinus on his march to Italy. In the third century cataphract units were stationed on the Rhine frontier and in Britain.

Cataphractarii and *clibanarii* presumably wore different types or different amounts of armour, since stelae of *cataphractarii* invariably show these soldiers riding unarmoured horses, which has given rise to the plausible idea that *cataphractarii* were heavily armoured horsemen, wearing for example long-sleeved mailcoats, vambraces, thigh protectors and greaves, and mounted on unarmoured horses. They seem to have derived from Sarmatian warriors, not Rome's eastern enemies (although it is an undeniable fact that wealthy Sarmatian warriors also rode barded horses). Such cavalry would basically have been suitable for the German campaign, but similar to the mediaeval knights, the tactical deployment of Roman heavy cavalry was in dense blocks of several ranks to maximise the sheer momentum and power of the charge. Thus flat terrain was essential to the cataphracts. In wooded or boggy country, their formation would easily have been disrupted and their long *contus* lances proved an encumbrance.

The problem is aggravated by the fact that *cataphractarii* is probably not just the name of a special mounted arm but also a general term simply denoting armour. The Greek term κατάφρακτοσ (*kataphraktos*) merely means "armoured, or "covered". Herodian thus speaks of armoured horsemen. Most Roman regular cavalry wore armour, so basically even every Roman medium cavalryman might have passed for a cataphract in the straightforward sense of the Greek word, but not necessarily for a *clibanarius* on an armoured horse. The introduction of the Greek word *cataphractarius* into the vernacular of the Roman army (and the explicit mentioning of these troops in the sources) does however seem to point to a special form of cavalry that had to be distinguished from their medium cavalry comrades. As said, these horsemen may have worn particularly heavy body armour and perhaps been armed with the *contus* (cf. the phrase *contarii*, a different unit altogether). To add to the confusion, both Arrian and Aelian call cavalrymen whose horses wore armour *cataphractarii*[174] .

172 DIXON/STEPHENSON, p. 115-116.

173 DIXON/STEPHENSON, p. 114. For a reconstruction see ibid., plates 11 and 14.

174 Quoted in ANDERSON, Erich B., *Cataphracts. Knights of the Ancient Eastern Empires*, Barnsley 2016, p. 104.

Clibanarii rode armoured horses. The first written source mentioning *clibanarii* in the Roman army is the inscription of a gravestone found in Bithynia dating from around 300 AD and commemorating Valerius Fuscianus from Klaudiopolis, who is referred to as a *cataphractarius clibanarius*[175] (the use of the two words implies they should not always be understood as synonyms). A controversial passage in the *Historia Augusta* (*Alexander Severus*, 56) claims that during Alexander Severus's Persian campaign the Romans seized enough Persian equipment to raise their own *clibanarii*[176]. We do know however that heavily armoured Roman cavalry were around much earlier. The word *clibanarius* is somewhat an etymological puzzler. It may be derived from a Persian term, or it may in fact be an example of a more sophisticated form of military humour. *Clibanus* was a mobile field oven, so *clibanarius* was indeed an appropriate name for a heavily armoured horseman plodding through the desert, always on the verge of sunstroke. To what extent the horsemen referred to as *cataphractarii* in the army of Maximinus were armoured, and whether their mounts were armoured as well, will probably remain a matter of debate due to the quibbles mentioned above. The Dura finds however do show that the Emperor's army in the East contained heavily armoured cavalry[177]. Roman cavalrymen wore either crescent-shaped spurs, a strap being passed through holes at both ends to attach the spur to the soldier's boot, or so-called studded spurs, whose straps were attached with the help of holes cut into the leather through which the studs were pushed.

The camel riders of the *alae dromedariorum* and *cohortes equitatae* used saddles very similar to modern ones. This fact can be ascertained with the help of numerous pictorial sources such as mosaics and carvings. Since a dromedary's hump cannot sustain pressure, the saddle consisted of a wooden construction integrating two cushions which sat on both sides of the hump and were joined by two cantles in the form of a reversed letter Y. To this saddle items of equipment like quivers, water bags, cloak, bowcase were attached.

175 https://de.wikipedia.org/wiki/clibanarius

176 FISCHER (2012), p. 100 f.

177 For queries regarding the tactical value of heavily armoured horse in Germany s. Chapter III.

STANDARDS AND MUSICAL INSTRUMENTS

Eagle lost, honour lost - honour lost, all lost.
Rosemary Sutcliff, *The Eagle of the Ninth*

An attempt has been made to show that despite some degree of artistic license the Ludovisi sarcophagus does in fact render a fairly accurate image of Roman military equipment in the 3rd century AD. At the top of the frieze the sculptor has depicted several standards. The Romans carry two Eagle standards (*aquilae*) and a flag (*vexillum*). A mounted officer holds a dragon standard (*draco*), while in the right foreground a standard bearer holds a standard (*signum*) decorated with several discs (*phalerae*) and surmounted by a pair of outstretched hands.

One of Marius' military reforms carried out in the 1st century BC had been to make the Eagle the sole legionary standard (previously there had also been the wolf, the bull, and the boar). The Eagle had been of silver at first, in the Principate it was made of gold or was at least gilded. Like all other military standards, the eagle was the object of religious veneration. On the anniversary of the founding of the legion, the standard was salved with precious ointments and decorated with wreaths, and in its hallowed presence the soldiers solemnly renewed their military oath to the Emperor (*sacramentum*). Numerous images of *aquilae* have survived on coins and Roman triumphal and funerary monuments. Depictions show the Eagle perched on a variety of bases, usually with lightning bolts in its talons, some examples with acorns in their beaks and laurel wreaths wound around upraised wings. The latter features may have been individual decorations for valour (on Trajan's column, one *aquila* is depicted with a *corona muralis* around its wings). The depiction of the Parthians' returning of the Eagles lost by Crassus at Carrhae in 53 BC on the cuirass of the Primaporta statue of Augustus in the Vatican shows the shaft of the standard decorated with several *phalerae*. This is unusual since shafts, which were commonly silvered, are frequently depicted quite bare. It certainly appears plausible that legionary eagles were individually manufactured and sculpted, since after all the individual legions varied in age and origin. The legion's First Cohort was responsible for the security of the sacred standard, ultimate responsibility resting with the *primus pilus* (First Centurion). The *aquila* standard remained with the legions right until the end of the Empire[178] and survived in mediaeval heraldry, becoming the shield blazon of the Holy Roman Emperor.

The Eagle served as a visible manifestation of the legion's *genius,* or protective spirit. It was a symbol of the legion itself; if it was lost, the legion commonly perished or was disbanded. Its loss was the ultimate disgrace, to save it from falling into enemy hands required acts of considerable personal heroism. Many well-known examples of outstanding bravery and sacrifice related in the sources have sufficiently been quoted in other works as to make repetition obsolete. Suffice it to say that the security and veneration of the legionary Eagle was crucial for the confidence, punch and military pride of any self-respecting Roman legion.

Several depictions of *aquilae* from the 3rd century AD have survived. The Emperor Septimius Severus commissioned a series of coins honouring his legions, the coins' obverse depicting an eagle standard with raised wings. The early 3rd century AD grave stele of *aquilifer* (Eagle bearer) Titus Flavius Surillio of *legio II Adiutrix* found and preserved at Istanbul depicts the officer in undress uniform (i. e. without helmet and cuirass) but carrying a small oval shield. The short shaft is decorated with two rams' heads, one at the bottom, while the other serves as a base for the box-shaped eagle's perch (*legio II Adiutrix*'s badges were Pegasus, capricorn and boar). The eagle itself is depicted frontally with slightly raised wings, but without lightning bolts. The gravestone of *aquilifer* Aurelius, like Surillio presumably soldier of *legio II Adiutrix*[179], was found at Budaörs (H). The eagle is shown in a similar posture to Surilio's standard, but the base of the figure is in this case a trapezoid capital broadening towards the top. The most unusual depiction of a legionary Eagle from the time of Maximinus however is surely the funerary stele of *aquilifer* Felsonius Verus of *legio II Parthica* from c. 240 AD excavated at Apamea (SYR). Verus too is shown in undress uniform, with a hook-shaped handle attached to the shaft of his *aquila* standard. This device, well-known from other Roman standards, served to carry the standard, but also to extract it from the ground and, most importantly, to fix it firmly into the ground without having to ram it into the soil and thereby possibly causing damage to the precious object. The eagle itself is shown inside a cage-like construction shaped like a box with two crossed bars through which the bird itself is visible. This has led COWAN to speculate that *legio II Parthica* allowed itself the extravagance of a live eagle[180]! Live birds are attested as regimental mascots in the American Civil War[181], but in the case of *legio II Parthica* such a standard seems highly improbable. One explanation which has been brought forward for the odd cage is that the sculptor attempted to show the so-called *aedicula*, a small shrine resembling a temple which could be placed over the eagle figure when the legion was on the march, the *aedicula* thus replacing the *sacellum*

178 TÖPFER; Kai Michael, *Signa Militaria. Die römischen Feldzeichen in der Republik und im Prinzipat*, Mainz 2011, S. 20.

179 Ibid., p. 381.

180 COWAN (2003), p. 38.

181 The 8th Wisconsin Volunteer Infantry carried a bald eagle on a perch, aptly named „Old Abe".

Tafel XXXV

Grave stele of *cornicen* Aurelius Bitus of *legio II Adiutrix*, 3rd century AD (detail)

This well-known gravestone depicting military musician Aurelius Bitus and his four-year-old son Vitalis was found at Aquincum (H), former base of the 2nd Adiutrix Legion, in 1899. According to the text carved under the depiction of the deceased, Bitus served for twenty years before being killed in action aged 38. He is shown wearing undress uniform according to 3rd century artistic convention, wearing a long-sleeved tunic, the *sagum*, breeches, and closed boots. His ring buckle belt is clearly discernible. The longish, pointed device protruding from under the cornu is hard to define. It cannot be the end of the *cingulum* strap, as what appears to be two straps with pendants are visible on the right. It is probably not the end of the balteus strap either, since none is visible across Bitus' chest between *cornu* and right hand. Possibly iit is a crude depiction of the *spatha*, or a knife, or dagger. Bitus has a small shield either strapped to his left arm or suspended by means of a strap to facilitate the handling of his instrument, which he carries over his left shoulder. The crude execution of the shield is somewhat puzzling, since it seems to depict either a small curved *scutum* lacking a boss, or a round *parma* buckler.

The grip of his *cornu* is decorated by two circular ornaments representing either scaled-down *phalerae*, or egg-shaped *ovula*, which are also shown on standards. In his left hand Bitus holds either the cornu's detachable mouthpiece (which is probable), or a scroll pointing to his citizenship.

Tafel XXXVI

Grave stele of *bucinator* Aurelius Surus (detail)

Surus served as a military musician with *legio I Adiutrix Pia Fidelis*. His grave stele, now on display at the Istanbul Archaeological Museum, gives his rank as *bucinator*. In accordance with contemporary fashion, Surus is shown in uniform without armour, but the sculptor has included his helmet and shield. The helmet resting at his feet has a large peak and seems to have a face mask or overlapping cheek guards, possibly defining it as of Niederbieber or Heddernheim type. His oval shield may be depicted as smaller than in real life, but then to manage his instrument efficiently, Surus would have required a smaller shield than the regular legionaries.

Surus is attired with the *sagum*, a tunic with ring buckle belt, breeches and boots. His *spatha* hangs from a *balteus* retained by clasp on the sheath. Surus held the rank of *bucinator* yet appears to be holding two *tubae* trumpets of different size, the longer being held with the mouthpiece up. The latter may also be some form of staff, but this appears doubtful. The straight and long instrument with bell and mouthpiece which could frequently be disassembled into several parts has been identified by scholars as the *tuba*, while the shape of the elusive *bucina* so far remains unclear.

Tafel XXXVII

Grave stele of eagle-bearer Titus Flavius Surillio of *legio II Adiutrix Pia Fidelis*

The aquilifer's gravestone, now on display at Istanbul's Archaeological Museum, shows the deceased wearing long-sleeved tunic, breeches, and *calcei* half-boots. His *sagum* cloak is secured by a round decorated fibula at the right shoulder. He wears the usual ring-buckle belt. In contrast to other depictions however, the ends are not tucked under the belt but pass vertically through the buckle itself almost in the manner of earlier studded aprons.

The *aquila* standard itself is in some respect an anomaly. Its shaft is remarkably short for a standard designed to be held high. The shaft itself broadens towards the top, supporting a box-shaped postament on which the eagle itself is perched. The postament is adorned with a ram's head, a decoration repeated at the end of the shaft. It remains unclear how exactly the standard was planted in the ground. Since the ram (*aries*) is not recorded otherwise as the Second *Adiutrix* Legion's blazon, it remains remotely possible to identify the ram's heads as awkward depictions of capricorns, which indeed were connected with this specific legion, but given the overall high artistic quality of the stele and the fine execution of the heads themselves this is extremely improbable.

Since no sidearm is discernible, several modern scholars have claimed that the *balteus* passing over Surillio's right shoulder is in fact a carrying device to support the heavy standard. Close scrutiny of the stele itself however reveals that this is simply not the case. The strap clearly passes behind the standard and is thus the soldier's *balteus* from which the sword was suspended. Possibly the sculptor for artistic reasons did not wish an actual depiction of the *spatha* to interfere with that of the standard. The ram's head at the bottom is evidently part of the standard and quite obviously attached to the shaft. Surillio's small round buckler rests on the ground to his left. The original red colour is still faintly visible. In his outstretched left hand he proudly displays a scroll. These scrolls are a common artistic feature on military tombstones not just of this epoch. Surillio died aged forty after serving for eighteen years. His comrade Aurelius Zanax, who succeeded him as *aquilifer*, had the stele erected for his predecessor.

at the legion's base[182]. Such an *aedicula*, mentioned by Cassius Dio (XL, 18), is probably what is depicted on the Portenaccio sarcophagus in Rome; another depiction of a legionary Eagle protected by an *aedicula* can be found at Trasacco (I)[183]. COWAN's and McBRIDE's reconstruction of Verus with a lion's pelt draped over his head and shoulders[184] follows present-day artistic convention; indeed, legionary *aquiliferi* are never depicted with this attribute (in contrast to the *signiferi* and musicians) but are often shown bareheaded. The wearing of animal skins seems to have gone out of fashion in the 3rd century, since pictorial evidence is lacking.

A *vexillum*, a flag hanging from a crossbar attached to a lance, is visible behind the cavalry officer charging into battle at the young general's right side on the Ludovisi sarcophagus. It is impossible to say if this specific example is an infantry standard or whether it belongs to a cavalry unit. *Vexilla* (carried by the *vexillarii*) served as standards for the horsemen of the *alae* and *cohorts equitatae*, and for the legionary cavalry. They were also employed as standards for the auxiliary infantry cohorts. Every legion had a *vexillum* alongside its Eagle. *Vexilla* were also the standards of legionary detachments serving away from their parent units (hence the term "vexillation" denoting these contingents), and for temporary units raised from veterans or recruits. The *vexillum* itself commonly consisted of a square fringed piece of cloth (the *stola* or *flamma*[185]) displaying number and name, honorary titles and badge of the legion or auxiliary regiment, occasionally also the Emperor's cypher. It was attached to a crossbar which in turn was attached to a shaft surmounted either by a decorated spearhead, a disc (*phalera*) or a figure representing either the legion's or unit's badge, *genius* or some other protective deity. From the ends of the crossbar flew decorative straps studded with ornamental discs (*siphara*) which terminated in *lunulae* or ivy-leaf pendants or fringes[186]. One example of a *flamma* found in Egypt (now in St Petersburg) is decorated with the image of a winged Victory standing on a globe and brandishing a wreath and a palm of victory. The fresco depicting a sacrificial ceremony of the officers and men of *cohors XX Palmyrenorum* at Dura shows the regiment's *vexillarius* standing beside the altar. The *vexillum* flag is red with a yellow frame, the bottom edge is decorated with fringes. The image on the flag is too strongly eroded to allow identification, it appears plausible to suppose the unit's emblem, an inscription is improbable. The flag is surmounted by a disc and possibly a spearhead. The *vexillum* was the origin of the magnificent *labarum* of late antiquity, the sacred standard of the Christian Roman Emperors.

In contrast to the Eagles, *vexilla* and *imagines* (s. below), whose function was primarily religious and ceremonial, the *signa* also served tactical purposes. They marked their units' position in the line of battle, and their movements transferred orders to the soldiers in the din of combat. Scholars tend to disagree about the number of *signa* in a legion. TÖPFER argues that during the Empire each century had one *signum* (accordingly in the *auxilia*, each infantry century and each *turma* likewise would have had a *signum*). Thus an Imperial legion would have had 60 *signa* – in contrast to the 30 manipular *signa* of the Republican legion. The *signum* of each cohort's first century (that of the *pilus prior*) would have doubled as the cohort standard. TÖPFER goes on to claim that the cohort standard had a spearhead tip instead of the usual raised hand[187]. JUNKELMANN is inclined to agree with TÖPFER but points to a source from the time of Septimius Severus, according to which each legion only had 36 *cornicines* (musicians assigned to the *centuriae*); since it is commonly supposed that these musicians were assigned to the *signa* to combine acoustic and visual signals in battle, this would mean that an Imperial legion would have resembled its Republican predecessor in that there was only one *signum* per *manipulus* (one *manipulus* = two *centuriae*)[188]. This issue must remain unresolved for the time being. It is interesting to note that the *signifer* depicted on the Ludovisi sarcophagus (in contrast to the *cornicen*, he wears no animal pelt) carries a *signum* surmounted by two hands instead of the usual one. This is unique and defies straightforward interpretation. It may be the standard of one of the double centuries of the legion's first cohort.

Images of *signa* on funerary monuments and coins from the 3rd century AD show no remarkable differences from the standards of the early Principate. The depiction of a *signifer* from the Severan era on a sarcophagus found at Aquincum shows a *signum* crowned by raised hand but lacking the familiar wreath surrounding it (as depicted, for example, on Trajan's Column). Underneath the hand hangs a small flag, presumably bearing the unit's name and badge. The shaft is decorated by five round *phalerae* discs, each shaped like a sacrificial dish (*patera*) of the type employed during religious ceremonies. Below the *phalerae* there is an upturned *lunula* to ward off evil spirits from the standard. The standard lacks the tassel familiar from earlier depictions but features a Gorgon's or lion's head instead, possibly a legionary emblem. TÖPFER assumes it to be the lion badge of *legio IV Flavia Felix*,

182 Cf. JUNKELMANN (2015), p. 317.

183 TÖPFER, p. 131.

184 COWAN (2003), plate F.

185 JUNKELMANN, Marcus, *Die Reiter Roms*, pt. II: *Reitweise und militärischer Einsatz*, Mainz 1991, p. 136.

186 Cf. D'AMATO, Raffaele, *Roman Standards and Standard-Bearers (1), 112 BC – AD 192*, Oxford 2018, p. 24-25.

187 TÖPFER, p. 136. This would also have applied to the *cohortes urbanae* and the *cohortes vigilum*.

188 JUNKELMANN (2015), p. 319.

which sent a vexillation to assist Septimius Severus' Parthian campaign. This detachment was stationed at Aquincum[189].

The grave stele of Alexandrus from the later Severan era excavated at Ramleh (EGY) depicts the deceased during a religious ceremony. Alexandrus is framed by two *signa*, whose tops are decorated – possibly for the sake of artistic symmetry – with a left and right hand respectively. Both signa have six *phalerae* attached to the shafts while lacking any other form of decoration. The decorations of the *signa* flanking the *aquilae* on the series of coins issued by Severus are frequently hard to make out exactly. All sport various *phalerae*, some have *lunulae* and tassels, some are topped by spearheads, others by laurel wreaths.

In the *cohortes praetoriae* every *centuria* had an individual *signum*[190]. The Guard also seems to have carried a *vexillum* besides. Interestingly, Praetorian standards seem to have included *aquilae* standards, e. g. as depicted on the relief in the Louvre, and on a coin issued by Gaius, which shows him addressing his Guard, from whose midst protrude four *aquilae* decorated with *coronae* and *phalerae*[191]. D'AMATO therefore presumes that every Praetorian cohort carried a decorated eagle standard as its cohort standard[192]. This appears plausible, since Praetorian *signa* are often shown surmounted with eagles, e. g. on a relief celebrating the submission of conquered German tribes to Marcus Aurelius, now on display in the Palazzo dei Conservatori in Rome[193]. This kind of standard combining an eagle with *phalerae*, *imagines* and *coronae* is peculiar to the Praetorians and seems only rarely to occur in other arms of the Roman Army (cf. the Eagle of the 4th Legion on the *Portenaccio sarcophagus*). The Guard's attached cavalry squadrons carried *vexilla* and *signa*[194]. The Imperial horse guard (*equites singulares augusti*) carried a *vexillum* as its regimental standard, and possibly also an *imago*, which was carried by an officer holding the rank of *tablifer*. This must be treated with caution however[195]. The individual *turmae* seem to have carried *signa* (see below).

Regarding the appearance of the Praetorian *signa* during the 2nd and 3rd centuries, we may turn to a funerary altar from Rome for reference (now in the Vatican Museum). The altar stems from the late Antonine period[196] and also shows a soldier engaged in religious sacrifice. To the left and right, two virtually identical *signa* are mounted on pilasters. Like earlier Praetorian *signa*, both are surmounted by eagles. Below the eagles are small flags, presumably inscribed with the unit's name and title. This followed on each standard by a *phalera* bearing the Emperor's bust and two *coronae* attached horizontally so that they run around the shaft itself.

These are followed by another *phalera* depicting two clasped hands (presumably signifiying the *concordia*, the unity of the troops and their commander-in-chief). Both sets of decorations are terminated by tassels. The standards thus depicted are conspicuously similar to the standards associated with the Praetorian Guard on Trajan's Column, and to the *signa* depicted on the famous funerary monument of former guardsman Pompeius Asper from the 1st century AD. The unfortunately heavily damaged gravestone of an *eques singularis* from Rome (3rd century AD) has the shape of an altar or temple. The deceased guardsman (possibly a *signifer*) is shown standing between originally two pilasters adorned with *signa*, of which only one has survived. The *signum* resembles an infantry standard rather than the type commonly associated with the cavalry. The *signum* is surmounted by a spearhead, followed by an upturned *lunula*, a horizontal *corona*, two *patera*-shaped *phalerae*, another *corona*, and two tassels. The standard, which is strikingly similar to other Praetorian standards, must have been quite unwieldy for a soldier mounted on a horse; to date, it is the only depiction of a standard of the Imperial horse guards to have survived.

The officer of horse riding next to the general on the Ludovisi sarcophagus carries a *draco* standard. A magnificent example of this type of standard was excavated by archaeologists from the charred rubble of the *limes* fortress at Niederbieber near Koblenz, destroyed ca. AD 260. It consists of a 30 cm long copper pipe in the form of a snarling dragon's head complete with scales and a jagged crest. The upper half of the standard was gilded, the lower silvered, causing the dragon to glitter in two different colours. The dragon was originally attached to the top of a spear shaft, at its rear end was a brightly-coloured conical wind-sock, which twisted and reared as it was carried ahead of the troop into action or on parade. The *draco* standard (carried by the *draconarius*) was adopted from the Dacians and Sarmatians and was employed at first only by the cavalry. It is mentioned by Arrian in the context of the *hippika gymnasia*. Later the *draco* also became popular with the infantry, presumably as a cohort stand-

189 TÖPFER, p. 380.

190 Ibid., p. 93.

191 TÖPFER, plate 3, caption p. 270 (British Museum).

192 D'AMATO (2018), p. 39.

193 It appears possible that the *signum* of a Praetorian cohort's first century was crowned by an eagle and functioned as the cohort standard (TÖPFER, p. 94; cf. D'AMATO (2018), p. 38 f.).

194 TÖPFER, p. 94.

195 D'AMATO (2018), p. 39. Illustration p. 50. While D'AMATO considers the Emperor's bust on a relief now in the Palazzo dei Uffici to be an *imago* carried by the horse guards, TÖPFER assumes that the bust is in fact the standard of some form of society, since it appears too small to pass for a standard. *Caveat emptor*.

196 TÖPFER, p. 379.

Plate XXXVIII

Cornicen of the Praetorian Guard

A Praetorian *cornicen* rallies his *centuria* with a blast from his instrument. He wears a red *tunica manicata* with purple decorations, and a short-sleeved *lorica hamata* over a linen *subarmalis*. The mail coat is decorated with several rows of bronze rings at sleeves and hem. Although Praetorians have come to be associated chiefly with the scale *lorica squamata* (they are depicted thus armoured on the Arch of Constantine[197]), it is fairly probable that other forms of body armour were also in use. His richly adorned belt is of Klosterneuburg type. The Künzing type dagger is suspended from the belt with the help of two decorated bronze studs. The soldier's *balteus* is decorated with stitchings depicting a dolphin inside an *aedicula* and was found at Vimose on the island of Fünen (DK). His *spatha* with its studded pommel and handguard is based on finds from Vimose and Illerup (DK). The swords excavated on these sites were probably of Roman manufacture but intended for export. The *cornicen*'s head is protected by a partly silvered masked helmet of Worthing type. The mask is on display at the Castle Museum, Norwich. A similar mask was found at Rodez (F). A wolf pelt is worn over the helmet. The headdress of the Ludovisi *cornicen* is heavily stylised, so one might substitute the upper half of a bear pelt instead. Whether or not Praetorian musicians wore the lion pelts so popular with illustrators remains a matter of considerable debate. The *cornicen* has slung a scarf (*focale*) around his neck and wears the typical breeches and puttees common among the Roman troops in the North.

To counteract the cold of the Germanic provinces, the *cornicen* has donned his *sagum* cloak and fastened it with a bronze fibula in the shape of a *cornu* (cf. FISCHER 2012, p. 236). His instrument has a wooden cross brace. The 3rd century grave stele of *cornicen* Aurelius Bitus of *legio II Adiutrix* from Aquincum (H) shows the grip decorated with what appear to be two small *phalerae* disks, but we have chosen not to depict these in our reconstruction. The fixtures attaching the grip to the instrument are on display at the Limesmuseum in Aalen (D). The bronze horn itself is silvered except for the bell and the detachable mouthpiece. In this we choose to follow the depiction of a *cornu* on the so-called *Gladiatorenmosaik* found in the remains of the Roman villa at Nennig, Saarland (D).

197 The soldiers wearing Spangenhelme and scale armour surrounding the Emperor on the Arch of Galerius at Thessaloniki have frequently been identified as Praetorians but may actually be *Equites Singulares Augusti*, or *Equites Promoti*.

Tafel XXXIX

Aquilifer of Legio IIII Flavia Felix

An eagle bearer faces the enemy. Guarded by the crack legionaries of the First Cohort and in the personal care of the *primus pilus*, the standard, focus of the soldiers' faith and *esprit de corps*, will be defended to the death. The eagle bearer's rank is emphasised by the splendour of his equipment. He wears a precious *tunica russata* with purple stripes, red woollen breeches and bright blue puttees. Over his *subarmalis*, whose *pteryges* are decorated with yellow or golden fringes, he wears a two-coloured scale cuirass (*lorica squamata*) with decorated chestplates; it is fastened with leather thongs running through holes on the wearer's left side, which is normally covered by the shield. Over his cuirass the eagle bearer wears his decorations, a simple set of silvered *patera*-shaped *phalerae* mounted on a red leather harness modelled on those worn by *aquilifer* Gnaeus Musius of *Legio XIV Gemina* on his tombstone in Mainz (1st century AD), and of centurion Lucius Refidius Bassus of *Legio XVI Gallica* , whose funerary stele is in the collection of the Rheinisches Landesmuseum in Mainz. He also wears a pair of Celtic neckrings (*torques*) slung round his neck, which are also shown on Musius's grave stele, and on the famous cenotaph of chief centurion Marcus Caelius of *Legio XVIII* found at Xanten (now in the RLM Bonn). He also wears an *armilla* bracelet on his wrist. The *aquilifer* is a highly respected member of the *principales*, an experienced soldier who can hope to be promoted centurion – if he survives. His sword is of Lauriacum-Hromówka type. The elaborate mountings of his *cingulum* have been produced in gilded silver according to the so-called *opus interrasile* technique; they were found at Cologne (D). The skullpiece of his helmet with a double eagle protome follows a specimen formerly in the Axel Guttmann collection, now on display at the Musée d'Art Classique at Mougins (F). The mask has been added and is based on conjecture following similar contemporary examples. Legionary *aquiliferi* are not shown wearing lion pelts in Roman art.

Roman pictorial sources tend to show the shafts of legionary (though not praetorian) eagle standards devoid of any form of decoration (e. g. on grave stelae, or Trajan's Column). There are, however, a few exceptions, the famous Portonaccio sarcophagus at Rome (Museo Nazionale) being one of them. The battle frieze from the late Antonine or Severan period definitely depicts an *aquila* adorned with a *phalera* and tuft. We cannot be entirely sure whether the standard is a legionary one, but it appears highly probable in the given context. KÜNZL (2010, p. 51) believes it is in fact the standard of *Legio IIII Flavia Felix*., since the medaillon on the eagle's crown-like perch bears the numeral IV. The illustrated *aquila* follows the sarcophagus in showing the eagle perched with spread wings on what resembles a *corona civica* of laurel or oak leaves adorned with a medallion denoting the legion's number, identifying it as the Fourth Flavian. The silvered shaft is decorated by three *phalerae* (there is only one on the sarcophagus standard) and a *corona muralis*, as it is frequently depicted on other monuments. Two red tufts also follow the sarcophagus, which shows only one however. These tufts may have evolved from the handfuls of grass attached to spears in the Republican period, thus improvising a simple standard. The fresh laurels are either a reminder of the recently celebrated birthday of the legion, or may be a recent decoration won on campaign. We cannot be entirely sure whether the entire legion accompanied Maximinus on his German campaign, but if the majority of the cohorts joined him, they will have taken their eagle standard with them. *Legio IIII* (or *IV*) *Flavia Felix* was awarded the epithet *Maximiniana* by the new Emperor.

S. Dorin '20

Plate XL

Roman standards c. 200 AD (clockwise; not to scale):

i) A *vexillum*. This standard, consisting of a flag suspended from a crossbar attached to a lance surmounted by a ball and spearpoint, follows a depiction on the grave stele of an unknown *vexillarius* found at Alexandria. TÖPFER (2011) dates this find to the Severan period. This standard belongs to a detachment of the Fourth Flavian Legion, which fought at the Harzhorn. Every legion also had its own *vexillum* alongside the *aquila*, it was thus not only a standard of a detachment. The flag of dark blue cloth has been painted with the legion's badge, the lion, and gives the legion's name and number. Several pictorial sources show *vexilla* thus adorned. A *vexillum* now in the collection of the Hermitage Museum in St. Petersburg shows that flags could have the devices painted on. While the Alexandria *vexillum* has no fringes, these have been added here according to numerous pictorial sources, e. g. a frieze from the time of Marcus Aurelius reused on the Arch of Constantine, and the column of Marcus Aurelius.

ii) The frieze on the Portonaccio sarcophagus shows the legionary eagle accompanied by an odd kind of standard. It is a pole surmounted by an object shaped like a conical cup with a round, pointed roof surmounted by a ball. It obviously seeks to depict some form of building since it shows brickwork design on the outside and has an aperture in the form of a fairly large window. This has led KÜNZL (2010) to presume that we are dealing with a *corona muralis*. Since however the mysterious standard is shown next to the legionary eagle, it may actually simply be the eagle's *aedicula*, or, which is more probable, the *aedicula* holding the Emperor's *imago* (although admittledly no *imago* is visible on the sarcophagus). We are giving this notion the benefit of the doubt and reconstruct it in this function.

iii) *Draco* standard.Standards of this category are depicted on the Portonaccio and Ludovisi sarcophagi. On the latter, the officer galloping alongside the general is holding a dragon standard aloft, which may signify it was carried by the *equites singulares*. On Trajan's Column, dragon standards fly above Dacian hill fortresses, and a Sarmatian cavalryman dying far from home at Deva (Chester) had himself depicted with a dragon standard on his grave stele. It is generally assumed that the Romans came into contact with these standards in the Danube area. Depictions of these standards, used by friend and foe, abound in Roman triumphal architecture. They were introduced into the Roman Army by irregular units and then found their way into the cavalry, Arrian making specific mention of them in the context of the *hippika gymnasia*. In late antiquity, they were adopted by the infantry, probably serving as cohort standards. The head of this standard is the famous find from the rubble of the *limes* fortress at Niederbieber near Koblenz (D), which was destroyed c. 260 AD. The head is made of gilded and silvered copper alloy, the colouring of the windsock and shaft is conjectural.

iv) Praetorian standard. A grave altar shows a soldier holding a *patera* and *virga* rod sacrificing at a small altar. The side pilasters are decorated with two virtually identical standards (the *imagines* differ slightly in appearance), on which this reconstruction is based. TÖPFER (2011, p. 379) identifies them as praetorian *signa* and dates them to the late Antonine period. The standard is crowned by an eagle perched above a *vexillum* denoting the unit (in this case *Cohors III Praetoria [pia vindex]*). Beneath the flag there is an *imago* (the two depicted in our illustration do not follow the stele and are an artist's error, but depictions of several members of the Imperial family, e. g. of the emperor and his son, were common on standards of the Guard). The *imagines* are followed by two *coronae civicae*, and a rather peculiar decoration, which may be either a solid *phalera* or a ring with two hands clutching the standard's shaft, which is clearly visible. This depiction of a pledging handshake between the Imperial family and the Guard (δειχώσις, *deichosis*, cf. TÖPFER (2011), ibid.), and of both sides holding the staff of the sacred standard, signifies the harmony and understanding (*concordia*) between the Emperor and his soldiers. The shaft is finally decorated with two fringed hemispherical bowls with embossed oak leaves.

v) Eagle of *Legio II Adiutrix*; reconstruction based on the funerary stele of aquilifer Titus Flavius Surillio (see commentary plate 6)

vi) Centurial *signum*. This is a reconstruction of a *signum* depicted on a sarcophagus of a *signifer* and his wife found at Aquincum and now in the collection of the Aquincum Museum, Budapest. The standard bearer is shown in dress uniform and cloak, the standard itself is the height of a man, though in reality it was probably larger. It is crowned by an open hand signifying the military oath and the soldiers' faith. Underneath is a small fringed flag akin to that of a *vexillum*. Since the stone shows strong signs of corrosion, it is impossible to decide whether the stone mason depicted a pair of streamers or whether the fabric billows at the sides. Below the flag is a set of five *patera*-shaped *phalerae*, a *lunula*, and a rather unusual decoration in the shape of a head. It has been identified as that of a goat or a lion, but close scrutiny reveals that the open mouth sports a pair of tusks or an outstretched tongue. There appear to be horns above the eyes; these features would point to a *Gorgoneion* to ward off harm from the unit and its standard. Depictions such as this may be found on Greek shield blazons.

vii) Centurial *signum*. Reconstruction based on the late Severan funerary stele of *signifer* Aurelius Alexandrus serving with *Legio II Traiana Fortis*, excavated in the military suburbs of Nicopolis outside Alexandria. The standard is of comparatively simple design, topped by an open right hand (the stele shows a second, virtually identical *signum* with a left hand also) and decorated with seven *patera* disks. These are not all shown in exactly the same size, but this is probably due to restricted space.

viii) Standard of the Imperial horse guard. This standard appears on a funerary altar discovered in the vicinity of the graveyard of the *Equites Singulares Augusti* in the Via Labicana at Rome. It has been dated to between c. 160 and 180 AD and identified as belonging to the horse guard (TÖPFER (2011), p. 37; SPEIDEL (*Kaiserreiter*, 1994), p. 118 f.). The standard, which is unusual for a cavalry *signum* in that its shaft is adorned with numerous decorations, is crowned by a spearpoint and a lunula to ward off harm. This is supplemented by a *corona muralis*, three *patera*-shaped *phalerae*, a *corona civica*, and two tufts.

LEG IIII FL F MAX
COH III PR
i
ii
iii
iv
v
vi
vii
viii

ard [198]. In late antiquity, high-ranking Roman commanders had personal *dracones* to mark their position in battle and in the line of march.

Apart from the *signa* discussed above, both legions and auxiliaries carried images of the Emperor (*imagines*) and of his family, which signified both the personal presence of the commander-in-chief with his troops and the allegiance of the soldiers. Thus the Emperor watched over and exhorted them to fight valiantly, and witnessed their military glory. If a unit mutinied, the standard bearers' first action would be to tear the Emperor's image from the standards. The *imagines* commonly consisted of a bust sheltered by a shell-shaped *aedicula*, supplemented in the case of the *cohortes praetoriae* by the above-mentioned *phalerae*.

Other standards included those depicting the legion's individual badge, e. g. a ram for *legio I Minervia*, a bull for *III Parthica*, a stork for *III Italica*, a centaur for *I Parthica*, a capricorn for *II Augusta*, or the famous charging boar of *legio XX Valeria Victrix*. Images of certain warlike deities were carried by the troops, e. g. of Hercules or Mars. Statuettes of the goddess Victory were carried into the late Roman era, as may be seen on the Arch of Constantine in Rome.

Like the legions, the auxiliaries carried *signa* and *vexilla*. The main standards of the infantry cohorts were the *vexillum* and the *imago*, while every century carried a *signum*. As in the infantry, the regimental standard of the cavalry regiments was the *vexillum*. JUNKELMANN suggests that the élite milliary cavalry regiments carried particularly ornate *vexilla* [199]. The individual squadrons carried *signa* whose design does not seem to have been universal, as numerous depictions on gravestones of cavalry standard bearers indicate. DOMASZEWSKI assumes that the cavalry squadron of the part-mounted cohorts only carried the *vexillum* [200], but it appears sensible to suppose that the individual squadrons also carried *signa* to mark their position and encourage *esprit de corps*.

As regards instruments, Roman military music of the 3rd century AD does not appear to have differed significantly from that of the early Principate. Music, an indispensable feature of modern military display, was not part of Roman military tradition, neither was the military step. Although the Romans did employ musical instruments to enhance the solemnity of religious rites, the army relied on acoustic signals merely to transmit orders in the chaos of battle and to communicate orders in camp and on parade. The Ludovisi sarcophagus features a trumpeter (*tubicen*) and a horn blower (*cornicen*) dressed in a (heavily stylised) animal pelt. His circular instrument's crossbar rests on his shoulder as he gives a blast to signal the charge. The previously mentioned grave stele of Aurelius Bitus from the 3rd century shows that the *cornu* had not changed in its appearance, the only peculiarity being two *phalerae* on the instrument's crossbar. The mouthpiece could be removed, since Bitus holds it in his hand. Some examples have been excavated at Straubing. The gravestone of trumpeter Aurelius Surus shows the deceased holding the two separate parts of his instrument (*tuba*). The *tuba* indeed seems to have been such an unwieldy affair that an example found at Zsámbék (H) has two rings in order to attach a cord or strap to pull it closer to the player's mouth, and perhaps to carry it slung across the back (such a strap is clearly visible in sc. VIII of Trajan's Column, and in the Piazza Armerina mosaics in Sicily).

Oddly enough, his gravestone refers to Surus as a *bucinator*. This instrument, frequently mentioned in the sources, has remained something of a mystery [201]. Possibly a trombone-like instrument (the word *bucina* resembles the German word for trombone, *Posaune*) on a gravestone from Remagen depicts a *bucina*. A curved bronze instrument found at the Saalburg (now in the LVR-Museum in Bonn) has been identified as a *lituus* [202] and may have been an instrument employed by the cohort's mounted troops.

198 KÜNZL associates the introduction of the *draco* with the worship of snakes as benevolent earth spirits. The snake is also depicted on military armour and domestic *lararia* altars. It assumes significant importance in the context of the legendary begetting of Alexander the Great. KÜNZL claims that the *draco* attained widespread popularity in the Roman army under Caracalla, who was an ardent admirer of the Macedonian (KÜNZL (2008), p. 32).

199 JUNKELMANN, *Reiter Roms* (2) (1991), p. 136 f.

200 Quoted in D'AMATO (2018), p. 41.

201 FISCHER (2012), p. 236.

202 FEUGERE, Michel, *Weapons of the Romans*, Stroud 2002, p. 57.

REWARDS AND PUNISHMENTS

The Roman army's appreciation of individual valour is well-attested. Many a soldier was careful to have himself depicted on his gravestone in the full splendour of his decorations (*dona militaria*). Grave stelae often show metal or glass medals (*phalerae*) in the form of simple *paterae*, while other decorations, as shown by the famous gravestone of senior centurion Marcus Caelius from Xanten, or the Lauersfort hoard, were magnificent affairs of sculpted and inlaid metalwork. *Phalerae* were commonly attached to a leather or fabric harness worn strapped to the torso on parade (and, given Roman love of display, possibly also in battle). These decorations were supplemented by bracelets (*armillae*) and Celtic-style torcs (*torques*) commonly worn attached to ribbons which were passed around the neck. It is fairly sure that richly decorated and precious weapons and armour were awarded in recognition of personal bravery. The range of honorary wreaths and crowns includes the *corona civica* for saving the life of a Roman citizen, the *corona vallaris* or *corona muralis* for the first man inside an enemy fortress (provided he survived his hour of triumph). The *donativa* principle proves that bonus payments and financial gratifications also numbered among the rewards at the army's disposal. In fact, these payments tended to be taken for granted in the progress of time (which tended to somewhat modify their exclusiveness). It remains a cynical footnote to observe that the corruption rampant in the army made the regular granting of *donativa* by the Emperors necessary to enable the soldiers to bribe their superior officers to escape extra duties and punishments.

Among the decorations restricted to high-ranking centurions and staff officers were awards like miniature *vexilla* and lances (*hastae purae*) made of silver or gold, but

Plate XLI

Two officers' staffs

Since early Republican times, the notorious *vitis* was both a badge of rank and instrument for the enforcement of discipline. While it could simply be a gnarled rod cut from a vine, centurions also often carried straight slender rods topped by knobs of hemispherical or disc shape, some tapering towards the top like the capital of a column. The illustrated staffs are modelled on depictions on grave stelae from the 2nd and 3rd centuries AD. Several centurions' gravestones show officers carrying these staffs, among them three examples from Aquileia which can be dated to the third and early fourth centuries AD. Grave stelae of centurions from Este, Italy (1st century BC) and Graz, Austria (2nd century AD) suggest that such canes were around much earlier however. An officer identified as a centurion on the famous Great Hunt mosaic at the Villa Casale at Piazza Armerina in Sicily (4th century AD) raises a rod with a hemispherical knob to chastise a subordinate while leaning on a long stick topped by a t-shaped crossbar (*virga*). Such separate signs of rank for centurions do not yet seem to have existed in Maximinus' army.

also the *corona navalis* (or *classica*) for naval victories, or the *corona obsidionalis* for the successful relief of a besieged fortress or city.

The adornment of the standards shows that decorations could also be awarded collectively to entire units. TÖPFER and JUNKELMANN however believe that the decorations on the shafts of the standards may very well have been the individual decorations of the units' respective commanding officers. This is not altogether convincing however, since in such a case the standard would have had to be redecorated every time there occurred a change in command. Collective rewards on the other hand enhance a unit's morale and *esprit de corps*, a notion which was surely not lost on a nation so deeply immersed in military thinking as the Romans. We hear of auxiliary units awarded titles such as *bis torquata* ("twice decorated with torcs"), *armillata* ("decorated with bracelets"), or *coram laudata* ("publicly acclaimed", something akin to "mentioned in dispatches"). GOLDSWORTHY also believes such titles to have been awarded to individual soldiers[203], but in this case every Roman unit would have sported several of these titles, which is not always the case, unless the Roman army had been more thrifty with its decorations of individual soldiers than would be considered appropriate. The honorary title *civium Romanorum* attests the collective granting of Roman citizenship to an auxiliary unit before the soldiers finished their regular service (whether collectively or individually is again a matter of debate). These units maintained the title even after all the original recipients had retired. The *Constitutio Antoniniana* made this title obsolete, even though it continued to be carried.

The variety of rewards was counterbalanced by a refined system of punishments. The fact that in the Roman army *disciplina* was worshipped as a deity shows the importance attached to order, conduct and discipline in the ranks. The brutality of the centurions, who were wont to exercise corporal punishment on their soldiers with the help of their vine canes (*vitis*), is such common knowledge that it is hardly worth mentioning in the context. The punishments administered for desertion, cowardice, mutiny, but also for neglection of sentry duty (due to the potentially extremely far-reaching consequences) could be savage. Decimation, a fate described in grisly detail by Christian chroniclers in the context of the martyrdom of the legendary Theban Legion, which involved the execution of every one man in ten, was probably no longer applied in the 3rd century AD[204]. Even individual capital punishment seems to have been the exception rather than the rule. As we have seen, it was left to a Septimius Severus to keep his soldiers in awe with draconian measures (he threatened the tribune of his horse guard with dreadful consequences if he failed to hunt down the notorious bandit Bulla Felix who was running rings around the army in Italy) and to dishonourably discharge entire units. In the knowledge that their soldiers' benevolence was a life insurance, later Emperors even went out of their way to exercise lenience by paying the troops' debts or letting the soldiers off punishments (as did Maximinus on his accession). These developments notwithstanding, there certainly existed a large catalogue of disciplinary measures to bring the disorderly to heel, e. g. reduction in rank, posting to a less prestigious unit, extra duties, fatigues, pay and forage cuts, cancellation of leave, and punishments designed to affect the soldier's sense of honour. Dishonourable discharge was frequent, since this not only ruined the individual's reputation but also meant painful financial hardship. For lesser offences, soldiers were made to stand outside the *praetorium* clad in their ungirded tunics and holding a measuring stick or a clod of turf, the laughing stock of any comrade who happened to pass by. After a regiment of cataphracts had disgraced itself by giving way at the battle of Argentoratum (Strasbourg) in AD 357, Emperor Julian the Apostate had the unit parade through camp in women's clothing. Zosimus, who recounts this incident, however remarks that this measure was the Emperor's personal whim and not common practice.

The names of units which had been dishonourably disbanded were frequently erased from the records and official monuments (*damnatio memoriae*). If an Emperor was unfortunate enough to suffer this fate, the troops' honorific titles honouring this Emperor's memory (*epitheta*) were likewise removed. Thus after Maximinus' assassination *legiones I Minervia, I and II Adiutrix, IV Flavia Felix, VII Claudia* and *XIV Gemina* lost their honorary epithets *Maximiniana*. This name had also been carried by a large number of auxiliary units. In fact, all units stationed in the province of Lower Pannonia seem to have summarily received the title in recognition of their loyal and valiant service. Many units including the above-mentioned legions were ordered to change their *epitheta* to *Gordiana* after Maximinus' death to demonstrate their new allegiance. [205]

Legio III Augusta, which had suppressed the rebellion of the Gordiani outside Carthage and been awarded the title *Maximiana* in recognition of this feat, suffered a particularly ignoble fate. It was dishonourably discharged under Gordian III and condemned to *damnatio memoriae*. Only in the year 253 AD was it re-raised as *legio III Augusta Valeriana Galliena*.[206]

203 GOLDSWORTHY (2003), p. 97.

204 Already in the 1st century, Tacitus notes that the *decimatio* had become more or less obsolete (Annales III, 21, quoted in JUNKELMANN (2015), p. 179).

205 HUND, Ragnar, „Maximiana – zu einem ehrenden Beinamen militärischer Formationen im frühen 3. Jh. n. Chr.", in PÖPPELMANN, Heike/DEPPMEYER, Korana/STEINMETZ, Wolf-Dieter (eds.): *Roms vergessener Feldzug. Die Schlacht am Harzhorn*. Darmstadt 2013, p. 208-216. The article contains an extensive and accessible approach to the granting of honorific titles in the Roman army of the 3rd century AD.

206 POLLARD/BERRY, p. 117.

ARTILLERY AND BAGGAGE TRAIN

Entire areas of the Harzhorn battlefield were virtually riddled with catapult bolts. When the German ambush commenced, the Romans must have reacted with breathtaking speed, bringing their catapults into action in very short time. It may be fairly safely assumed that Maximinus' army only had only taken the smaller, bolt-shooting *scorpiones* on campaign to engage human targets, since sieges were not to be expected. Since speed and flexibility on the march were a top priority, the baggage train will have been reduced to a minimum, which would have meant that the heavy stone-throwers, the *onagri* ('wild asses' because of their 'kick' when fired) and *ballistae* capable of hurling stones of up to 26 kilograms[207], remained in the fortresses on the Rhine. Many of the *scorpiones* (probably thus named because of the 'flick' of the firing mechanism and the lethal 'sting' of the bolt) were mounted on carts to ensure mobility (hence *carroballistae*, of which some are depicted on Trajan's Column).

Heavy torsion stone-throwers were mostly, but not exclusively, employed in siege warfare. In his account of the Jewish War, which developed into a series of sieges, Josephus gives nauseating evidence of the efficiency of these machines. In battle catapults were placed behind the battle line, from where they bombarded the enemy (Arrian positioned his artillery on the flanks). Vegetius gives the number of bolt-throwing catapults per legion as 55, thus each *centuria* would have been assigned one. Also according to Vegetius, every cohort was in charge of one heavy *onager*. Earlier works on the topic claim that the Romans were reluctant to entrust their auxiliary regiments with artillery for fear of finding themselves at the receiving end in the case of rebellion. Two inscriptions from the fortress of High Rochester north of Hadrian's Wall however (one of them from the time of Alexander Severus) refer to a *ballistarium*, which clearly denotes some kind of facility to shelter artillery, and the auxiliaries of Dura's gallant *cohors XX Palmyrenorum* manned catapults on the fortress's turrets and walls. Thus we may conclude that in the 3rd century AD the auxiliaries had at least limited access to the army's catapults.[208]

While the *onagri*, which came in various sizes, were one-armed stone-throwers (they can be attested as forming part of the Roman arsenal only from AD 359 onwards, Ammianus Marcellinus mentioning them in his account of the siege of Amida[209], but they were probably around much earlier), the *ballistae* were two-armed affairs resembling oversized crossbows. The Romans adopted the latter from the Greeks and Macedonians. Calibre is determined by the size of the washers used to twist two synchronised bundles of sinew or horsehair in such a manner as to make them develop the necessary torsion power to hurl a missile over a certain distance. According to BAATZ, the one-armed *onagri* began to supersede the two-armed stone-throwing *ballistae* as the Roman army's standard siege artillery from the 3rd century AD onwards[210], possibly because they were less sophisticated and as such easier to construct, operate and maintain. Maximum range of the heavy stone-throwers is believed to have been ca. 400 metres if we may trust Josephus, but Philon claims average effective range was commonly only around 160[211].

For reasons of space, it is possible only to provide a brief summary of how *ballistae* worked. The weapon was spanned by first engaging a claw into the weapon's bowstring. Two hand-operated winches then pulled back the string together with the slider which passed freely to and fro along the catapult's pipe, this part being comparable to a modern artillery piece's barrel. The operating of the winches pulled back the two limbs of the catapult's 'bow' and thus increased the torsion power of the twin sinew springs. The weapon was then loaded, aimed, and fired. When the claw was released, the springs caused the twin limbs to swing forwards, hurling the missile towards its target. At Dura Europos, catapult bolts have been excavated, whose slighlty conical bolts measured up to 45 cm. The pyramid-shaped points, capable of piercing armour, measured ca. 4, 6 cm.

Right into the high Imperial era, the Romans had incorporated the washers and sinew bundles (sometimes protected by bronze cylinders) into the catapult's massive wooden frame, which stood at an angle of ninety degrees towards the pipe. These frames were often decorated with bronze shields. Around the beginning of the 2nd century AD, a new type of catapult appeared, which possessed a simple iron frame.

Some examples from a slightly later date point to the introduction of a new technology. Several examples of metal frame parts have been found, among them pieces from Lyon (F), Hatra (IQ), and Orsova (RO). All of these examples are remarkably broad, the Orsova frame measuring 1, 48 metres, the Hatra find even measuring 2, 40 metres. This fact seems to suggest that these catapults' limbs no longer swung outside but inside the frame.

207 CAMPBELL, Duncan, *Greek and Roman Artillery 399 BC-AD 363*, Oxford 2003, p. 37.

208 MOOSBAUER, Günther, „Torsionsgeschütze. Antike Wunderwaffen", in PÖPPELMANN, Heike/DEPPMEYER, Korana/STEINMETZ, Wolf-Dieter (eds.), *Roms vergessener Feldzug. Die Schlacht am Harzhorn*, Darmstadt 2013, p. 242-248, p. 160.

209 23.4. 4-7

210 BAATZ, Dietwulf, „Catapults", in LE BOHEC (2015), p. 154-166, p. 160.

211 Duncan CAMPBELL, *Greek and Roman Artillery*, Oxford 2003, p. 33.

LEG I ADIV P F MAVRM
LEG I
ADIV
P F MAX

Tafel XLII

Legionaries of *Legio I Adiutrix* with *scorpio* catapult

Two legionaries of *legio I Adiutrix Pia Fidelis* campaigning with Emperor Maximinus on the Danube have cast aside their spears and shields and are operating a light catapult. Catapults of this size were called *scorpiones*, but the names *ballistae* or *manuballistae* had also become common by this time. These were highly effective anti-personnel weapons and could be easily disassembled and transported by mule when on campaign. They were employed in siege towers and fortresses, but could also be mounted on carts and used at a minute's notice (*carroballistae*). Bolt-throwers of this type can be seen on Trajan's Column, and on the Column of Marcus Aurelius. Effective range was ca. 100 to 150 metres when aimed horizontally, but was considerably higher (between 300 and 400 metres) if the weapon was fired parabolically.

From the late 1st century AD onwards, the Romans began to use catapults with iron frames. These can clearly be seen in various scenes on Trajan's Column. Metal frames facilitated aiming due to improved vision and prevented accidents caused by the bolt hitting the back of the shield if the springs were unevenly wound.

The so-called Orsova type, named after the Romanian town where specimens of iron frame parts (*kamaria* and *kambestria*) were found, presumably possessed arms swinging inwards instead of outwards, since the Orsova frame measured 1, 25 metres across (CAMPBELL, 2003)). However, bolt-throwers of older construction with outwards-swinging arms and metal or wooden frames (the latter often decorated with bronze shields) do not seem to have fallen out of use (MOOSBAUER in PÖPPELMANN/DEPPMEYER/STEINMETZ (2012), p. 242-248).

As said, catapults of *scorpio* type were of particularly light construction, which allowed them to be disassembled and loaded onto mules for transport. If action was imminent, they could be rapidly assembled and brought to bear against the enemy; this is what occurred at the Harzhorn. It remains doubtful if the Romans would have been able to employ *carroballistae* in the hilly and wooded terrain of the Harzhorn. The soldiers will have jogged up the slopes carrying the scorpions and mounted them to drive off the German tribesmen harrying their beleaguered comrades. The necessary ammunition was probably carried in baskets.

Legio I Adiutrix was not part of the Roman forces engaged at the Harzhorn but would have been just as effective in the use of their bolt-throwers as their fellow soldiers in Germany. Every *centuria* possessed one *scorpio* and a crew of specially trained artillerymen (*ballistarii*) whose duty it was to maintain the piece and man it in battle. According to Vegetius, each *scorpio* had a crew from one specific *contubernium*, but it could be operated effectively by two. Presumably the frames were painted to protect the wood from the elements. *Legio I Adiutrix* was originally recruited from marines and its soldiers have variously been reconstructed wearing blue tunics. Thus we choose to depict the catapult painted a faded blue. Since the pieces would have required some form of identification, it has been decorated with the legion's mascot, the capricorn, and the name of the *centuria*'s commanding officer (note the centurion's mark <).

The legionaries' discarded shields display the legion's two devices, the capricorn and the Pegasus. Moreover, the *ballistarii* are identified by the legion's title *Legio I Adiutrix Pia Fidelis Maximiniana*, "The Emperor Maximinus's Own First Supporting Legion, Pious and Faithful"). The two legionaries wear bronze-decorated iron helmets of Niederbieber type. Contrary to the depiction here, the bar running down the front of this specific helmet and the centre of the peak were attached to the skull with one and the same rivet.

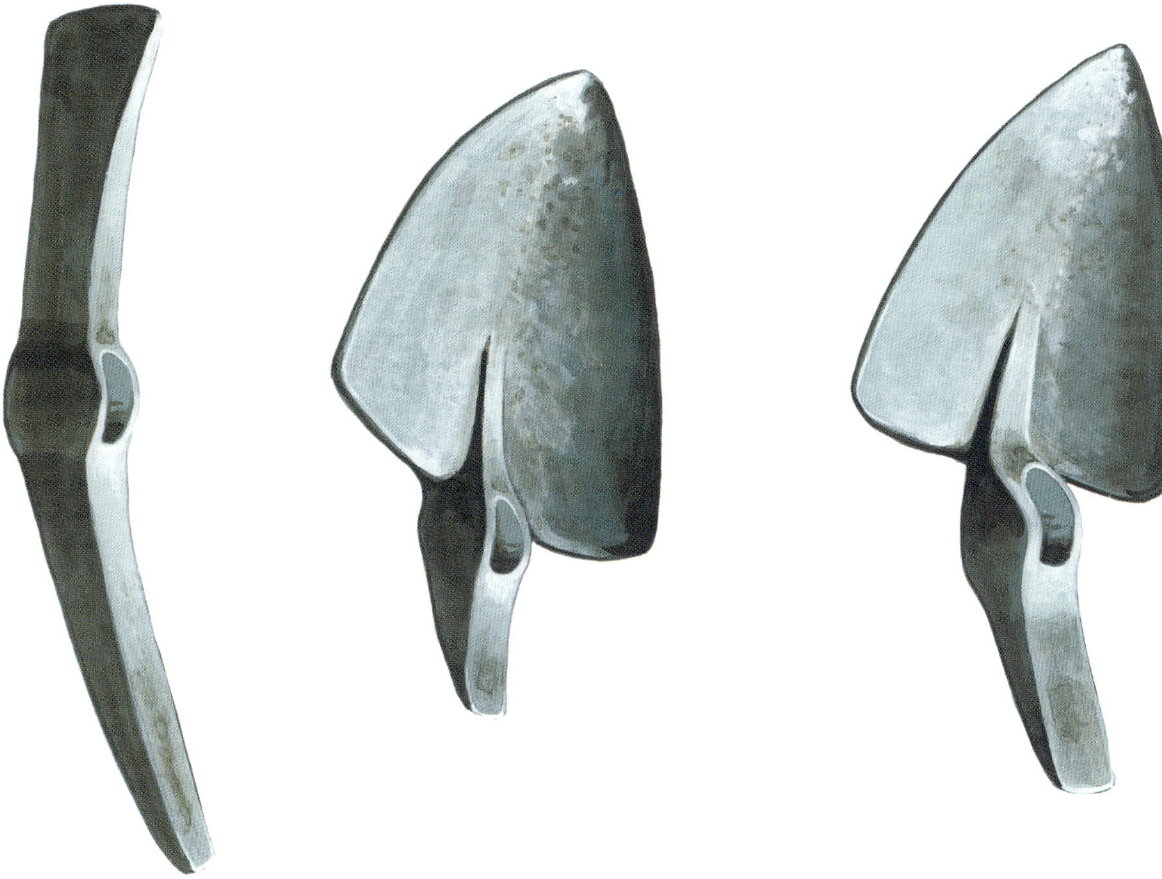

Tafel XLIII

Roman entrenching tools from the Harzhorn battlefield

Together with baskets, sickles and axes, tools like these formed part of the soldiers' marching equipment. They were necessary to swiftly build fieldworks and marching camps. The pioneer's axe (*dolabra*, left) also made an excellent improvised weapon when required. The *dolabra* found in the Kahlberg area of the battlefield, which almost certainly fulfilled this purpose handsomely, bears the (slightly muddled) inscription *LEG IIII SA FA IV V IIII* (i. e. *Legio IIII Severiana Alexandriana Flavia* [*Felix*]); cf. M. GESCHWINDE, „Die *dolabra* vom Kahlberg", in Deppmayer, K./Pöppelmann, H./Steinmetz, W.-D. (eds.) 2013, p. 310.

Frames of similar type excavated at Gomea (RO) suggest that there also existed *manuballistae* ('hand catapults', i. e. crossbows operated by one man) of this type.[212]

Even if the heavy siege artillery was left behind, the army's baggage train must have been enormous. The Romans had good reason to call an army's baggage train *impedimenta*, 'obstacles' bogging the soldiers down. Surrounded by swarms of light infantry and cavalry whose job it was to screen the army's march from enemy reconnaissance and attack, the huge column of a Roman army on the march wound its way through the countryside. In his account of the Jewish War, Flavius Josephus has provided a detailed if description of Roman troops marching in enemy territory (III, 6). The afore-mentioned advance guard was followed by engineers whose duty it was to clear the way and at the end of the day's march (which JUNKELMANN gives as 20-25 km per day in reasonably passable terrain[213]) to begin with the construction of a marching camp for the night. The engineers were followed by the general and his staff and personal baggage secured by bodyguards. After them marched the legionary cavalry guarding the disdmantled siege engines. Then came the legions, each headed by its tribunes, standard bearers and musicians. Terrain permitting, the legionaries marched six or eight abreast, which made it possible for them to turn about into battle order in case of an attack from either side. Every legion was followed by its baggage train, which was taken care of by the baggage attendants, the *contubernia* slaves, and the officers' servants (*calones*). Cursing and coughing dust, auxiliary infantry and cavalry secured the rear. If an enemy attack appeared imminent, the army could march in the *agmen quadratum*, a formation which thanks to the protection of the baggage train by troops prepared for immediate action marching on the flanks, in the van and rear enabled the army to immediately engage the enemy. This was a strategy adopted by Maximinus' army while marching through the Harzhorn defile. The impending crisis of a German breakthrough in the area of the baggage train was resolved by the drawing up of strong legionary units coming from the rear of the column, and the soldiers who had been forced to temporarily abandon the baggage were able to rally when they encountered friendly troops approaching from the front of the column.

Apart from their armour and weapons, the *muli mariani* were obliged to carry rations, casserole, saucepan, flask, cloak, personal items, rope, chain, water bag, and smaller pieces of equipment like knife, saw, and sickle. If we are to believe the *Historia Augusta*'s description of Alexander Severus' Persian campaign, each soldier carried a full 17 days' rations. A *contubernium*'s more unwieldy equipment was transported by two mules, which were loaded with baskets and entrenching tools, the eight-man leather tent, the stone handmill designed to grind the tent section's corn ration, palisade stakes, extra rations and cooking utensils. The centurions were entitled to an individual mule (they had, after all, their own tents), and were mounted on the march. The imposing tents and the baggage of the staff officers were transported in wagons, which were, like the officers themselves, heavily guarded by élite troops. Wagons were also used to transport the field forge, field dispensary and hospital (including the wounded and footsore cases), artillery, heavy tools, equipment and clothing, surveying instruments, rations both for man and beast, and, most importantly, ammunition in the form of arrows, javelins, catapult bolts and other spare weapons. The Arch of Severus shows that one- and two-axled wagons were used. Christina ERKELENZ gives the presumed number of mules required to carry the baggage of a 6,000-strong legion as 1,400[214]. These would have been supplemented by spare horses for officers and mounted troops and additional mules. To the baggage of a Roman army returning from a successful season of campaigning we must further add prisoners, captured livestock and other spoils of war. Herodian places emphasis on the huge amount of booty and prisoners which formed part of Maximinus' baggage train (VII, 2, 9). Archaeological finds at the Harzhorn battlefield show that the Romans employed wagons, among them parts of yokes, guiding rings for bridles, axle rings, and finally the famous hippo sandal which originally caused the archaeological bombshell in 2008 (it had been excavated illegally by two amateur archaologists in 2000). These iron horseshoes were attached with leather thongs to the unshod hooves of Roman horses and mules to provide footing on unstable ground. Christina ERKELENZ observes that due to the fact that archaeological evidence shows that Maximinus' troops used wagons, the Roman staff officers must have been informed of passable routes when planning the campaign[215].

As regards the soldiers' staple rations on campaign, these were much more paltry than at base. Finds and archaeological sites such as refuse and latrine pits in legionary and auxiliary forts provide extensive evidence for the Roman soldiers' peacetime rations. To keep the *contubernia* well-fed, various sorts of meat, fruit and vegetables as well as cheese, onions, garlic, olives and olive oil were supplemented by wheat, which was baked in ovens often incorporated into the fortress walls to reduce the risk of fire. To these were added fish, mussels, bacon, the universally popular *garum* (a sauce, also known as

212 S. also MOOSBAUER, Günther „Torsionsgeschütze. Antike Wunderwaffen", in Pöppelmann, Heike/Deppmeyer, Korana/Steinmetz, Wolf-Dieter (eds.), *Roms vergessener Feldzug. Die Schlacht am Harzhorn*, Darmstadt 2013, p. 242-248.

213 JUNKELMANN (2015), p. 336.

214 ERKELENZ, Christina, „Die Logistik und die medizinische Versorgung", in PÖPPELMANN; Heike/DEPPMAYER, Korana/ STEINMETZ, Wolf-Dieter (eds.), *Roms vergessener Feldzug. Die Schlacht am Harzhorn*, Darmstadt 2013, p. 249-255, p. 251.

215 Ibid., p. 251.

liquamen, made of fermented fish entrails which in its popularity resembled modern ketchup), and venison, which the soldiers hunted themselves in their free time. On campaign the soldiers received iron rations of bacon and cheese. The omnipresent grain ration was ground by means of a stone handmill and baked to provide hardtack or *puls*, a kind of gruel. Captured food items were used to enhance the soldiers' diet. During the German campaign, Maximinus passed all captured livestock to the soldiers, who will have had no inhibitions to make immediate good use of it. To quench their thirst, the soldiers were forced to rely on the notorious *posca*, a sour-tasting vinegar-water mix with disinfectant qualities, which nevertheless had the advantage of serving as an effective and surprisingly refreshing drink when throats became parched[216].

216 JUNKELMANN (2015), p. 176.

Plate XLIV

Ballista of *Legio I Adiutrix Pia Fidelis Maximiniana*

Under the watchful eyes of an *optio*, two legionaries make ready to load a *ballista* stone-thrower.

The city of Hatra in modern Iraq was sacked by the Persians in 241 AD. In the rubble archaeologists made a remarkable find that pointed to an extraordinary weapon (the following technical information closely follows BAATZ (1994) and CAMPBELL (2003)): finds comprised three washers and bronze plating once covering a catapult's torsion frame ca. 1, 5 metres wide (we have depicted it engraved with the legion's badges, name and titles, as well as the number of the cohort to which it was assigned). Apart from the extraordinary width of the frame, the fact that the insides had semicircular holes for the arms gave rise the conclusion that in contrast to conventional stone-throwers the Hatra catapult's arms swung inwards and would have been arrested only when at right angles to the frame and parallel with the pipe and slider. Thus the arms' swinging radius would have been almost double in proportion compared to conventional *ballistae*, and developed more power accordingly.

This medium *ballista* is being operated by two legionary *ballistarii* wearing Newstead *loricae segmentatae*. The *optio* wears a mail coat with chestplates. His Niederbieber helmet is adorned with a horsehair crest (*crista*) and two feathers at the side (*geminae pennae*, attributed to Mars himself) denoting his rank. He is proud of his splendid dagger sheath of Künzing type (cf. FISCHER (2012), p. 86), now on display at the museum in Mougins (F). The decorative bronze plating belonged to a scabbard of earlier construction and was later incorporated.

As *duplicarii*, the *optiones* received double pay. A ring belonging to an *optio* of *Legio I Minervia Pia Fidelis* found at Bonn suggests that the *optiones*, who were of *principalis* rank, wore rings as a badge of rank, possibly to seal important documents in the context of the *centuria*'s administration. The centurion's second-in-command also carried the *hastile*, a ball-tipped staff which not unlike the half-pikes of 18th-century NCOs served to dress ranks and shove potentially reluctant or wavering *bellatores* back into line! This is shown lying under the shields in the background. *Optio* Caecilius Avitus of *Legio XX Valeria Victrix* is shown on his grave stele carrying a *hastile* in his right hand while holding a set of writing tablets in his left (Grosvenor Museum, Chester). Clearly the *optiones*, who must have been fairly educated men, were entrusted with administrative duties in the *centuria*'s incessant daily round.

LEG I ADIV P F COH III

S. Borini

Plate XLV

Manuballistarius of Legio I Adiutrix

In 1999, a 1st century AD Roman catapult frame was excavated from a gravel pit outside Xanten, formerly the base of *legio XXX Ulpia Victrix*. Due to its small size, it has been reconstructed in various recent works and re-enactment groups as a hand-held *ballista*, and such a reconstruction is on display at the *Römermuseum* in Xanten. FISCHER (2012) casts doubt on this specific interpretation though himself admitting that some hand-held catapults lacking a tripod must have existed. The remarkably good condition of the Xanten frame provided scholars with vital details regarding the construction of these weapons (MOOSBAUER in PÖPPELMANN/DEPPMEYER/STEINMETZ (2012); cf. plate XX)

Comparatively light hand-held catapults were already in use by the Greeks in the 4th century BC. The famous "belly catapult", the *gastraphetes* (γαστραφέτης) described by Heron of Alexandria, relied on the body weight of its operator, who in order to span it was required to push down on the weapon to force back the bowstring and slider.

The Romans were familiar with the crossbow (which was probably known as *arcuballista*). Two Gallo-Roman reliefs found at Sarignac and Saint Marcel (F) prove that it was used as a hunting weapon. These weapons were however clearly not torsion catapults since they did not rely on a pair of twisted bundles of sinew or hair for power but in fact resemble mediaeval crossbows in their construction.

In the second book of his work on the Roman military, Vegetius mentions that soldiers armed with *manuballistae* (the exact definition of this word is as yet unclear) and *arcuballistae* were positioned behind the legion's second battle line. The *Notitia Dignitatum* lists several regiments of *ballistarii* but whether these were missile troops or heavy artillery units is impossible to tell.

The legionary operates a hand-held torsion catapult. In contrast to the classic crossbow, which derives its power from the bow limbs alone, it relies on the power of the twisted sinew or hair bundles controlled by pairs of washers on both sides of the slider. Due to this we choose to follow the notion that his weapon is indeed a *manuballista* in the literal sense of the word. The reconstruction is based on the Xanten example. However *manuballistae* at this time could also have metal frames like the example depicted in the previous plate to facilitate aiming and to make the weapon easier to handle. Iron frames belonging to *manuballistae* were found at Gornea (RO).

The soldier is a legionary of the First *Adiutrix* Legion based at Brigetio (Szöny in modern Hungary). He is on campaign with Maximinus on the Danube, and is fighting Sarmatian cataphracts. Even at a considerable distance, the bolts of his *manuballista* are capable of effortlessly penetrating the armour of horses and riders. *Manuballistae* may also have been employed in the Harzhorn fighting. His equipment is based on various contemporary finds. A soldier of a legion formerly raised from marines, he wears the blue tunic of the scouting galleys, but this is admittedly guesswork.

S Borin 19

AFTERWORD

Res ad triarios rediit – a typically Roman euphemism for impending crisis. If the first two battle lines of infantry were beaten, it had been up to the battle-scarred veterans of the third line to save the day for Rome. Although the *triarii* had long passed into history by the time the Emperor Maximinus took the purple, the situation at home and abroad will have caused many a Roman to uneasily remember the old saying.

In the course of the 3rd century AD a profound crisis bore down on the Roman Empire. This crisis was the result of previous blunders in foreign affairs but also of dynamics working beyond the borders and therefore far from Roman control. To this was added domestic and dynastic strife and economic decline, all of which combined to a situation to which the rapidly changing rulers of the mid-3rd century were only able to react inappropriately. Strong rulers like Gallienus, Aurelian and Probus were able to stem the tide until Diocletian introduced a series of far-reaching and radical political, economic and military reforms. The establishment of the Tetrarchy once again put Roman power on solid ground.

This little volume has tried to provide a small amount of insight into organisation and equipment of the Roman army of the late 2nd and first half of the 3rd century AD. In this time of profound political and strategic change the army itself was undergoing a series of changes. These changes, be they in the structure of command or the soldiers' equipment, were the result of various developments to which the army was forced to adapt, but it should not be forgotten that indeed the soldiers themselves exercised considerable influence on the rapidly changing face of the Empire in this crucial phase of its history. Proud, efficient and highly professional fighting men, increasingly appreciated and humoured by Emperors and generals alike, rapidly found themselves rising socially and financially. Conscious of this new position, they did not hesitate to interfere with politics, either in the form of careers enhanced by military achievement, or with actions which presented the Empire and its people with many a political *fait accompli*. Rome's armies made Emperors at the same breakneck speed with which they dispensed with them. The crisis which began to set in was thus caused to a considerable extent by themselves. But it was also these soldiers who followed Emperors into the bloody conflicts, putting their lives at risk either to crush a renegade general ambitious enough to contest the Imperial purple, or against enemies abroad in the deserts of Mesopotamia and the German forests. The soldiers of the Emperor Maximinus Thrax, and those of his predecessors and successors, formed a proud and efficient military link between the height of Empire and Late Antiquity.

Plate XLVI

The approach of a new era: Grave stele of an unknown cavalry officer, mid- to late 3rd century AD.

The fragment of a grave stele of slightly later date is on display at the Museo Archeologico Nazionale at Aquileia (I) and shows the incipient change in certain features of military fashion towards the middle of the 3rd century AD. It depicts an officer of cavalry, possibly even of the *Equites Singulares Augusti*, since the depiction of the deceased is strikingly similar to the guardsmen's stelae found in Rome. The bearded officer is shown unarmoured, holding his horse's reins. He is dressed in a long-sleeved tunic and the *sagum*, breeches, and boots. The *sagum* is fastened with what already appears to be a crossbow fibula with its typical onion-shaped buttons (hence the German word *Zwiebelknopffibel*), a form of clasp which developed out of early 3rd century types and became fashionable in the second half of the 3rd century AD. A presumably scaled-down oval shield rests against his left leg. He wears a conspicuous belt which resembles the broad belts of Germanic origin which began to be fashionable in the Roman military towards the end of the third century AD. It appears to be decorated alternatingly with rectangular and rhomboid metal plates and has no visible buckle. The *spatha* at his left hip is not suspended by a *balteus* but gunslinger fashion from a narrow strap as is the case with 4th-century *baltei*. His staff with its conical grip is of particular interest – is it a form of the *vitis*, or a badge of rank denoting senior officer status just as the staffs of the officers on the early 4th-century mosaics at the Villa del Casale in Piazza Armerina in Sicily? It is actually quite probable that the deceased soldier was a squadron commander (*decurio*) of the *Equites Singulares Augusti*, and that the staff was a rank distinction. A similar staff with conical knob (*virga*; cf. SPEIDEL, *Kaiserreiter*, 1994, p. 290) is depicted on the grave stele of 3rd century AD Imperial Horse Guard decurion Natalinius Natalianus, now at the Museo Gregoriano in the Vatican.

S.Bajinko

GLOSSARY OF IMPORTANT LATIN MILITARY TERMS

aedicula	"little temple"; small shrine to shelter the legionary Eagle or *imago*.
ala	"wing"; auxiliary cavalry regiment
antesignani	light troops operating "ahead of the standards"
aquila	legionary Eagle standard. Most important standard of the legion
aquilifer	Eagle bearer; senior standard bearer
armilla	bracelet awarded for valour
auxilia	auxiliaries originally recruited from non-citizens
ballista	torsion catapult
balteus	baldric
beneficiarius	NCO assigned to special duties (literally a "recipient of benefaction"). *Beneficiarii* were recognisable by their special lances and served on the governor's staff. As military policemen, they manned street police stations.
bracae	breeches with attached footlets
bucinator	military musician; player of the *bucina*
calceus	military boot
caliga	military sandal
calo	cavalryman's or officer's servant; baggage attendant
campidoctor	officer in charge of military training
capsarius	medical orderly named after the bandage box (*capsa*) carried by these troops
cassis	helmet
cataphractarius	armoured cavalryman
carroballista	catapult mounted on a cart
centuria	"a hundred"; during the Empire, unit of eighty infantrymen commanded by a *centurio*.
cingulum militare	military belt
classis	fleet
clibanarius	"oven man"; heavy cavalryman mounted on an armoured horse
clipeus	oval shield
cohors	cohort; tactical sub-unit of the legion consisting of six *centuriae* (= three maniples). The élite first cohort was double strength. Also: auxiliary regiment
cohors equitata	part-mounted auxiliary regiment
cohors praetoria	Praetorian Cohort, named after the general's tent (*praetorium*, headquarters of the *praetor*); lifeguards of republican generals, later of the Emperors
cohors urbana	Urban Cohort; regiment of Rome's paramilitary police force
cohors vigilum	Cohort of the Watch; regiment of Rome's fire service and night watch
commilito	"fellow fighter", comrade
contubernium	tent section numbering eight soldiers
contus	heavy cavalry lance of Iranian origin up to five metres in length
cornicularius	office orderly with administrative duties; senior military clerk
cornu	military horn played by a *cornicen*; also a wing of a deployed force
corona	miltary decoration in the form of a crown or wreath
crista	helmet crest
decanus	commander of ten
decurio	in the army, officer commanding a squadron of horse
diploma	document recording a soldier's honourable discharge
dona militaria	military decorations
donativum	financial gratification
draco	dragon standard carried by a *draconarius*
dromedarius	cavalryman mounted on a dromedary
duplicarius	soldier on double pay
dux	officer in overall command of military forces in a specific province
equites sagittarii	mounted archers
equites singulares	"individually chosen" mounted bodyguards of the Emperors and provincial governors (in this case named *equites singulares legati Augusti pro praetore*). Élite foot guards were referred to as *pedites singulares*.
evocatus	veteran recalled to the standards
fasciae crurales	puttees
feminalia	(*femur* (l)=thigh); knee breeches
focale	scarf
fulcum	shield wall
funditor	slinger
genius legionis	a legion's protective spirit

gladius hispaniensis	"Spanish" short sword carried by the legions during the Republic and early Empire
hasta	spear
hippika gymnasia	cavalry games
imago	standard displaying the bust of the Emperor, carried by an *imaginifer*
impedimenta	"obstacles", baggage train
immunis	soldier excused heavy duty
humeralia	shoulder pieces of mail armour
lancea	lance or light javelin
lanciarius	light infantryman equipped with the *lancea*
legatus	senatorial legionary commander
legio	"levy"; infantry unit consisting entirely of Roman citizens, usually between 3, 000 and 6, 000 strong. The word has survived in place names such as León (E) and Caerleon (GB).
librarius	military clerk belonging to the *immunes*
lituus	military instrument; possibly a curved signal instrument for mounted use; played by a *liticen*
lorica hamata	coat of mail
lorica musculata	muscle cuirass imitating the idealized shape of a human torso, usually made of bronze.
lorica segmentata	plate armour
lorica squamata	scale armour
lunula	"little moon"; crescent-shaped decoration
manica	laminated armour protecting the soldier's arm and hand
manipulus	tactical unit composed of two *centuriae*
manuballista	"hand ballista", crossbow
mater castrorum	"Mother of the Camp"; honorary title for the Empress
Mauri	North African light horse
miles gregarius	private soldier
muli mariani	"Marius's Mules"; legionary on the march (*mulus marianus*), so called because the consul Gaius Marius had ordered the soldiers to carry large parts of their personal equipment themselves in order to reduce the size of the baggage train.
munifex	soldier lacking special qualifications, usually on heavy duties
navarchus	ship's captain
ocreae	greaves
onager	"wild ass"; one-armed catapult which "kicked" when fired
optio	centurion's deputy-in-command, originally elected (*optare* (l) = to choose)
origo castris	"from the camp"; rather vague statement of origin during recruitment
paenula	military cloak of the early Principate
panis militaris	military bread
patera	sacrificial dish
pelta	originally a crescent-shaped buckler employed by Thracian light troops; later a crescent-shaped pendant
peregrinus	free-born inhabitant of the Empire without Roman citizenship
phalera	medal, ornamental disk
pilum	legionary javelin
pilus prior	centurion leading a cohort's first century. The rank was named in accordance with the Republican structure of command. Originally officer in command of the First Century of the spear-armed veteran *triarii* (also termed *pilani*) who formed the third battle line.The cohort`s centurial hierarchy ran as follows (from bottom to top): *hastatus posterior, hastatus prior, princeps posterior, princeps prior, pilus posterior, pilus prior*. The Tenth Cohort's *hastatus posterior* was thus the legion's lowest-rank centurion, the *primus pilus*, commander of the First Cohort, the most senior.
praefectus	staff officer, often of equestrian rank. The *praefectus castrorum* was responsible for the legion's logistics, and its third-in-command. *Praefecti* also commanded auxiliary regiments, and later replaced the *legati* as legionary commanders
praetorium	commander's quarters; originally tent of the *praetor*
primi ordines	"first rankers"; centurions of the First Cohort

primus pilus	"First Spear"; most senior centurion and commander of the legion's double-strength First Cohort; responsible for the safety of the Eagle
principales	junior officers (*optio*, *signifer*, and others)
principia	headquarters building
protector	member of the army's officer academy; also a bodyguard
pteryges	strips of leather or fabric protecting the soldier's shoulders and groin
pugio	military dagger
sacellum	shrine housing the standards
sacramentum	military oath
sagittarius	archer
sagum	military cloak
sarcina	soldier's personal baggage and equipment carried on a forked or t-shaped staff (*furca*)
scorpio	small catapult employed against human targets
scutum	curved oval or rectangular legionary shield
semispatha	"half-sword" carried in place of the military dagger
sesquiplicarius	soldier who received one and a half times the regular amount of pay
signaculum	metal identity disc worn around the neck
signum	(pl. *signa*); standard carried by a *signifer*
spatha	Celtic long sword originally employed by auxiliary infantry and cavalry; adopted by the legions in the course of the 3rd century AD
stator	military policeman or provost
subarmalis	(or *thoracomachus*); padded jerkin worn underneath a soldier's armour
tesserarius	officer of the watch whose duty it was to receive the watchword on a tablet (*tessera*) at headquarters
tibialia	puttees (*tibia* (l) = shinbone)
tiro	recruit
tribunus	officer of senatorial or equestrian rank; legionary staff officer or commander of a large or élite auxiliary regiment (*ala* or *cohors milliaria*)
tuba	trumpet played by a *tubicen*
tunica manicata	long-sleeved military tunic, also named *tunica dalmatica*
turma	squadron of horse numbering 30 cavalrymen
udones	socks
umbo	shield boss
urbaniciani	soldiers of the Urban Cohorts
vexillum	flag carried by the *vexillarius*; the unit carrying the standard was called *vexillatio*
virga	officer's cane
vitis	centurion's vine cane

BIBLIOGRAPHY

Primary Sources:

Lucius Flavius Arrianus, *Arrian's Array against the Alans* (http://members.tripod.com/~S_van_Dorst/Ancient_Warfare/Rome/Sources/ektaxis.html#translation)

Cassius Dio, *Dio's Roman History*, vol. IX, Books LXXI-LXXX (transl. E. Cary), Loeb Classical Library, Cambridge, Mass./London 1982.

Herodian, *History of the Empire*, Books 5-8 (transl. C. R. Whittaker), Loeb Classical Library, Cambridge, Mass./London 1970.

Flavius Josephus, *Der Jüdische Krieg* (transl. H. Endrös), Munich2 1980.

Ammianus Marcellinus, *The Later Roman Empire (A.D. 354-378)* (transl. Walter Hamilton), London 1986.

Maurice's Strategikon. Handbook of Byzantine Military Strategy (transl. George T. Dennis), Philadelphia 1984.

Scriptores Historiae Augustae, vol. II (transl. David Magie), Loeb Classical Library, Cambridge, Mass./London 1980.

Flavius Vegetius Renatus, *The Military Institutions of the Romans* (transl. John Clark), Harrisburg/Penn. 1944.

Tacitus, *Historien* (transl. Helmuth Vretska), Stuttgart 1986.

Secondary sources:

Anderson, Erich B., *Cataphracts. Knights of the Ancient Eastern Empires*, Barnsley 2016

Archäologisches Landesmuseum Baden-Württemberg (ed.), *Caracalla. Kaiser, Tyrann, Feldherr*, Darmstadt/Mainz 2013.

Baatz, Dietwulf, *Bauten und Katapulte des römischen Heeres*, Stuttgart 1994.

Baatz, Dietwulf: „Catapults", in Le Bohec, Yann (ed.): *The Encyclopedia of the Roman Army*, 3 Bde., Chichester 2015, p. 154-166.

Baatz, Dietwulf, *Der Limes. Archäologische Ausflüge zwischen Rhein und Donau*, Berlin 1974.

Baatz, Dietwulf, "Die Römische Jagdarmbrust", *Archäologisches Korrespondenzblatt* 21(1991), pp. 283-290.

Bätz, Alexander, „Sieg im Sumpf. Eine große Ausstellung in Braunschweig erhellt die Beziehungen zwischen Römern und Germanen und erzählt die Geschichte eines vergessenen Feldzugs", in *Die Zeit* Nr. 39 (19. 9. 2013), p. 22.

Bingham, Sandra, *The Praetorian Guard. A History of Rome's Elite Special Forces*, London/New York 2013.

Bishop, M./Coulston, C., *Roman Military Equipment*, Aylesbury 1989.

Bishop, M. C./Coulston, J. C. N., *Roman Military Equipment from the Punic Wars to the Fall of Rome*, Oxford2 2011.

Bishop, M. C., "Armas y armaduras en la Roma del siglo II d. C.", in *Desperta Ferro (Numero especial XIII): La legión romana (IV): El auge del Imperio*, Madrid 2017/18, p. 30-37.

Bishop, M. C., *The Gladius. The Roman Short Sword*, Oxford 2016.

Bishop, M. C., *The Pilum. The Roman Heavy Javelin*, Oxford 2017.

Börm, Henning, „Die Herrschaft des Kaisers Maximinus Thrax und das Sechskaiserjahr 238. Der Beginn der „Reichskrise?", in *Gymnasium*, vol. 115, 2008, p. 69 ff.

Breeze, David J., *The Roman Army*, London/New York2 2017.

Brzezinski, Richard/Mielczarek, Mariusz/Embleton, Gerry, *The Sarmatians 600 BC-AD 450*, Oxford 2002.

Busch, Alexandra, *Militär in Rom. Militärische und paramilitärische Einheiten im kaiserzeitlichen Stadtbild*, Wiesbaden 2011.

Campbell, Brian/Trittle, Lawrence A. (Hrsg.), *The Oxford Handbook of Warfare in the Classical World*, Oxford 2013.

Campbell, Duncan, *Greek and Roman Artillery 399 BC-AD 363*, Oxford 2003.

Campbell, Duncan, *Siege Warfare in the Roman World 146 BC – AD 378*, Oxford 2005.

Cascarino, Giuseppe, *L'esercito Romano. Armamento e Organizzazione, vol. II: Da Augusto ai Severi*, 2010.

Cascarino, Giuseppe, *L'esercito Romano. Armamento e Organizzazione, vol. III: Dal III Secolo alla Fine dell'Imperio d'Occidente*, Rimini 2009.

Cheesman, G. L., *The Auxilia of the Roman Imperial Army*, Oxford 1914.

Clauss, Manfred, *Lexikon lateinischer militärischer Fachausdrücke*. Schriftenreihe des Limesmuseum Aalen, vol. 52, Stuttgart 1999.

Connolly, Peter, *Greece and Rome at War*, London 1981.

Cowan, Ross, *Imperial Roman Legionary AD 161-284*, Oxford 2003.

Cowan, Ross, *Roman Battle Tactics 109 BC – AD 313*, Oxford 2007.

Cowan, Ross, *Roman Guardsman 62 BC-AD 324*, Oxford 2014.

Cowan, Ross, *Roman Legionary AD 69-161*, Oxford 2013.

Cowan, Ross, *Roman Legionary AD 284-337. The Age of Diocletian and Constantine the Great*, Oxford 2015.

Dabrowa, E. (Hrsg.), *The Roman and Byzantine Army in the East*, Cracow 1994.

D'Amato, Raffaele, *Imperial Roman Naval Forces 31 BC-AD 500*, Oxford 2009.

D'Amato, Raffaele, *Roman Heavy Cavalry (1): Cataphractarii & Clibanarii, 1st Century BC – 5th Century AD*, Oxford 2018.

D'Amato, Raffaele, *Roman Standards and Standard-Bearers (1), 112 BC – AD 192*, Oxford 2018.

D'Amato, Raffaele/Negin, Andrey Evgenevich, *Decorated Roman Armour. From the Age of the Kings to the Death of Justinian the Great*, Barnsley 2017.

M. Dawson (ed.), *Roman Military Equipment: The Accoutrements of War. Proceedings of the Third Roman Military Equipment Research Seminar* (British Archaeological Reports International Series 336), 1987

De la Bédoyère, Guy, *Praetorian. The rise and fall of Rome's imperial bodyguard*, New Haven/London 2017.

Demandt, Alexander, *Marc Aurel. Der Kaiser und seine Zeit*, München 2018.

Deppmayer, Korana, „Maximinus Thrax – vom thrakischen Soldaten zum römischen Kaiser", in Pöppelmann, Heike/Deppmeyer, Korana/Steinmetz, Wolf-Dieter (eds.), *Roms vergessener Feldzug. Die Schlacht am Harzhorn*, Darmstadt 2013, p. 103-109.

Dixon, Karen/Stephenson, Ian, *Roman Cavalry Equipment*, Stroud 2003.

Dixon, Karen/Southern, Patricia, *The Roman Cavalry*, London 1992.

v. Domaszewski, Alfred, *Die Rangordnung des römischen Heeres*, Bonn 1908. Reprint with an introduction, corrections and additions by Brian Dobson. *Beihefte der Bonner Jahrbücher*, vol. 14, Cologne/Vienna3 1981.

Drinkwater, J. F., *The Alamanni and Rome 213-496: Caracalla to Clovis*, Oxford 2007.

Elliott, Paul, *Legions in Crisis. Transformation of the Roman Soldier AD 192-284*, 2014.

Elliott, Simon, "Arms to armour. Adapting to new opponents", in *Ancient Warfare* XII/3, 2018, p. 33-37.

Elton, Hugh: „Military Forces", in: SABIN, Philip/VAN WEES, Hans/WHITBY, Michael (eds.): *The Cambridge History of Greek and Roman Warfare, Vol. II: Rome from the late Republic to the late Empire, Part II: The Late Empire*, p. 270-309.

Elton, Hugh, *Warfare in Roman Europe AD 350-425*, Oxford 1997.

Erdkamp, Paul (Hrsg.), *A Companion to the Roman Army*, Malden/Oxford/Victoria 2007.

Erkelenz, Christina, „Die Logistik eines Feldzuges und die medizinische Versorgung", in Pöppelmann, Heike/Deppmeyer, Korana/Steinmetz, Wolf-Dieter (eds.), *Roms vergessener Feldzug. Die Schlacht am Harzhorn*, Darmstadt 2013, p. 249-255.

Eschbach, Jan: "Patrolling the Desert Frontier. Roman Dromedary Troops", in: *Ancient Warfare* XI/5 (2018), pp. 18-22.

Feugère, Michel, *Weapons of the Romans*, Stroud 2002.

Fischer, Thomas, *Der Römische Limes in Bayern. Geschichte und Schauplätze entlang des UNESCO-Weltkulturerbes*, Regensburg2 2017.

Fischer, Thomas, *Die Armee der Caesaren. Archäologie und Geschichte*, Regensburg 2012.

Fischer, Thomas, „Die Soldaten des Maximinus Thrax. Die Einheiten und ihre Bewaffnung", in Pöppelmann, Heike/Deppmeyer, Korana/Steinmetz, Wolf-Dieter (eds.), *Roms vergessener Feldzug. die Schlacht am Harzhorn*, Darmstadt 2013, p. 198-206.

Fischer, Thomas, „Zur Bewaffnung und Ausrüstung der Kavallerieformationen Roms in der Zeit des Maximinus Thrax", in Pöppelmann, Heike/Deppmeyer, Korana/Steinmetz, Wolf-Dieter (eds.), *Roms vergessener Feldzug. die Schlacht am Harzhorn*, Darmstadt 2013, p. 228-234.

Fontana, Eszter, „Die Tuba aus Zsámbék, in Limesmuseum Aalen (eds.), *Von Augustus bis Attila. Leben am ungarischen Donaulimes*, Stuttgart 2000, p. 41-44.

Fuentes, N., „The Roman Military Tunic", in M. Dawson (Hrg.), *Roman Military Equipment: The Accoutrements of War. Proceedings of the Third Military Research Seminar; British Archaeological Report*, Int. Ser. 336, Oxford 1987, p. 41-75.

Fuhrmann, Jens/Steinmetz, Wolf-Dieter, „Nach seiner Ankunft ließ er das ganze Land verheeren. Germanische Besiedlung entlang des römischen Marschweges", in Pöppelmann, Heike/Deppmeyer, Korana/Steinmetz, Wolf-Dieter (eds.), *Roms vergessener Feldzug. die Schlacht am Harzhorn*, Darmstadt 2013, p. 135 ff.

Geschwinde, Michael: „Die *dolabra* vom Kahlberg", in: Pöppelmann, Heike/Deppmeyer, Korana/Steinmetz, Wolf-Dieter (eds.): *Roms vergessener Feldzug. Die Schlacht am Harzhorn*, Darmstadt 2013, p. 311.

Geschwinde, Michael, „La batalla olvidada. La *expeditio germanica* del emperador Maximino el Tracio y los hallazgos arquelógicos de Harzhorn", in: *Desperta Ferro (Numero Especial XVII): La legión romana (V): La anarquía militar*, Madrid 2018-2019, p. 44-51.

Geschwinde, Michael/Lönne, Petra/Meyer, Michael et al., „Das Harzhorn-Ereignis. Die Archäologie einer römisch-germanischen Konfrontation im 3. Jhd. n. Chr.", in: Pöppelmann, Heike/Deppmeyer, Korana/Steinmetz, Wolf-Dieter (eds.), *Roms vergessener Feldzug. die Schlacht am Harzhorn*, Darmstadt 2013, p. 294 ff.

Geschwinde, Michael/Lönne, Petra/Meyer, Michael: „Eingefrorene Zeit. Das Harzhorn-Ereignis – Archäologie einer römisch-germanischen Konfrontation 235 n. Chr.", in: Wemhoff, Matthias/Rind, Michael M. (eds.): *Bewegte Zeiten. Archäologie in Deutschland* (exhibition catalogue), Berlin 2018, p. 283-293.

Geschwinde, Michael/ Lönne, Petra, „Relikte einer Schlacht. Die Funde vom Harzhorn", in Pöppelmann, Heike/Deppmeyer, Korana/Steinmetz, Wolf-Dieter (eds.), *Roms vergessener Feldzug. die Schlacht am Harzhorn*, Darmstadt 2013, p. 272-284.

Gilliver, Catherine M.: „Battle", in: Sabin, Philip/van Wees, Hans/Whitby, Michael (eds.): *The Cambridge History of Greek and Roman Warfare, Vol. II: Rome from the late Republic to the late Empire, Part II: The Late Empire*, Cambridge 2007, p. 122-157

Goldsworthy, Adrian, *The Complete Roman Army*, London 2003.

Goldsworthy, Adrian, *The Roman Army at War 100 BC-AD 200*, Oxford 1996.

Gräf, Julia, „Hingegen bereiteten ihm die Germanen keine Freude", in: Archäologisches Landesmuseum Baden-Württemberg (ed.): *Caracalla. Kaiser, Tyrann, Feldherr*, Darmstadt/Mainz 2013., p. 71-87.

Gunnison, Anne Turner and Passeri, Irma, *An Investigation of Painted Wood Shields from 3rd Century Dura-Europos*, Yale 2014 (https://www.culturalheritage.org/docs/default-source/annualmeeting/2014am_poster14_an_investigation_of_painted.pdf?sfvrsn=2)

Haynes, Ian: *Blood of the Provinces. The Roman* Auxilia *and the Making of Provincial Society from Augustus to the Severans*, Oxford 2013.

Head, Duncan: "Numidian and Moorish Cavalry: The Cavalry's New Clothes", in: Ancient Warfare XII/3, Rotterdam.

Holder, Paul, "Auxiliary Deployment in the Reign of Hadrian", in: J.J. Wilkes (ed.), *Documenting the Roman army: Essays in honour of M. Roxan*. Institute of Classical Studies; 2003, p. 101-145.

Hose, Martin, „Ausgelöschte Geschichte. Der Feldzug des Maximinus Thrax in das Innere Germaniens 235/236 in der historischen Überlieferung", in: Pöppelmann, Heike/Deppmeyer, Korana/Steinmetz, Wolf-Dieter (eds.), *Roms vergessener Feldzug. die Schlacht am Harzhorn*, Darmstadt 2013, p. 111-115.

Hund, Ragnar, „Maximiniana. Zu einem ehrenden Beinamen militärischer Formationen im frühen 3. Jh. n. Chr.", in: PÖPPELMANN, Heike/DEPPMEYER, Korana/STEINMETZ, Wolf-Dieter (eds.), *Roms vergessener Feldzug. die Schlacht am Harzhorn*, Darmstadt 2013, p. 108-116.

James, Simon, *Excavations at Dura Europos 1928-1937. Final Report VII: Arms and Armour and other Military Equipment*, Oxford 2010.

James, Simon, *Rome and the Sword. How Warriors and Weapons Shaped Roman History*, London 2011.

Junkelmann, Marcus, *Die Legionen des Augustus*, Munich15 2015.

Junkelmann, Marcus, *Panis Militaris. Die Ernährung des römischen Soldaten oder der Grundstoff der Macht*, Mainz 1997.

Junkelmann, Marcus, *Die Reiter Roms*, vols. 1-3, Mainz 1990-92.

Junkelmann, Marcus, *Reiter wie Statuen aus Erz*, Mainz 1996.

Kemkes, Martin/Scheuerbrandt, Jörg/Willburger, Nina, *Am Rande des Imperiums. Der Limes, Grenze Roms zu den Barbaren*, Stuttgart/Ulm 2002.

Kemkes, Martin/Scheuerbrand, Jörg: *Zwischen Patrouille und Parade. Die römische Reiterei am Limes*, Stuttgart 1997.

Keppie, Lawrence, *The Making of the Roman Army. From Republic to Empire*, London 1984.

Koepfer, Christian, „Guarding the Gates to Italy. The Raetian Army in the 3rd Century", in *Ancient Warfare* II/6 (2009), p. 12-17.

Künzl, Ernst, *Der Traum vom Imperium. Der Ludovisisarkophag – Grabmal eines Feldherrn Roms*, Regensburg/Mainz 2010.

Künzl, Ernst, *Unter den goldenen Adlern. Der Waffenschmuck des römischen Imperiums*, Regensburg/Mainz 2008.

Küßner, Mario/Schüler, Tim: „Truppen in Thüringen. Nordöstlichste römische Militäranlage entdeckt", in: *Archäologie in Deutschland* 3/2014, S. 6.

Küßner, Mario/Walter, Diethard: „Ur- und frühgeschichtliche Besiedlung und archäologische Denkmalpflege im Kyffhäuserkreis", in: *Denkmaltopographie Bundesrepublik Deutschland. Kulturdenkmale in Thüringen, vol. 5. 1.: Kyffhäuserkreis, Überblicksdarstellungen,* Altenburg 2014, S. 32-69.

Kulikowski, Michael, *Imperial Triumph. The Roman World from Hadrian to Constantine AD 138-363*, London 2016.

Le Bohec, Yann, *Die Römische Armee. Von Augustus zu Konstantin dem Großen*, Stuttgart 1993.

Le Bohec, Yann, *Das römische Heer in der Späten Kaiserzeit*, Stuttgart 2010.

Le Bohec, Yann (ed.), *The Encyclopedia of the Roman Army*, 3 vols., Chichester 2015.

Lehmann, Gustav Adolf, *Imperium und Barbaricum. Neue Befunde und Erkenntnisse zu den römisch-germanischen Auseinandersetzungen im norddeutschen Raum – von der augusteischen Okkupationsphase bis zum Germanien-Zug des Maximinus Thrax (235 n. Chr.)*, Wien 2011.

Limesmuseum Aalen (ed.), *Von Augustus bis Attila. Leben am ungarischen Donaulimes*, Stuttgart 2000.

Loades, Mike, *The Composite Bow*, Oxford 2016.

Luttwak, Edward, *The Grand Strategy of the Roman Empire*, Baltimore/London 1976

MacDowall, Simon, „The Roman Army in Transition. Legions of Marcus Aurelius", in *Ancient Warfare* VII/6, p. 12-16.

Märtin, Ralf-Peter, „Die Rache der Römer. Neues Schlachtfeld am Harz entdeckt", in *National Geographic Deutschland* VI/2010, p. 66-93.

Marsden, E. W., *Greek and Roman Artillery. Historical Development*, Oxford 1969.

Menéndez Argüín, Adolfo Raúl: "La doctrina militar romana durante la crisis del siglo III", in: *Desperta Ferro (Numero Especial XVII): La legión romana (V): La anarquía militar*, Madrid 2018-2019, p. 52-56.

Menéndez Argüín, Adolfo Raúl, „Las reformas militares de Septimio Severo", in *Desperta Ferro (Antigua y Medieval)* 35, Madrid 2016, p. 24-29.

Meyer, Michael/Moosbauer, Günther, „Der Weg zum Harzhorn", in: Pöppelmann, Heike/Deppmeyer, Korana/Steinmetz, Wolf-Dieter (eds.), *Roms vergessener Feldzug. Die Schlacht am Harzhorn*, Darmstadt 2013, p. 265-268

Meyer, Michael/Moosbauer, Günther, „Osrhoener, Mauren und Germanen.Bogenschützen und Speerschleuderer“, in: Pöppelmann, Heike/ Deppmeyer, Korana/Steinmetz, Wolf-Dieter (eds.), *Roms vergessener Feldzug. Die Schlacht am Harzhorn*, Darmstadt 2013, p. 223-226.

Miks, Christian, Studien zur römischen Schwertbewaffnung in der Kaiserzeit (2 vols.), Rahden 2007.

Miks, Christian: „Zum Wandel der römischen Schwertausrüstung im 2. Jh. n. Chr. und seinem Stand z. Zt. der Markomannenkriege“ in: *Studijné Zvesti Archeologického Ústavu* SAV 62 (2017), p. 113-136.

Moosbauer, Günther, *Die vergessene Römerschlacht: Der sensationelle Fund am Harzhorn*, Munich 2018.

Moosbauer, Günther, „Torsionsgeschütze. Antike Wunderwaffen“, in Pöppelmann, Heike/Deppmeyer, Korana/Steinmetz, Wolf-Dieter (eds.), *Roms vergessener Feldzug. Die Schlacht am Harzhorn*, Darmstadt 2013, p. 242-248.

Németh, Margit, „Pannonien und die römischen Kaiser“, in: Limesmuseum Aalen (ed.),*Von Augustus bis Attila. Leben am ungarischen Donaulimes*, Stuttgart 2000, p. 19-22.

Nosch, Marie-Louise (ed.), *Wearing the Cloak. Dressing the Soldier in Roman Times*, Oxford/Oakville 2012.

Nüsse, Hans-Jörg, „Germanien im 3. Jahrhundert. Eine Zeit des Wandels“, in Pöppelmann, Heike/Deppmeyer, Korana/Steinmetz, Wolf-Dieter (eds.), *Roms vergessener Feldzug. die Schlacht am Harzhorn*, Darmstadt 2013.

Paulys Realencyclopädie der Klassischen Altertumswissenschaft, Stuttgart 1893-1980.

Pearson, Paul N., *Maximinus Thrax. From Common Soldier to Emperor of Rome*, Barnsley 2016.

Pérez Rubio, Alberto, *„Acies contra Alanos“*, in *Desperta Ferro (Antigua y Medieval)* 11/2, Madrid2 2015, p. 40-45.

Pferdehirt, Barbara/Scholz, Markus (eds.), *Bürgerrecht und Krise. Die* Constitutio Antoniniana *212 n. Chr. und ihre innenpolitischen Folgen*, Mainz 2012.

Pferdehirt, Barbara/Scholz, Markus, „Die Epoche der Severischen Kaiser“, in: Archäologisches Landesmuseum Baden-Württemberg (ed.): *Caracalla. Kaiser, Tyrann, Feldherr*, Darmstadt/Mainz 2013, p. 33-52.

Pitassi, Michael, *The Roman Navy. Ships, Men and Warfare 350 BC-AD 475*, Barnsley 2012.

Pöppelmann, Heike/Deppmeyer, Korana/Steinmetz, Wolf-Dieter (eds.), *Roms vergessener Feldzug. die Schlacht am Harzhorn*, Darmstadt 2013.

Pollard, Nigel/Berry, Joanne, *The Complete Roman Legions*, London 2012.

Potter, David S., *The Roman Empire at Bay AD 180-395*, London/New York2 2014.

Rathbone, Dominic: „Welfare and the State: A: Military Finance and Supply“, in: Sabin, Philip/van Wees, Hans/ Whitby, Michael (eds.): *The Cambridge History of Greek and Roman Warfare, Vol. II: Rome from the late Republic to the late Empire, Part II: The Late Empire*, Cambridge 2007, p. 158-197.

Rance, Philip: “Camels: Late Empire”, in: Le Bohec, Yann (ed.), *The Encyclopiedia of the Roman Army*, 3 vols., vol. 1, Chichester 2015, pp. 125-126.

Rankov, Boris, *The Praetorian Guard*, Oxford 1994.

Rau, Andreas: “Der unsichtbare Gegner. Größe und soziale Zusammensetzung germanischer Kampfverbände“, in Pöppelmann, Heike/Deppmeyer, Korana/Steinmetz, Wolf-Dieter (eds.), *Roms vergessener Feldzug. die Schlacht am Harzhorn*, Darmstadt 2013, p.167-171.

Riesch, Holger, *Pfeil und Bogen in der Römischen Kaiserzeit*, Ludwigshafen 2017.

Ross, Ian, “An invulnerable enemy. Countering the *clibanarii* at Turin”, in *Ancient Warfare* XII/3, 2018, p. 22-32

Russell Robinson, Henry, *The Armour of Imperial Rome*, New York 1975.

Sabin, Philip/van Wees, Hans/Whitby, Michael (eds.): *The Cambridge History of Greek and Roman Warfare, vol. II: Rome from the Late Republic to the Late Empire*, Cambridge 2007.

Saddington, Denis B.: “Moors, Mauri: Principate”, in Le Bohec, Yann (ed.): *The Encyclopedia of the Roman Army*, 3 vols., Chichester 2015, p. 664-665.

Sim, David/Kaminski, Jaime, *Roman Imperial Armour. The Production of Early Imperial Roman Armour*, Oxford 2012.

Sommer, Michael, *Die Soldatenkaiser*, Darmstadt3 2014.

Soria Molina, David: „Jinetes de hierro. La caballería pesada del ejército romano en el siglo II d. C.“, in *Desperta Ferro (Numero especial XIII): La legión romana (IV): El auge del Imperio*, Madrid 2017/18, p. 40-45

Southern, Patricia/Dixon, Karen, *The Late Roman Army*, London 1996.

Southern, Patricia, *The Roman Army. A History 753 BC-AD 476*, Stroud 2014.

Southern, Patricia, *The Roman Army. A Social and Institutional History*, Oxford 2007.

Southern, Patricia, *The Roman Empire from Severus to Constantine*, Abingdon/New York2 2014.

Spaul, John, COHORS 2, The evidence for and a short history of the auxiliary infantry units of the imperial Roman Army. British Archaeological Report Series No. 841, 2000.

Speidel, Michael: Die Denkmäler der Kaiserreiter Equites Singulares Augusti. Beihefte der Bonner Jahrbücher, Bd. 50 (Bonner Jahrbücher des Rheinischen Landesmuseums Bonn und des Rheinischen Amtes für Boden- und Denkmalpflege im Landschaftsverband Rheinland und des Vereins von Altertumsfreunden im Rheinlande). Köln: Rheinland-Verlag; Bonn: Habelt, 1994.

Speidel, Michael, “Faustina – mater castrorum. Ein Beitrag zur Religionsgeschichte”, in: Tyche. Beiträge zur Alten Geschichte, Papyrologie und Epigraphik, 27 (2012), https://tyche-journal.at/tyche/index.php/tyche/article/view/42/html_24, accessed on 11th May 2017.

Speidel Michael: "Maximinus and the Thracians. Herodian on the Coup of 235, and Ethnic Networks in the Roman Army of the Third Century CE", in: Victor Cojocaru, Alexander Rubel (eds.): *Mobility in Research of the Black Sea Region*. Cluj-Napoca 2016, p. 339 ff.

Speidel, Michael, *Riding for Caesar. The Roman Emperors' Horse Guards*, London 1994.

Stephenson, Ian, *Roman Infantry Equipment. The Later Empire*, Stroud 1999.

Strobel, Karl, „Strategy and Army Structure between Septimius Severus and Constantine the Great", in: Paul Erdkamp (ed.), *A Companion to the Roman Army*, Malden/Oxford/Victoria 2007, p. 267-285.

Sumner, Graham, "Del *cingulum* al *balteus*. El atuendo militar en el siglo III" in: *Desperta Ferro (Numero Especial XVII): La legión romana (V): La anarquía militar*, Madrid 2018-2019, p. 18-25.

Sumner, Graham: "Roman Camel Corps. Dromedarii in the Roman Middle East", in: *Military Illustrated* 90 (1996), p. 19 ff.

Sumner, Graham, *Roman Military Clothing (2), AD 200-400*, Oxford 2003.

Sumner, Graham, *Roman Military Dress*, Stroud 2009.

Syvänne, Ilkka: *Caracalla. A Military Biography*, Barnsley 2017.

Syvänne, Ilkka: *Military History of Late Rome, vol. I: 284-361*, Barnsley 2015.

Thomas, Mike, "Lorica Segmentata. Facts and Myths about Roman Sheet Armour", in *Ancient Warfare* XI/1, Rotterdam 2017,p. 48-50.

Töpfer, Kai Michael, *Signa Militaria. Die römischen Feldzeichen in der Republik und im Prinzipat*, Mainz 2011.

Travis, Hilary & John, *Roman Body Armour*, Stroud 2012.

Travis, Hilary & John, *Roman Helmets*, Stroud 2014.

Travis, Hilary & John, *Roman Shields. Historical Development and Reconstruction*, Stroud 2014.

Webster, Graham, *The Roman Imperial Army*, London3 1985.

Wemhoff, Matthias/Rind, Michael M. (eds.): *Bewegte Zeiten. Archäologie in Deutschland* (exhibition catalogue), Berlin 2018.

Wiegels, Rainer, „Die Reitergrabstele aus Stuttgart-Bad Cannstatt", in Pöppelmann, Heike/Deppmayer, Korana/Steinmetz, Wolf-Dieter (eds.), *Roms vergessener Feldzug. die Schlacht am Harzhorn*, Darmstadt 2013, p. 358

Wiegels, Rainer, „Reiter Roms an Germaniens Grenzen im frühen 3. Jh. n. Chr.", in Pöppelmann, Heike/Deppmeyer, Korana/Steinmetz, Wolf-Dieter (eds.), *Roms vergessener Feldzug. die Schlacht am Harzhorn*, Darmstadt 2013, p. 235-241.

Wolters, Reinhard, „Der Feldzug des Maximinus Thrax in das Innere Germaniens 235/236 n. Chr. in der numismatischen Überlieferung", in Pöppelmann, Heike/Deppmeyer, Korana/Steinmetz, Wolf-Dieter (eds.), *Roms vergessener Feldzug. die Schlacht am Harzhorn*, Darmstadt 2013, p. 116-123.

Websites:

anneeepigraphique.msh-paris.fr

culturalheritage.org

members.tripod.com

roman-britain.co.uk

romanarmytalk.com

wikipedia.org

http://tastesofhistory.blogspot.com/2016/12/arcuballista-late-roman-crossbow.html

https://tyche-journal.at

INDEX OF NAMES AND PLACES

GENERAL INDEX